PANDEMIC 2020
The U.S. Edition

A Statistical Keepsake

MARY MARLOW

PANDEMIC 2020
The U.S. Edition

A Statistical Keepsake

GATEWAY TO BEING

MARY MARLOW

ISBN-13: 978-0-9824123-3-6
ISBN-10: 0-9824123-3-9

~ CONTENTS *~*

III. U.S. TERRITORIES

IV. U.S. COMMUNITIES

V. YEAR-END SUMMARIES

VI. REFERENCES & RESOURCES

~ INTRODUCTION *~*

The story of the novel coronavirus begins, perhaps, with the first suspected but unconfirmed case in a 55 year-old Chinese male resident in Hubei Province, traced back to November 17, 2019.[1] It would be mid-December before Chinese scientists would come to realize they were dealing with a brand new (novel), highly contagious virus which would soon spark the birth of a global pandemic. Little did we know we were about to be plunged into one of the most severe health and economic crises the world has ever seen—a crisis that would forever change the landscape of life on planet Earth and threaten to plummet us all into civil war or worse... World War III.

Enter COVID-19—a disease caused by the never-before-seen virus, SARS-CoV-2, that, according to data gathered so far, sports a fatality (death) rate of 30 times that of seasonal influenza. Initial estimates would place the fatality rate at around 2%. However, on March 3, 2020, the World Health Organization (WHO) made the announcement that the fatality rate was calculating at 3.4% globally. And, as of 10/25/20, the fatality rate calculated at 3.0%, where it has remained throughout the remainder of the year. In comparison, the fatality rate for seasonal influenza is around 0.1%.[2,3,4]

Many of the world's scientists believe the pandemic originated as a naturally-occurring zoonotic (animal-based) virus present within the Huanan Wholesale Seafood Market in Wuhan (often called the "wet market"), where illegal wildlife is sold and animals are slaughtered on site.[5] China's earliest *acknowledged* confirmed patient would become symptomatic on December 1st—notably, a man who had never been to the market.[6] Coincidentally, the Wuhan Institute of Virology, part of the China Academy of Sciences and China's only biosafety level 4 lab (BSL-4), is located just eight miles away from the market. What's more, the Wuhan Center for Disease Control and Prevention is located just 300 yards from the market. Both are known locations of bat coronavirus research.[7]

Soon, many would speculate that the virus—which they claim may have been bio-engineered—possibly leaked from one of these labs, most likely by accident via a contaminated researcher. Despite no accusations of malice inherent in such a speculation—the U.S. itself has over 200 such labs—this is a theory China vehemently refutes. Since China did not allow the U.S. and other international scientists and researchers to investigate for the first full year, the world may never know the true origins of the disease.[8]

The fact that the first confirmed patient never set foot in the Huanan market is significant, and casts doubt as to the virus' wet market origin story.[9] It does not, however, prove a lab origin. China's original theory was as follows: a diseased horseshoe bat infected an intermediary animal such as a pangolin or a snake, which, in turn, infected the first human. However, it seems bats were never for sale at the market, nor do we have confirmation of the sale of pangolins or snakes.[5]

In mid-March, China would shift gears and begin accusing the U.S. military of originating the virus. Lijian Zhao, a spokesman for the Chinese ministry of foreign affairs would tweet: "When did patient zero begin in U.S.?... Be transparent! Make public your data! U.S. owe us an explanation!"[10]

The original SARS—Severe Acute Respiratory Syndrome (SARS-CoV for "SARS-Associated Coronavirus)—was an acute viral respiratory illness caused by a specific type of virus known as a *coronavirus*. Coronaviruses are in no way new to mankind. The common cold, for example, is caused by a wide range of some of the more harmless coronaviruses. In November, 2002, the SARS outbreak began in China and spread to more than two dozen countries until disappearing in July, 2003. A total of 8,098 people in 26 countries were infected, and of those, 774 died—a shockingly high case fatality rate (CFR) of approximately 10%.[11,12]

Of those who die of COVID-19, the most frequent complication resulting in death is sepsis (blood infection), followed by respiratory failure (including pneumonia, acute respiratory distress syndrome (ARDS), heart failure, septic shock (multiple organ and system failure) and sudden death arising from blood clots.[13,14]

Of those who test positive, 80% will either be asymptomatic or have mild symptoms. However, the "mild" category includes those who often describe the ordeal as "the worst flu of my life" and "the sickest I've ever been," despite avoiding hospitalization. The more we learn about this disease, the more we understand it can affect nearly every system of the body, with symptoms ranging from the typical fever, dry cough and shortness of breath, to sore throat, headache, body aches and extreme fatigue, to gastrointestinal upset, appetite loss and even more bizarre symptoms such as rashes, nerve pain of the skin, depression, memory loss and loss of the sense of smell and taste.[15,16,17]

Of the roughly 20% that suffer severe disease and require hospitalization, one quarter will die and the majority of the rest often struggle to recover fully. Even those with mild disease are at risk of suffering from what's become known as "long hauler syndrome," people who report prolonged, debilitating symptoms which may or may not be permanent.[18] Among the sickest victims, the median time between symptom onset and hospitalizations is 7 days, the median time between symptom onset and ICU admission is 12 days, and the median time between symptom onset and death is 18.5 days. For those who survive hospitalization, the median time spent as an inpatient is 22 days. Of patients placed on a ventilator, a full 80% will lose their lives.[19]

Besides its alarming fatality rate and potential to create life-long disability, the novel coronavirus possesses several defining characteristics which make it more concerning than seasonal flu. First, the coronavirus is completely new to the human race. Since no one has ever been exposed, no one has any immunity.[20] Second, it has an R0 ("R naught") infection contagion rating of 3.8–8.9 (explained below). Third, it has an unusually long incubation period of 2–14 —with outliers of up to 27 days. Fourth, it is capable of asymptomatic spread, meaning that even people without symptoms may shed the virus and can spread the infection to others. And finally, the novel coronavirus is capable of airborne transmission.[21] Let's look more closely at these factors.

The R0 is the reproduction number of a virus, which means the average number of people one infected person is expected to infect. The R0 is partially intrinsic to the virus, as a characteristic of its contagion, and partially based on human behavior. For example, if everyone goes on lockdown, wears masks and maintains a significant social distance, the R0 will be drastically reduced. If, on the other hand, people gather in large crowds inside buildings with few wearing masks, the R0 will increase. Reducing the R0 is all about taking away the opportunity for the virus to jump from one person to another. The goal is to get the R0 below 1, causing the virus to eventually die out and disappear from the population. Initially, the R0 was calculating at around 2.2–2.7, however mathematical models from the CDC in April, 2020 updated the R0 to 3.8–8.9, with a median of 5.7.[8,21]

Next, the incubation period is the time between the moment of infection (the moment the virus is introduced into the body) and the moment symptoms first appear. The longer the incubation period, the more efficiently the virus can spread. This is because people incubating the virus, who feel fine and have no idea they are infected or infectious, are likely to interact freely in their communities.[22] Some are asymptomatic, while others are pre-symptomatic, meaning they will go on to develop symptoms within two weeks. It has been postulated that children may even be asymptomatic carriers, capable of bringing the virus home from school and daycare to parents, grandparents and other more vulnerable populations. Until evidence proves otherwise, some advise it's best to assume children are infectious and take the appropriate precautions.[23]

This highly aggressive novel coronavirus is spread through various means, including droplets from the nose and mouth (coughing, sneezing, talking, shouting, singing), the touching of objects and surfaces (known as "fomites") then touching nose, mouth and eyes, and most disturbingly, airborne transmission (aerosolization). The virus can linger on various surfaces such as door handles, light switches, elevator buttons and mobile phones for hours or even days. It can remain suspended in the air for up to two hours where an individual coughed or sneezed, waiting to be inhaled by the next person who walks by.[24] It is present in urine and feces, and may become airborne with every flush of the toilet. There is some evidence the virus may spread through indoor ventilation such as heating and cooling systems.[25] In fact, simply standing and breathing less than six feet away from an infected individual while indoors without both donning masks can spread the disease.[26]

There are two methods for calculating the fatality/death rate—the "case fatality rate" (CFR) and the "infection fatality rate" (IFR). The CFR equals the number of confirmed deaths divided by the number of confirmed cases *which have had an outcome*. There are only two possible outcomes—recovery or death. The denominator for the CFR equation is found by subtracting the number of active cases from the number of total cases. Keep in mind, the CFR will be artificially high at the beginning of the pandemic, growing more accurate as data accumulates. Also useful but artificially low, is the "infection fatality rate" (IFR). This is the number of confirmed deaths divided by the total number of confirmed cases, with or without progressing to a final outcome.

The IFR will be artificially low at the beginning of the outbreak, grow higher over a period of time, then level off. In the end, when every confirmed case has resolved, the CFR and the IFR will match exactly. The CFR and IFR are not to be confused with the "mortality rate," which is the number of deaths divided by the total population, most of whom never had the disease—hardly a useful statistic.[27]

A retrospective CDC study in November 2020 found COVID-19 specific antibodies in donated blood in three states between December 13-16, 2019. This means that before the CDC became aware of the cases in China on December 31, 2019, the virus was already here, circulating in the U.S.[28] In early January 2020, warnings about the "mysterious respiratory illness in China" were included in President Trump's Daily Brief, which he largely downplayed and ignored.

China then released the genetic code of the virus to the world on January 9, 2020, allowing scientists to begin work on treatments and a vaccine.[29,30] On January 9, the novel coronavirus was given its official name—COVID-19. On January 10, the WHO confirmed human-to-human transmission. Limited airport screenings began on January 17. On January 18, President Trump accused HHS Secretary Alex Azar of being an "alarmist" after receiving his briefing on the status of the epidemic. On January 20, the U.S. recorded its first case, an American citizen traveling from Wuhan.[31] It was at this moment every opportunity to stop the virus should have been immediately deployed—an opportunity we sorely missed.[32]

The U.S. Coronavirus Task Force was formed on January 29 and included Robert Redfield of the CDC, Alex Azar of HHS, and Dr. Anthony Fauci of the NIAID. Not until February 26 was Vice President Mike Pence named as head and Dr. Deborah Birx brought on board as response coordinator.[33]

The CDC's coronavirus test developed in mid January was soon found to contain a defective component, setting the U.S. back in its efforts toward early virus containment.[34] On January 22, a reporter asked President Trump if he was concerned about the virus. He replied, "No, not at all. And we have it totally under control. It's one person coming in from China. It's going to be just fine."[35] Nothing could have been further from the truth. Throughout the entire first year of the pandemic, President Trump flouted science, refuted evidence, and created an extreme division in this country in which even wearing or refusing a mask became a statement of political affiliation. This, combined with the lack of a federalized coordinated response, led to the U.S. becoming (and remaining) by far the #1 most infected nation on Earth.[36]

Whenever the very first signs of a contagious disease emerge, non-pharmaceutical interventions (NPIs) must be employed right away to find, isolate and eradicate the virus by eliminating the opportunity for it to jump from person to person. Every single day lost can result in the exponential spread of disease until the point of no return is reached.[37] Prevention actions taken during the first two weeks, for example, will have far greater impact than mitigation efforts taken during the next two months. NPIs include things like surveillance testing, health screening, contact tracing, isolation or quarantine, mask wearing, social distancing and frequent hand washing. These measures are remarkably effective if implemented *immediately* and *aggressively*, such as was demonstrated in the approach of some of the most successful countries, like South Korea, Taiwan, Singapore, Hong Kong, New Zealand and Finland—some of whom took action even before confirming a single case.[38,39]

On January 31, 2020, HHS Secretary Azar declared a Public Health Emergency.[40] Only seven cases had been confirmed in the United States, though experts knew we likely had thousands more undetected. United, American and Delta airlines announce the temporary suspension of all flights to and from mainland China. Simultaneously, President Trump signs a formal order denying entry to foreign nationals who have traveled to China within the past two weeks—to take effect on February 2nd. This travel restriction was nowhere near a "ban," and did not apply to US citizens, lawful permanent residents nor their immediate family.[41]

Though clearly not his own brainchild, President Trump would boast of this "travel ban" through self-praise in nearly every press conference for the months to come, especially when confronted with pointed questions by reporters about what, exactly, steps he took to prepare the U.S. from January through March. Chinese officials called the travel restrictions "an overreaction, which would greatly hurt global tourism and hinder people to people exchanges."[42] Democratic president nominee and former Vice President Joe Biden's top coronavirus adviser Ron Klain also took issue with the travel restrictions, calling them "premature."[43] Biden himself opposed travel bans in the beginning, but would quickly change his tune.

It's important to note that Trump's extremely loose travel restrictions weren't implemented until after floods of travelers had already entered the U.S. from China between December and February—and *after*. In fact, nearly 430,000 people traveled to the U.S. via direct flights from China between December 31 and March 31—40,000 of whom were allowed in after the so-called travel ban. In fact passengers flooded in to the U.S., flying directly from Wuhan and Beijing into New York, Newark, Detroit, Chicago, Seattle, Los Angeles and San Francisco. Chinese travelers would also report they could easily enter the U.S. indirectly by simply flying to another country first. What's more, airport screening procedures (temperature checks and questioning about potential symptoms) for arrivals were reported to be very hit or miss.[44]

For any epidemic, once containment fails, virus control measures move into the next phase, known as mitigation. Although containment efforts continue to be employed during this phase, mitigation adds new strategies such as school closures, shutting down non-essential businesses, canceling sporting events and banning large gatherings. In addition, stay-at-home orders may be mandated.[45] The goal of both containment and mitigation efforts is summed up in the popular catch phrase—"flatten the curve." The curve refers to the shape of the graph depicting the daily increases and decreases in cases. When it comes to infectious disease, the expected trajectory takes the general shape of a bell curve—a rapid incline, followed by a leveling off or plateau, followed by a decline. A pandemic can have many "waves," one after the other. Some graphs also display a horizontal line representing the capacity of local health-care systems to accept and treat new and critical patients. If cases increase too rapidly, hospitals can become overwhelmed and no longer able to handle the increased load, resulting in patients being turned away and, inevitably, higher casualties. The goal of flattening the curve, therefore, is to avoid exceeding hospital capacity by slowing the rate of increase of infection in the population.[46]

The U.S. testing criteria was initially very narrow, testing only highly symptomatic individuals who also had a travel history to China or a known exposure to a confirmed case. In the critical early days, the U.S. missed the majority of cases, especially asymptomatic and pre-symptomatic people who were unwittingly spreading the virus to family, friends, co-workers and local communities.

In the early days, we embarked on the cumbersome task of contact tracing every single confirmed infection in an attempt to prevent additional outbreaks and lose control over this highly contagious virus through what is known as "community spread." Unfortunately, we were not successful, mainly because mass testing came far too late.[47] Compare and contrast the United States with South Korea, which confirmed its first case just one day after us. They *immediately* deployed mass drive-through testing of around 10,000 patients per day, aggressive contact tracing and mandatory mask wearing. In so doing, they contained the virus successfully and avoided any major disease or death toll.[48] By the end of 2020, South Korea had a total of only 60,740 cases and 900 deaths. That calculates to 1,145 cases per million population, and 17 deaths per million population. The U.S., on the other hand, ended the year with 20,451,302 cases and 354,316 deaths—that's 60,176 cases per million population and 1,044 deaths per million population.[4]

Some people believe that U.S. death counts are artificially inflated or worse, totally false. Such beliefs are politically charged.[49,50] While 100% accuracy is of course impossible, it's important to keep in mind that both the number of deaths *and* the number of confirmed infections are *under*-represented, not over-inflated. Deaths—because many deaths (especially those at home, in nursing homes, or months after "recovery" from Covid-related heart attacks, strokes and blood clots) were never counted, and cases—because many mild and asymptomatic cases never seek testing and are thus never discovered.[51]

Also mission from the equation are what is known as indirect deaths—deaths from an inability to obtain emergency care for any critical event (heart attacks, strokes, car accidents, etc.) due to health care systems operating beyond capacity, as well as deaths due to economic collapse, delays in exams and procedures for other diseases, starvation, suicide and so forth.[52]

Perhaps the most objective method of estimating COVID-19's true death count can be gleaned by studying the "excess deaths" charts for the United States and other hard-hit countries. The New York Times maintains an updated page of such graphs under the title: "Tracking the True Toll of the Coronavirus Outbreak."[52,53,65] When you compare the average numbers of daily deaths of all causes in 2020 to averages over the past five years, large spikes can be seen across the board, corresponding perfectly with the pandemic outbreaks in each area. The *only* thing that explains this is COVID-19 direct and indirect deaths. In fact, these charts may be *under*-

representing the true COVID-19 death toll when you take into account the fact that, during the same timeframe, there were far fewer traffic accident fatalities as people telecommute and follow stay-at-home orders.

The statistics provided in this book were recorded from official counts provided by the website worldometers.info.[4] Any gaps in my records or missing information on the specific first cases and first deaths for each state were found on Wikipedia's extensive coronavirus pages, the statistics for which I found match exactly with my data from worldometers.[54] Whether you believe the statistics to be accurate or not, one thing's for sure: This disease is ruthless, it's vicious, and it appears to be unstoppable. As of the publishing of this book, the U.S. (and the world) are in the midst of their third wave, with each wave reaching new heights. As we struggle to vaccinate as quickly as possible, the virus mutates, and we begin 2021 with three new concerning strains: The UK variant, the South African variant and the Brazilian variant—each far more contagious than the original.[55]

Sadly, the United States has become a tragic accounting of what *not* to do during the early, late and end stages of any pandemic. Under former president Donald Trump, politics became dangerously intertwined in all our decisions, with him and his most ardent supporters flouting science every step of the way. The U.S. lacked true leadership and a federalized response, even resulting in states competing with one another for life-saving PPE (personal protective equipment—masks, face shields, gloves and gowns) in short supply. Half the country was determined to wear masks, practice social distancing and follow expert advice, whereas the other half became pandemic deniers, refusing these measures, some even believing Trump's accusation that the virus was the Democrat's newest hoax.[56] The result: The U.S. became the Divided States of America. Although our country, our families and our friendships will not likely be healed from these divisions within our lifetimes, it is my hope that under President Joe Biden, we will find a way to begin to work together and promote the true healing we so desperately need.

This book is an accurate statistical account of various data points throughout the year 2020, featuring weekly case and death counts, weekly increases in each and daily averages calculations. Also included are notable events such as initial school closures, stay-at-home orders, mask mandates, holidays, and mass protests and rallies which promoted the spread of the disease. In addition, you will find testing counts, fatality rates, data on hospitalizations and deaths/million population and a year-end summary for each state in the back of the book.[57,58,59,60,61,62,63,64,65]

Coming in Spring of 2021 is my next book, PANDEMIC 2020: The Global Edition. And, if the virus continues to mutate, cause mass infection, death and disability, evading our best efforts, you can expect to see 2021 U.S. and global editions as well. Please enjoy this statistical keepsake. Use it as a tool to make predictions and gauge human behavior and its consequences, and pass it down through the generations in the hope that humankind can learn from this historic event.

~ TIMELINE *~*
THE BIRTH OF A PANDEMIC

11/17/19: Possible "patient zero" from Hubei Province, China retroactively identified[1]

12/01/19: Debate rages as to whether virus originated in wet market or bio-safety lab[2,3]

12/07/19: Several Chinese health-care workers fall ill, but China refuses to confirm contagion[4]

12/22/19: China silences whistleblowers, destroys virus samples and under-reports statistics[5,6,7,15]

12/23/19: China rules out original SARS, MERS and influenza as cause of outbreak[8,9]

12/27/19: China designates 100,000 hospital beds to the epidemic[10]

12/27/19: Shocking photos are leaked of crowded emergency rooms and long lines outside[11,55]

12/31/19: Between 12/31/19 and 4/04/20, 430,000 people flew to U.S. directly from China[12]

01/02/20: Complete genetic sequence mapped by China, shared worldwide one week later[13,14,28]

01/02/20: Wuhan labs ordered to stop testing samples and destroy existing samples[16,17]

01/02/20: China notifies U.S. CDC's Dr. Robert Redfield of the "serious situation"[18,19]

01/02/20: After being notified by HHS Alex Azar, Trump accuses him of being "alarmist"[20]

01/03/20: Chest x-rays show unique ground glass opacities that differ from typical pneumonia[21]

01/04/20: China denies official U.S. requests to study the virus origins on site[22]

01/04/20: "Panic buying" begins of non-perishable foods, hand sanitizers, toilet paper, etc.[23]

01/06/20: The the U.S. CDC issues a Level 1 Travel Watch (the lowest of 3 levels).[24]

01/07/20: Hong Kong, S. Korea, Taiwan and Singapore take aggressive containment action[25]

01/09/20: The World Health Organization (WHO) recommends against travel restrictions[26]

01/10/20: The first known/recognized COVID-19 death occurs in China[27]

01/10/20: It is reported that people over age 65 and those with comorbidities at highest risk[28]

01/11/20: China announces it has mapped the SARS-CoV-2 genome, 16 days after the fact[29]

01/13/20: First case outside China is recorded in Taiwan[30]

01/14/20: The WHO finally announces that the coronavirus *may* be contagious[31]

01/16/20: German researchers develop the first PCR test for detecting the virus[32,33]

01/17/20: Three U.S. airports begin screening (not testing) passengers traveling from China[34]

01/17/20: Dr. Nancy Messonnier warns the U.S. about the "serious situation" of the outbreak[35]

01/18/20: China hosts a massive potluck dinner with 40,000 families[36]

01/19/20: China's official (grossly inaccurate) tally stands at 201 cases and 3 deaths[27]

01/19/20: Trump sidelines Alex Azar for his repeated stark warnings about the virus[37]

01/19/20: Trump tells Americans the virus will "go away" and "magically disappear"[38]

01/20/20: First human-to-human transmission officially confirmed in China[39]

01/20/20: The U.S., U.K. Italy and Brazil fail to take immediate containment measures[40]

01/20/20: The very first case is confirmed in the U.S.[41]

01/20/20: Five million panicked citizens flee Wuhan as massive lockdown announced[42,43]

01/20/20: The U.S. requires all virus samples to be sent to and tested at the CDC headquarters[44]

01/20/20: Chinese CDC confirms at least 3 distinct strains of the virus (rapid mutation)[45]

01/21/20: Dr. Anthony Fauci announces virus is "not a major threat" to the U.S. at this time[46]

01/22/20: The virus is in 13 countries. China claims a total of 481 cases and 17 deaths[27]

01/22/20: Trump tells CNBC during an interview, "We have it totally under control"[47,48,49,50]

01/22/20: The U.S. realizes it has a severe mask shortage; stockpile equipment is expired[51,52]

01/22/20: Several pharmaceutical companies announce they have begun working on a vaccine[53]

01/22/20: Chinese woman reports morgues and crematoriums are operating 24/7, can't cope[54]

01/22/20: Senator Tom Cotton urges Trump to implement an immediate travel ban[56]

01/23/20: U.S. deploys faulty coronavirus test kits, setting testing efforts back significantly[57,58]

01/23/20: Social distancing and hand washing are encouraged; mask wearing is debated[59,60]

01/23/20: China quarantines Wuhan (11 million people) in biggest lockdown in history[61]

01/24/20: China's lockdown extends to all of Hubei province (59 million people)[62]

01/24/20: The WHO continually praises China, calling its efforts "unprecedented"[63]

01/24/20: Trump and right-wing media refer to outbreak as "hoax," "hype" and "fake news"[64]

01/24/20: Free speech is touted as authorities strive to shut down dangerous disinformation[65]

01/24/20: Countries around the world evacuate their citizens from China on chartered flights[66]

01/24/20: Chinese whistleblowers try to report the extreme severity of their situation[7,15,67,68]

01/24/20: China rapidly builds 1,000 bed and 1,600 bed hospitals; rooms resemble jail cells[69,70]

01/24/20: Trump praises and thanks China and President Xi for "efforts and transparency"[71]

01/25/20: HHS Alex Azar falsely promises U.S. will be able to test 75K people by end of week[72]

01/25/20: South Korea leads the world in testing, 10,000/day using drive through testing[73]

01/25/20: With only 5 cases, Hong Kong closes schools, implements lockdown[74]

01/26/20: The incubation period is announced as 1-14 days with outliers up to 27 days[27,75]

01/26/20: Dr. Nancy Messonnier announces U.S. needs to prepare "as if this is a pandemic"[76]

01/26/20: China readies 409,000 hospital beds while claiming only 2,000 total cases[77]

01/27/20: The WHO increases Global Risk Assessment from "moderate" to "high"[78]

01/27/20: The DOW plunges 453 points, wiping out all 2020 gains[79]

01/27/20: Presidential candidate Joe Biden calls Trump "unqualified to handle" the situation[80]

01/28/20: Experts estimate there are upwards of 44,000 infected residents in Wuhan alone[81]

01/28/20: An average of 8,000 people are flying to the U.S. from China each day[82]

01/28/20: Presidential candidate Elizabeth Warren releases her plan to tackle the coronavirus[83]

01/29/20: Trump announces the formation of the White House Coronavirus Task Force[84]

01/29/20: Health officials lie to the American public, stating masks do not prevent spread[85,86]

01/29/20: Officials close to Trump state he is disinterested in hearing about the coronavirus[87]

01/29/20: Peter Navarro states, worst case scenario, the virus could take 583,000 U.S. lives[88]

01/29/20: With the virus circulating in 17 countries, WHO asks world to be on high alert[89]

01/30/20: The WHO declares the virus a Public Health Emergency of International Concern[90]

01/30/20: As Trump travels the U.S. conducting rallies, the virus is confirmed in 5 U.S. states[91]

01/30/20: Russia closes its 2,600-mile border with China[92]

01/30/20: As Azar warns of impending pandemic, Trump claims it's "under control"[93]

01/31/20: Trump announces his U.S. "travel ban" that wasn't—excludes U.S. citizens, lawful permanent residents and their families. 40,000 Chinese traveled to U.S. after the "ban"[94]

01/31/20: Trump squanders the time bought and takes little to no further action[95]

02/01/20: The world has 14,000 confirmed cases in 24 countries; 1st death outside China[27]

02/01/20: In a short-sighted move, the U.S. donates nearly all its PPE to China[96,97]

02/01/20: The U.S. declares a Public Health Emergency[98]

02/01/20: Chorus line coming from White House: "the risk to the American public remains low" (a blatant lie)[98]

02/01/20: Trump and right-wing news media falsely claim the virus is no worse than the flu[99]

02/01/20: Trump escalates his vendetta against mainstream media, calling it "fake news" every time factual reporting disagrees with his constant disinformation[100]

02/04/20: The Diamond Princess cruise ship docks in Japan with 40 infected passengers[101]

02/04/20: Two drugs—hydroxychloroquine and Remdesivir—show promising results[102]

02/05/20: Trump is acquitted in his first impeachment trial[103]

02/05/20: Crippled by the defective kits, the U.S. still has no effective mass testing strategy[104]

02/07/20: Chinese whistleblower, hero and martyr, Dr. Li Wenliang, dies of coronavirus[105]

02/07/20: U.S. health-care workers cry out for personal protective equipment (PPE)[106]

02/08/20: The death toll for SARS-CoV-2 surpasses that of the original 2003 SARS[107]

02/10/20: Trump declares that come April with the heat, virus will "miraculously disappear"[108]

02/10/20: The disease caused by SARS-CoV-2 gets its official name: COVID-19[109]

02/12/20: The global case count surpasses 60,000 and global deaths surpass 1,100[27]

02/13/20: Cases aboard the Diamond Princess reach 218, the largest cluster outside China[110]

02/14/20: The U.S. CDC reports that COVID-19 might be around for at least another year[111]

02/14/20: The world grows nervous about its drug supplies, most manufactured in China[112,113]

02/15/20: Of 56,249 cases in China, 73.6% are in mild condition, 21.4% serious, 5% critical[114]

02/15/20: Talks begin about the potential for the U.S. Olympics to be postponed or cancelled[115]

02/20/20: HHS reports its running out of money due to the flawed $250-apiece testing kits[116]

02/20/20: One infected parishioner infects up to 600 fellow members of a S. Korean church[117]

02/22/20: With 79 confirmed cases, Italy becomes the epicenter of the virus in Europe[118]

02/23/20: The virus is now present in 30 countries with 79,000 confirmed cases[27]

02/24/20: China permanently bans trade and consumption of live wild animals[119]

***

This ends my note-taking on the main events during the early days of the pandemic. My focus from this point on became recording cases and deaths every day for all 50 states and any country with 3,000 or more confirmed cases. When this became overwhelmingly time consuming (approximately 4 hours/day), I eventually switched to weekly recording every Friday.

The WHO declared COVID-19 an official global pandemic on March 11, 2020.[120] The United States has experienced three distinct waves thus far—the first and smallest wave peaking the first week in April, the second medium-sized wave peaking in mid-July, and a third, much larger wave peaking the first week in January, 2021.[27]

On December 14, the U.S. began vaccinating its citizens.[121] First, we have the Pfizer-BioNTech vaccine which is said to be 95% effective after two doses. It requires sub-zero storage which can make distribution costly and tedious.[122] In addition, we have the Moderna vaccine at 94% effective after two doses, requiring regular freezer temperature storage.[123] On the horizon is the Johnson & Johnson vaccine, slightly less effective at 85%, but requiring only one dose and allowing for storage at regular refrigerator temperatures.[124]

As we strive to deploy vaccinations as quickly as possible, with President Biden's goal of 100 million vaccines in the first 100 days of his presidency, we are trying to outrun the virus' ability to mutate and change significantly enough to make our vaccines less effective or worse, ineffective.[125] The new U.K. variant, a mutation of COVID-19, was first discovered to be present in the United States on December 22, 2020. The Brazilian variant was discovered here on January 25, 2021, and on January 28 came the South African variant.[126]

Although there are countless variants in circulation, as of February 2021, these are the three causing the most concern. The U.K. variant is 30-50% more contagious than the original and does appear to also be more lethal—causing more severe disease and death. The Brazilian and South African variants are even more concerning, with up to 70% more transmissible and even more lethality, plus the likelihood of evading our current vaccines. Scientists are already working on modifications to the vaccines and this may end up being an ongoing process in the years to come.[126] There is much debate and disagreement as to the safety of these new vaccines, and of vaccines in general. However, this debate is not within the scope of this book.

The next section of the book, "Guide to the Statistical Data," will assist you in understanding the main statistical sections to come, so you can get the most benefit possible when using this book as a reference and as a COVID-19 pandemic keepsake.

~ GUIDE TO THE *~* STATISTICAL DATA

This is a book of weekly COVID-19 statistics for the United States of America, its individual states, territories and communities. Global statistics are also included for frame of reference. Data shown in **bold font** is taken each Friday and includes:

~ weekly cumulative number of cases and deaths in the format: cases / deaths
~ weekly increase in number of cases and deaths in the format: cases / deaths
~ the daily average number of cases and deaths, in the format: cases / deaths

The daily averages are rounded to the nearest whole person. At the top of each new state's page, you will also find the population as of March, 2020 (which, coincidentally, reduced in nearly every state by the end of the year), the political affiliation of the state, the name of the state's current governor, and the presidential election results for that state. In addition, the timeline includes additional data in italics such as:

~ date of the very first case and date of very first death for each state
~ major announcements and declarations by WHO, President Trump and individual states
~ the monthly infection fatality rate (IFR = total deaths divided by total cases)
~ the year-end case fatality rate (CFR = total deaths divided by cases with an outcome.)
~ monthly tally of total number of coronavirus tests performed
~ dates of initial school closures, stay-at-home orders, mask mandates and more
~ current and cumulative COVID-19 hospitalizations
~ monthly test positivity rate (the % of performed coronavirus tests that come back positive)
~ national holidays and rallies which, due to social gatherings, often increased infection rates

This book serves as a comprehensive reference as well as a keepsake to be passed down generation after generation. Its companion book, set to release the first quarter of 2021, is PANDEMIC 2020: The Global Edition. The contrast between how the United States handled the virus compared to many countries in Asia and Europe is stark and heart-wrenching, especially when you realize it didn't have to be this way. Instead of taking decisive, federalized action, the United States politicized the coronavirus, pitting Republicans against Democrats, with the former tending not to believe in the necessity for mask wearing, social distancing and other life-saving precautions. This book's data shows exactly how that belief system turned out.

It has been a century since the world endured the 1918 Spanish Flu pandemic which ended with a death toll of over 50 million people. As of December 31, 2020, the global death toll for COVID-19 has reached 1,834,484, and the U.S. death toll has reached 354,316. We rank first in the world for total case counts, and first in the world for total death counts. In countries with at least 20 million people, we rank #1 in cases/million and #3 in deaths/million.

In addition, there is a stark contrast between red states—who don't tend to believe in following expert health directives—and blue states, who do. Of the top 25 highest states for cases/million, 18 of them are red states, while only 7 are blue. No matter what anyone "believes": Masks work, social distancing works, avoiding crowds works and avoiding indoor gatherings works. Our very survival depends on these and other factors.

I will continue gathering data as we move into the next phase of our fight against this virus, keeping an eye on all the various vaccinations that are becoming available around the world and other promising treatments that we all hope might bring an end to this nightmare. If the pandemic continues as expected, there will be 2021 versions of this and the global edition books.

Thank you for your purchase of this book. Please know that 3% of the profits of each sale will be donated to my favorite charity, Hope for Paws animal rescue. Not only do they do amazing work driving all across the country rescuing dogs and other animals who have been lost or abandoned, they also get them into foster homes and loving forever homes. I don't know where we'd all be without the love of our precious pets as we have suffered through the isolation and loneliness of this pandemic.

SECTION I

GLOBAL & U.S. STATS

CHAPTER 1

~ GLOBAL *~*

DATE	CASES / DEATHS	WEEKLY INCREASE	DAILY AVERAGE
11/17/2019	1 / 0 ← probable "patient zero"		
12/31: China reports cluster of mysterious pneumonia cases to WHO			
01/01: Huanan Wholesale Seafood Market closes			
01/11: China reports its first death from the virus			
(01/22)	(609 / 17) ← *earliest available data on worldometers.info*		
01/23: Wuhan is placed under quarantine, followed by Hubei Province soon thereafter			
01/24	1,349 / 41	+1,348 / +41	193 / 6
01/30: WHO declares Public Health Emergency of International Concern			
01/31	12,001 / 259	+10,652 / +218	1,522 / 31
02/07: Chinese whistleblower Dr. Li Wenliang dies of coronavirus			
02/07	35,021 / 724	+23,020 / +465	3,289 / 66
02/09: death toll of 811 surpasses original SARS outbreak of 2002-03			
02/11: the novel coronavirus gets its official name: COVID-19			
02/14	67,363 / 1,526	+32,342 / +802	4,620 / 115
02/15: IFR (infection fatality rate) = 2.40%			
02/21	78,188 / 2,360	+10,825 / +834	1,546 / 119
02/28	86,136 / 2,923	+7,968 / +563	1,138 / 80
03/06	109,587 / 3,493	+23,431 / +570	3,347/ 81
03/08: Italy goes on lockdown			
03/11: WHO declares COVID-19 a pandemic			
03/13	178,900 / 5,445	+69,313 / +1,952	9,902 / 279
03/15: IFR (infection fatality rate) = 3.05%			
03/20	355,981 / 11,610	+177,081 / +6,165	25,297 / 881
03/27	684,392 / 28,861	+328,411 / +17,251	46,916 / 2,464
03/30: over 01/3rd of the world's population now under lockdown			
04/03	1,172,917 / 63,195	+488,525 / +34,334	69,789 / 4,905
04/15: IFR (infection fatality rate) = 6.87%			
04/17	2,254,113 / 159,686	+1,081,196 / +96,491	154,457 / 13,784

DATE	CASES / DEATHS	WEEKLY INCREASE	DAILY AVERAGE
04/24	2,804,681 / 204,580	+550,568 / +44,894	78,653 / 6,413
05/01	3,356,393 / 244,917	+551,712 / +40,337	78,816 / 5,762
05/08	3,956,976 / 282,826	+600,583 / +37,909	85,798 / 5,416
05/15: IFR (infection fatality rate) = 6.95%			
05/15	4,564,111 / 317,071	+607,135 / +34,245	86,734 / 4,892
05/22	5,246,390 / 348,384	+682,279 / +31,313	97,468 / 4,473
05/29	5,981,211 / 378,561	+734,821 / +30,177	104,974 / 4,311
06/05	6,820,846 / 410,048	+839,635 / +31,487	119,948 / 4,498
06/12	7,717,301 / 441,597	+896,455 / +31,549	128,065 / 4,507
06/15: IFR (infection fatality rate) = 5.59%			
06/19	8,720,566 / 475,799	+1,003,265 / +34,202	143,324 / 4,886
06/26	9,870,274 / 509,101	+1,149,708 / +33,302	164,244 / 4,757
07/03	11,182,184 / 541,925	+1,311,910 / +32,824	187,416 / 4,689
07/10	12,625,144 / 576,660	+1,442,960 / +34,735	206,137 / 4,962
07/15: IFR (infection fatality rate) = 4.39%			
07/17	14,196,521 / 613,501	+1,571,377 / +36,841	224,482 / 5,263
07/24	15,950,073 / 653,330	+1,753,552 / +39,829	250,507 / 5,690
07/31	17,784,534 / 693,961	+1,834,461 / +40,631	262,066 / 5,804
08/07	19,574,351 / 735,361	+1,789,817 / +41,400	255,688 / 5,914
08/14	21,433,962 / 776,883	+1,859,611 / +41,522	265,659 / 5,932
08/15: IFR (infection fatality rate) = 3.73%			
08/21	23,200,792 / 817,353	+1,766,830 / +40,470	252,404 / 5,781
08/28	25,014,521 / 856,551	+1,813,729 / +39,198	259,104 / 5,600
09/04	26,912,190 / 895,049	+1,897,669 / +38,498	271,096 / 5,500
09/11	8,803,842 / 930,643	+1,891,652 / +35,594	270,236 / 5,085
09/15: IFR (infection fatality rate) = 3.16%			
09/18	30,837,737 / 966,897	+2,033,895 / +36,254	290,556 / 5,179
09/25	32,878,144 / 1,002,331	+2,040,407 / +35,434	291,487 / 5,062
10/02	34,949,832 / 1,037,342	+2,071,688 / +35,011	295,955 / 5,002
10/09	37,174,857 / 1,074,448	+2,225,025 / +37,106	317,861 / 5,301
10/15: IFR (infection fatality rate) = 2.82%			
10/16	39,644,748 / 1,110,919	+2,469,891 / +36,471	352,842 / 5,210
10/23	42,543,489 / 1,151,292	+2,898,741 / +40,373	414,106 / 5,768
10/30	45,957,327 / 1,195,724	+3,413,838 / +44,432	487,691 / 6,347
11/06	49,704,145 / 1,249,190	+3,746,818 / +53,466	535,260 / 7,638
11/13	53,803,878 / 1,309,018	+4,099,733 / +59,828	585,676 / 8,547
11/15: IFR (infection fatality rate) = 2.42%			
11/20	57,907,364 / 1,377,015	+4,103,486 / +67,997	586,212 / 9,714

DATE	CASES / DEATHS	WEEKLY INCREASE	DAILY AVERAGE
11/27	61,980,680 / 1,448,307	+4,073,316 / +71,292	581,902 / 10,185
12/04	66,213,774 / 1,523,646	+4,233,094 / +75,339	604,728 / 10,763
12/11	71,454,215 / 1,600,483	+5,240,441 / +76,837	748,634 / 10,977
12/15: IFR (infection fatality rate) = 2.22%			
12/18	75,992,777 / 1,680,360	+4,538,562 / +79,877	648,366 / 11,411
12/25	80,257,970 / 1,757,249	+4,265,193 / +76,889	609,313 / 10,984
01/01/2021	84,418,109 / 1,834,807	+4,160,139 / +77,558	594,306 / 11,080

BONUS: Enjoy additional week from upcoming book: PANDEMIC 2021: The U.S. Edition

DATE	CASES / DEATHS	WEEKLY INCREASE	DAILY AVERAGE
01/08	89,337,765 / 1,920,914	+4,919,656 / +86,134	702,808 / 12,305

GLOBAL YEAR-END STATS
TOTAL CASES = 84,361,826
CASES/MILLION = 10,823
TOTAL DEATHS = 1,834,484
DEATHS/MILLION = 235.3
IFR (INFECTION FATALITY RATE) = 2.18%
CFR (CASE FATALITY RATE) = 3.00%

*The daily average column is rounded to the nearest whole person. The infection fatality rate (IFR) is the number of deaths divided by the number of confirmed cases. The case fatality rate (CFR), shown only at the end of the year, is the number of deaths divided by the number of confirmed cases *which have had an outcome* (either recovery or death). The CFR excludes active cases.

CHAPTER 2

~ THE UNITED STATES *~*

POPULATION AS OF MARCH, 2020: 330,568,224
PRESIDENTIAL ELECTION RESULTS: Biden 51.0% / Trump 47.1%

DATE	CASES / DEATHS	WEEKLY INCREASE	DAILY AVERAGE
	01/20: first case in the U.S.		
01/24	**2 / 0**	**N/A**	**N/A**
	01/30: WHO declares Public Health Emergency of International Concern		
	01/31: Trump issues a China "travel ban"		
01/31	**7 / 0**	**+5 / +0**	**1 / 0**
02/07	**12 / 0**	**+5 / +0**	**1 / 0**
02/14	**14 / 0**	**+2 / +0**	**0 / 0**
02/21	**14 / 0**	**+0 / +0**	**0 / 0**
02/28	**62 / 0**	**+48 / +0**	**7 / 0**
03/06	**233 / 14**	**+171 / +14**	**24 / 2**
	03/11: WHO declares COVID-19 a pandemic		
	03/13: Trump declares a National Emergency		
	03/13: Trump issues a Europe "travel ban"		
03/13	**1,832 / 41**	**+1,599 / +27**	**228 / 4**
03/20	**14,371 / 218**	**+12,539 / +177**	**1,791 / 25**
	03/22: NEW! test positivity rate = 14.55%		
03/27	**85,755 / 1,304**	**+71,384 / +1,086**	**10,198 / 155**
	03/31: total tests = 1,084,228		
04/03	**245,442 / 6,098**	**+159,687 / +4,794**	**22,812 / 685**
04/10	**502,876 / 18,747**	**+257,434 / +12,649**	**36,776 / 1,807**
	04/12: Easter		
	04/15: IFR (infection fatality rate) = 4.43%		
04/17	**709,735 / 37,154**	**+206,859 / +18,407**	**29,551 / 2,630**
	04/22: test positivity rate = 19.20%		

DATE	CASES / DEATHS	WEEKLY INCREASE	DAILY AVERAGE
04/24	**925,232 / 52,193**	**+215,497 / +15,039**	**30,785 / 2,148**
	04/30: total tests = 6,579,680		
	NEW! 05/01: deaths/million population = 199		
05/01	**1,131,030 / 65,753**	**+205,798 / +13,560**	**29,400 / 1,937**
05/08	**1,321,785 / 78,615**	**+190,755 / +12,862**	**27,251 / 1,837**
	05/10: Mother's Day		
	05/15: IFR (infection fatality rate) = 5.96%		
05/15	**1,484,285 / 88,507**	**+162,500 / +9,892**	**23,214 / 1,413**
	05/22: test positivity rate = 11.87%		
05/22	**1,645,094 / 97,647**	**+160,809 / +9,140**	**22,973 / 1,306**
	05/25: Memorial Day		
	05/26: George Floyd protests begin		
05/29	**1,793,530 / 104,542**	**+148,436 / +6,895**	**21,205 / 985**
	05/31: total tests = 17,672,567		
	06/01: deaths/million population = 319		
06/05	**1,965,708 / 111,390**	**+172,178 / +6,848**	**24,597 / 978**
06/12	**2,116,922 / 116,825**	**+151,214 / +5,435**	**21,602 / 776**
	06/15: IFR (infection fatality rate) = 5.42%		
06/19	**2,297,190 / 121,407**	**+180,268 / +4,582**	**25,753 / 655**
	06/21: Father's Day		
	06/22: test positivity rate = 24.67%		
06/26	**2,552,956 / 127,640**	**+255,766 / +6,233**	**36,538 / 890**
	06/30: total tests = 34,198,027		
	07/01: deaths/million population = 392		
07/03	**2,890,588 / 132,101**	**+337,632 / +4,461**	**48,233 / 637**
	07/04: Independence Day		
07/10	**3,291,786 / 136,671**	**+401,198 / +4,570**	**57,314 / 653**
	07/15: IFR (infection fatality rate) = 3.87%		
07/17	**3,770,012 / 142,064**	**+478,226 / +5,393**	**68,318 / 770**
	07/22: test positivity rate = 22.98%		
07/24	**4,248,327 / 148,490**	**+478,315 / +6,426**	**68,331 / 918**
07/31	**4,705,889 / 156,747**	**+457,562 / +8,257**	**65,366 / 1,180**
	07/31: total tests = 58,591,052		
	08/01: deaths/million population = 473		
08/07	**5,095,524 / 164,094**	**+389,635 / +7,347**	**55,662 / 1,050**
08/14	**5,476,266 / 171,535**	**+380,742 / +7,441**	**54,392 / 1,063**
	08/15: IFR (infection fatality rate) = 3.12%		
08/21	**5,797,599 / 179,200**	**+321,333 / +7,665**	**45,905 / 1,095**

DATE	CASES / DEATHS	WEEKLY INCREASE	DAILY AVERAGE
	08/22: test positivity rate = 18.89%		
08/28	**6,096,235 / 185,901**	**+298,636 / +6,701**	**42,662 / 957**
	08/31: total tests = 86,759,202		
	09/01: deaths/million population = 580		
09/04	**6,389,057 / 192,111**	**+292,822 / +6,210**	**41,832 / 887**
	09/07: Labor Day		
09/11	**6,636,247 / 197,421**	**+247,190 / +5,310**	**35,313 / 759**
	09/15: IFR (infection fatality rate) = 2.95%		
09/18	**6,925,941 / 203,171**	**+289,694 / +5,750**	**41,385 / 821**
	09/22: test positivity rate = 20.55%		
09/25	**7,244,355 / 208,440**	**+318,414 / +5,269**	**45,488 / 753**
	09/30: total tests = 107,536,225		
	10/01: deaths/million population = 645		
10/02	**7,549,323 / 213,524**	**+304,968 / +5,084**	**43,567 / 726**
10/09	**7,894,478 / 218,648**	**+345,155 / +5,124**	**49,308 / 732**
	10/15: IFR (infection fatality rate) = 2.71%		
10/16	**8,288,278 / 223,644**	**+393,800 / +4,996**	**56,257 / 714**
	10/22: test positivity rate = 9.35%		
10/23	**8,746,953 / 229,284**	**+458,675 / +5,640**	**65,525 / 806**
10/30	**9,316,297 / 235,159**	**+569,344 / +5,875**	**81,335 / 839**
	10/31: total tests = 144,186,274		
	11/01: deaths/million population = 714		
	11/03: Election Day		
11/06	**10,058,586 / 242,230**	**+742,289 / +7,071**	**106,041 / 1,010**
	11/07: Biden wins election		
11/13	**11,064,462 / 249,977**	**+1,005,876 / +7,747**	**143,697 / 1,107**
	11/15: IFR (infection fatality rate) = 2.22%		
11/20	**12,274,726 / 260,283**	**+1,210,264 / +10,306**	**172,895 / 1,472**
	11/22: test positivity rate = 18.81%		
	11/26: Thanksgiving		
11/27	**13,454,254 / 271,026**	**+1,179,528 / +10,743**	**168,504 / 1,535**
	11/30: total tests = 198,258,153		
	12/01: deaths/million population = 835		
12/04	**14,774,591 / 285,575**	**+1,320,337 / +14,549**	**188,620 / 2,078**
12/11	**16,295,714 / 302,762**	**+1,521,123 / +17,187**	**217,303 / 2,455**
	12/14: first COVID-19 vaccinations given in the U.S.		
	12/15: IFR (infection fatality rate) = 1.81%		
12/18	**17,888,353 / 320,845**	**+1,592,639 / +18,083**	**227,520 / 2,583**

DATE	CASES / DEATHS	WEEKLY INCREASE	DAILY AVERAGE
12/22: new U.K. variant identified in the U.S.			
12/22: test positivity rate			
12/25: Christmas			
12/25	**19,210,166 / 338,263**	**+1,384,890 / +17,668**	**197,841 / 2,524**
12/31: total tests = 250,170,250			
12/31: deaths/million population = 1,044			
01/01: New Year's Day			
01/01: CFR (case fatality rate) = 2.89% (28.9X more deadly than influenza at 0.1%)			
01/01/2021	**20,672,474 / 356,575**	**+1,344,103 / +17,932**	**192,015 / 2,562**

BONUS: Enjoy additional week from upcoming book: PANDEMIC 2021: The U.S. Edition

DATE	CASES / DEATHS	WEEKLY INCREASE	DAILY AVERAGE
01/06: right-wing mob insurrection at U.S. Capitol as Joe Biden confirmed president			
01/08: Twitter permanently bans Trump's account			
01/08	**22,461,696 / 378,204**	**+1,789,222 / +21,629**	**255,603 / 3,090**

USA: YEAR-END STATS
GLOBAL CASE COUNT RANK = #1
TOTAL CASES = 20,451,302
CASES/MILLION = 60,176
TOTAL DEATHS = 354,316
DEATHS/MILLION = 1,044
TOTAL TESTS = 250,170,250
TESTS/MILLION = 753,603
IFR (INFECTION FATALITY RATE) = 1.73%
CFR (CASE FATALITY RATE) = 2.89%

*The daily average column is rounded to the nearest whole person. The infection fatality rate (IFR) is the number of deaths divided by the number of confirmed cases. The case fatality rate (CFR), shown only at the end of the year, is the number of deaths divided by the number of confirmed cases *which have had an outcome* (either recovery or death). The CFR excludes active cases.

SECTION II

50 U.S. STATES & D.C.

CHAPTER 3

~ ALABAMA *~*

POPULATION AS OF MARCH, 2020: 4,908,621
Republican Governor Kay Ivey
VOTED RED: Trump 62.0% / Biden 36.6%

DATE	CASES / DEATHS	WEEKLY INCREASE	DAILY AVERAGE
01/30: WHO declares Public Health Emergency of International Concern			
01/31: Trump issues a China "travel ban"			
03/11: Alabama's first 3 cases			
03/11: WHO declares COVID-19 a pandemic			
03/13: Alabama declares State of Emergency			
03/13: Trump declares a National Emergency			
03/13: Trump issues a Europe "travel ban"			
03/13	8 / 0	N/A	N/A
03/19: schools close			
03/20	109 / 0	+101 / +0	14 / 0
03/25: Alabama's first death			
03/27	643 / 1	+534 / +1	76 / 0
03/27: non-essential services close			
03/31: total tests = 6,553			
04/03: stay-at-home order			
04/03	1,550 / 21	+907 / +20	130 / 3
04/10	3,008 / 80	+1,458 / +59	208 / 8
04/12: Easter			
04/15: IFR (infection fatality rate) = 2.90%			
04/15: hospitalizations current = 402			
04/15: hospitalizations cumulative = 525			
04/17	4,572 / 141	+1,564 / +61	223 / 9
04/24	6,026 / 209	+1,454 / +68	208 / 10

DATE	CASES / DEATHS	WEEKLY INCREASE	DAILY AVERAGE
04/30: total tests = 96,860			
05/01	7,294 / 289	+1,268 / +80	181 / 11
05/08	9,375 / 383	+2,081 / +94	297 / 13
05/10: Mother's Day			
05/15: IFR (infection fatality rate) = 4.26%			
05/15: hospitalizations current = 519			
05/15: hospitalizations cumulative = 1,377			
05/15	11,373 / 483	+1,998 / +100	285 / 14
05/22	13,670 / 541	+2,297 / +58	328 / 8
05/25: Memorial Day			
05/26: George Floyd protests begin			
05/29	17,031 / 610	+3,361 / +69	480 / 10
05/31: total tests = 214,876			
NEW! 06/01: deaths/million population = 132			
06/05	19,387 / 676	+2,356 / +66	337 / 9
06/12	23,710 / 769	+4,323 / +93	618 / 13
06/15: IFR (infection fatality rate) = 2.95%			
06/15: hospitalizations current = 641			
06/15: hospitalizations cumulative = 2,259			
06/19	29,002 / 822	+5,292 / +53	756 / 8
06/21: Father's Day			
06/26	34,183 / 907	+5,181 / +85	740 / 12
06/30: total tests = 406,143			
07/01: deaths/million population = 198			
07/03	41,865 / 1,006	+7,682 / +99	1,097 / 14
07/04: Independence Day			
07/10	50,508 / 1,104	+8,643 / +98	1,235 / 14
07/15: IFR (infection fatality rate) = 2.05%			
07/15: hospitalizations current = 1,332			
07/15: hospitalizations cumulative = 7,291			
07/16: mask mandate			
07/17	63,091 / 1,265	+12,583 / +161	1,798 / 23
07/24	76,005 / 1,438	+12,914 / +173	1,845 / 25
07/31	87,723 / 1,580	+11,718 / +142	1.674 / 20
07/31: total tests = 687,022			
08/01: deaths/million population = 327			
08/07	98,301 / 1,735	+10,578 / +155	1,511 / 22
08/14	106,309 / 1,894	+8,008 / +159	1,144 / 23

DATE	CASES / DEATHS	WEEKLY INCREASE	DAILY AVERAGE
	08/15: IFR (infection fatality rate) = 1.76%		
	08/15: hospitalizations current = 1,259		
	08/15: hospitalizations cumulative = 12,607		
08/21	**112,770 / 1,990**	**+6,461 / +96**	**923 / 14**
08/28	**122,185 / 2,107**	**+9,415 / +117**	**1,345 / 17**
	08/31: total tests = 1,021,456		
	09/01: deaths/million population = 464		
09/04	**130,393 / 2,257**	**+8,208 / +150**	**1,173 / 21**
	09/07: Labor Day		
09/11	**136,703 / 2,333**	**+6,310 / +76**	**901 / 11**
	09/15: IFR (infection fatality rate) = 1.70%		
	09/15: hospitalizations current = 716		
	09/15: hospitalizations cumulative = 15,756		
09/18	**142,863 / 2,428**	**+6,160 / +95**	**880 / 14**
	NEW! 09/22: test positivity rate = 14.0%		
09/25	**150,658 / 2,491**	**+7,795 / +63**	**1,114 / 9**
	09/30: total tests = 1,204,459		
	10/01: deaths/million population = 520		
10/02	**156,598 / 2,550**	**+5,940 / +59**	**849 / 8**
10/09	**163,465 / 2,653**	**+6,867 / +103**	**981 / 15**
	10/15: IFR (infection fatality rate) = 1.63%		
	10/15: hospitalizations current = 844		
	10/15: hospitalizations cumulative = 18,635		
10/16	**170,374 / 2,786**	**+6,909 / +133**	**987 / 19**
	10/22: test positivity rate = 16.9%		
10/23	**180,916 / 2,859**	**+10,542 / +73**	**1,506 / 10**
10/30	**190,496 / 2,932**	**+9,580 / +73**	**1,369 / 10**
	10/31: total tests = 1,410,946		
	11/01: deaths/million population = 606		
	11/03: Election Day		
11/06	**200,714 / 3,049**	**+10,218 / +117**	**1,460 / 17**
	11/07: Biden wins election		
	Alabama votes: 62.0% Trump / 36.6% Biden		
11/13	**213,617 / 3,231**	**+12,903 / +182**	**1,843 / 26**
	11/15: IFR (infection fatality rate) = 1.49%		
	11/15: hospitalizations current = 1,195		
	11/15: hospitalizations cumulative = 22,275		
11/20	**228,373 / 3,451**	**+14,756 / +220**	**2,108 / 31**

DATE	CASES / DEATHS	WEEKLY INCREASE	DAILY AVERAGE
11/22: test positivity rate = 23.2%			
11/26: Thanksgiving			
11/27	**242,874 / 3,572**	**+14,501 / +121**	**2,072 / 17**
11/30: total tests = 1,676,710			
12/01: deaths/million population = 757			
12/04	**264,199 / 3,831**	**+21,325 / +259**	**3,046 / 37**
12/11	**288,775 / 4,086**	**+24,576 / +255**	**3,511 / 36**
12/14: first COVID-19 vaccinations given in the U.S.			
12/15: IFR (infection fatality rate) = 1.37%			
12/15: hospitalizations current = 2,353			
12/15: hospitalizations cumulative = 29,259			
12/18	**315,683 / 4,296**	**+26,908 / +210**	**3,844 / 30**
12/22: new U.K. variant identified in the U.S.			
12/22: test positivity rate = 40.4%			
12/25: Christmas			
12/25	**342,426 / 4,680**	**+26,743 / +384**	**3,820 / 55**
12/31: total tests = 1,973,198			
12/31: deaths/million population = 994			
01/01: New Year's Day			
01/01: CFR (case fatality rate) = 2.35% (23.5X more deadly than influenza at 0.1%)			
01/01/2021	**365,747 / 4,872**	**+23,321 / +192**	**3,332 / 27**

BONUS: Enjoy additional week from upcoming book: PANDEMIC 2021: The U.S. Edition

01/06: right-wing mob insurrection at U.S. Capitol as Joe Biden confirmed president
01/08: Twitter permanently bans Trump's account

01/08	**394,287 / 5,191**	**+28,540 / +319**	**4,077 / 46**

*The daily average column is rounded to the nearest whole person. The infection fatality rate (IFR) is the number of deaths divided by the number of confirmed cases. The case fatality rate (CFR), shown only at the end of the year, is the number of deaths divided by the number of confirmed cases *which have had an outcome* (either recovery or death). The CFR excludes active cases.

CHAPTER 4

~ ALASKA *~*

POPULATION AS OF MARCH, 2020: 734,002
Republican Governor Mike Dunleavy
VOTED RED: Trump 52.8% / Biden 42.8%

DATE	CASES / DEATHS	WEEKLY INCREASE	DAILY AVERAGE
01/30: WHO declares Public Health Emergency of International Concern			
01/31: Trump issues a China "travel ban"			
03/03: Alaska's first 3 cases			
03/06	**6 / 0**	**N/A**	**N/A**
03/09: Alaska declares Public Health Emergency			
03/11: WHO declares COVID-19 a pandemic			
03/13: Trump declares a National Emergency			
03/13: Trump issues a Europe "travel ban"			
03/13	**23 / 0**	**+17 / +0**	**2 / 0**
03/15: hospitalizations current = 0			
03/15: hospitalizations cumulative = 1			
03/16: schools close			
03/20	**114 / 0**	**+91 / +0**	**13 / 0**
03/24: Alaska's first death			
03/27	**200 / 2**	**+86 / +2**	**12 / 0**
03/28: non-essential services close / stay-at-home order			
03/31: total tests = 5,117			
04/03	**263 / 3**	**+63 / +1**	**9 / 0**
04/10	**312 / 7**	**+49 / +4**	**7 / 1**
04/12: Easter			
04/15: IFR (infection fatality rate) = 2.74%			
04/15: hospitalizations current = 0			
04/15: hospitalizations cumulative = 33			

DATE	CASES / DEATHS	WEEKLY INCREASE	DAILY AVERAGE
04/17	338 / 9	+26 / +2	4 / 0
04/24	359 / 9	+21 / +0	3 / 0
04/30: total tests = 21,399			
05/01	375 / 9	+16 / +0	2 / 0
05/08	385 / 10	+10 / +1	1 / 0
05/10: Mother's Day			
05/15: IFR (infection fatality rate) = 2.55%			
05/15: hospitalizations current = 8			
05/15: hospitalizations cumulative = 43			
05/15	393 / 10	+8 / +0	1 / 0
05/22	404 / 10	+11 / +0	2 / 0
05/25: Memorial Day			
05/26: George Floyd protests begin			
05/29	430 / 10	+26 / +0	4 / 0
05/31: total tests = 51,695			
NEW! 06/01: deaths/million population = 14			
06/05	524 / 10	+94 / +0	13 / 0
06/12	625 / 12	+101 / +2	14 / 0
06/15: IFR (infection fatality rate) = 1.81%			
06/15: hospitalizations current = 21			
06/15: hospitalizations cumulative = 60			
06/19	722 / 12	+97 / +0	14 / 0
06/21: Father's Day			
06/26	836 / 14	+114 / +2	16 / 0
06/30: total tests = 112,185			
07/01: deaths/million population = 19			
07/03	1,063 / 15	+227 / +1	32 / 0
07/04: Independence Day			
07/10	1,323 / 17	+260 / +2	37 / 0
07/15: IFR (infection fatality rate) = 1.04%			
07/15: hospitalizations current = 32			
07/15: hospitalizations cumulative = 102			
07/17	1,733 / 17	+410 / +0	59 / 0
07/24	2,249 / 19	+516 / +2	74 / 0
07/31	2,990 / 23	+741 / +4	106 / 1
07/31: total tests = 233,106			
08/01: deaths/million population = 33			
08/07	3,536 / 25	+546 / +2	78 / 0

DATE	CASES / DEATHS	WEEKLY INCREASE	DAILY AVERAGE
08/14	**4,073 / 27**	**+537 / +2**	**77 / 0**

08/15: IFR (infection fatality rate) = 0.67%
08/15: hospitalizations current = 36
08/15: hospitalizations cumulative = 197

08/21	**4,588 / 30**	**+515 / +3**	**74 / 0**
08/28	**5,092 / 37**	**+504 / +7**	**72 / 1**

08/30: total tests = 385,002
09/01: deaths/million population = 57

09/04	**5,586 / 40**	**+494 / +3**	**71 / 0**

09/07: Labor Day

09/11	**6,113 / 43**	**+527 / +3**	**75 / 0**

09/15: IFR (infection fatality rate) = 0.69%
09/15: hospitalizations current = 44
09/15: hospitalizations cumulative = 278

09/18	**6,658 / 45**	**+545 / +2**	**78 / 0**

NEW! 09/22: test positivity rate = 2.4%

09/25	**7,254 / 51**	**+596 / +6**	**85 / 1**

09/30: total tests = 469,290
10/01: deaths/million population = 78

10/02	**8,074 / 57**	**+820 / +6**	**117 / 1**
10/09	**9,182 / 60**	**+1,108 / +3**	**158 / 0**

10/15: IFR (infection fatality rate) = 0.63%
10/15: hospitalizations current = 60
10/15: hospitalizations cumulative = 365

10/16	**10,549 / 66**	**+1,367 / +6**	**195 / 1**

10/22: test positivity rate = 5.2%

10/23	**12,118 / 68**	**+1,569 / +2**	**224 / 0**
10/30	**14,837 / 81**	**+2,719 / +13**	**338 / 2**

10/31: total tests = 604,207
11/01: deaths/million population = 113
11/03: Election Day

11/06	**17,597 / 84**	**+2,760 / +3**	**394 / 0**

11/07: Biden wins election

11/13	**21,275 / 97**	**+3,678 / +13**	**525 / 2**

11/15: IFR (infection fatality rate) = 0.43%
11/15: hospitalizations current = 141
11/15: hospitalizations cumulative = 550

11/20	**25,369 / 100**	**+4,094 / +3**	**585 / 0**

DATE	CASES / DEATHS	WEEKLY INCREASE	DAILY AVERAGE
11/26: Thanksgiving			
11/27	**29,554 / 118**	**+4,185 / +18**	**598 / 3**
11/30: total tests = 1,024,643			
12/01: deaths/million population = 165			
12/04	**34,041 / 141**	**+4,487 / +23**	**641 / 3**
12/11	**38,584 / 157**	**+4,543 / +16**	**649 / 2**
12/14: first COVID-19 vaccinations given in the U.S.			
12/15: IFR (infection fatality rate) = 0.44%			
12/15: hospitalizations current = 140			
12/15: hospitalizations cumulative = 908			
12/18	**41,905 / 182**	**+3,321 / +25**	**474 / 4**
12/22: new U.K. variant identified in the U.S.			
12/22: test positivity rate 4.5%			
12/25: Christmas			
12/25	**43,629 / 198**	**+1,724 / +16**	**246 / 2**
12/31: total tests = 1,275,750			
12/31: deaths/million population = 280			
01/01: New Year's Day			
01/01: CFR (case fatality rate) = N/A (active case counts are not available)			
01/01/2021	**45,461 / 205**	**+1,832 / +7**	**262 / 1**

BONUS: Enjoy additional week from upcoming book: PANDEMIC 2021: The U.S. Edition

01/06: right-wing mob insurrection at U.S. Capitol as Joe Biden confirmed president			
01/08: Twitter permanently bans Trump's account			
01/08	**48,063 / 222**	**+2,602 / +17**	**372 / 2**

*The daily average column is rounded to the nearest whole person. The infection fatality rate (IFR) is the number of deaths divided by the number of confirmed cases. The case fatality rate (CFR), shown only at the end of the year, is the number of deaths divided by the number of confirmed cases *which have had an outcome* (either recovery or death). The CFR excludes active cases.

CHAPTER 5

~ ARIZONA *~*

POPULATION AS OF MARCH, 2020: 7,378,494
Republican Governor Doug Ducey
VOTED BLUE: Biden 49.4% / Trump 49.0%

DATE	CASES / DEATHS	WEEKLY INCREASE	DAILY AVERAGE
01/26: Arizona's first case			
01/30: WHO declares Public Health Emergency of International Concern			
01/31: Trump issues a China "travel ban"			
03/06	**5 / 0**	**+4 / +0**	**1 / 0**
03/11: Arizona declares Public Health Emergency			
03/11: WHO declares COVID-19 a pandemic			
03/13: Trump declares a National Emergency			
03/13: Trump issues a Europe "travel ban"			
03/13	**9 / 0**	**+4 / +0**	**1 / 0**
03/15: hospitalizations current = 0			
03/15: hospitalizations cumulative = 36			
03/16: schools close			
03/20	**63 / 0**	**+54 / +0**	**8 / 0**
03/21: Arizona's first death			
03/27	**665 / 13**	**+602 / +13**	**86 / 2**
03/30: non-essential services close / stay-at-home order			
03/31: total tests = 21,438			
04/03	**1,769 / 41**	**+1,104 / +28**	**158 / 4**
04/10	**3,112 / 97**	**+1,343 / +56**	**192 / 8**
04/12: Easter			
04/15: IFR (infection fatality rate) = 3.58%			
04/15: hospitalizations current = 590			
04/15: hospitalizations cumulative = 1,213			

DATE	CASES / DEATHS	WEEKLY INCREASE	DAILY AVERAGE
04/17	4,507 / 169	+1,395 / +72	199 / 10
04/24	6,045 / 266	+1,538 / +97	220 / 14
04/30: total tests = 77,997			
05/01	7,962 / 330	+1,917 / +64	274 / 9
05/08	10,526 / 517	+2,564 / +187	366 / 27
05/10: Mother's Day			
05/15: IFR (infection fatality rate) = 4.92%			
05/15: hospitalizations current = 808			
05/15 hospitalizations cumulative = 2,636			
05/15	13,169 / 651	+2,643 / +134	378 / 19
05/22	15,608 / 775	+2,439 / +124	348 / 18
05/25: Memorial Day			
05/26: George Floyd protests begin			
05/29	18,465 / 885	+2,857 / +110	408 / 16
05/31: total tests = 307,715			
NEW! 06/01: deaths/million population = 124			
06/05	24,332 / 1,012	+5,867 / +127	838 / 18
06/12	32,918 / 1,144	+8,586 / +132	1,227 / 19
06/15: IFR (infection fatality rate) = 3.25%			
06/15: hospitalizations current = 1,449			
06/15: hospitalizations cumulative = 4,182			
06/19	46,689 / 1,312	+13,771 / +168	1,967 / 24
06/21: Father's Day			
06/23: Trump rally			
06/26	66,458 / 1,535	+19,769 / +223	2,824 / 32
06/30: total tests = 701,834			
07/01: deaths/million population = 236			
07/03	91,858 / 1,788	+25,400 / +253	3,629 / 36
07/04: Independence Day			
07/10	116,892 / 2,082	+25,034 / +294	3,576 / 42
07/15: IFR (infection fatality rate) = 1.85%			
07/15: hospitalizations current = 3,493			
07/15: hospitalizations cumulative = 6,103			
07/17	138,523 / 2,583	+21,631 / +501	3,090 / 72
07/24	156,301 / 3,142	+17,778 / +559	2,540 / 80
07/31	174,010 / 3,694	+17,709 / +552	2,530 / 79
07/31: total tests = 1,161,640			
08/01: deaths/million population = 515			

DATE	CASES / DEATHS	WEEKLY INCREASE	DAILY AVERAGE
08/07	185,053 / 4,081	+11,043 / +387	1,578 / 55
08/14	191,721 / 4,423	+6,668 / +342	953 / 49

08/15: IFR (infection fatality rate) = 2.33%
08/15: hospitalizations current = 1,282
08/15: hospitalizations cumulative = 20,795
08/18: Trump rally

08/21	196,899 / 4,688	+5,178 / +265	740 / 38
08/28	200,658 / 4,978	+3,759 / +290	537 / 41

08/31: total tests = 1,522,472
09/01: deaths/million population = 715

09/04	204,681 / 5,171	+4,023 / +193	575 / 28

09/07: Labor Day

09/11	207,523 / 5,288	+2,842 / +117	406 / 17

09/14: Trump rally
09/15: IFR (infection fatality rate) = 2.55%
09/15: hospitalizations current = 550
09/15: hospitalizations cumulative = 21,800

09/18	212,942 / 5,451	+5,419 / +163	774 / 23

NEW! 09/22: test positivity rate = 6.4%

09/25	216,367 / 5,587	+3,425 / +136	489 / 19

09/30: total tests = 1,773,468
10/01: deaths/million population = 782

10/02	219,763 / 5,693	+3,396 / +106	485 / 15
10/09	224,084 / 5,746	+4,321 / +53	617 / 8

10/15: IFR (infection fatality rate) = 2.53%
10/15: hospitalizations current = 726
10/15: hospitalizations cumulative = 20,462

10/16	229,486 / 5,806	+5,402 / +60	772 / 9

10/19: 2 Trump rallies
10/22: test positivity rate = 9.1%

10/23	235,882 / 5,865	+6,396 / +59	914 / 8

10/28: 2 Trump rallies

10/30	244,054 / 5,934	+8,172 / +69	1,167 / 10

10/31: total tests = 20,091,090
11/01: deaths/million population = 822
11/03: Election Day

11/06	254,764 / 6,109	+10,710 / +175	1,530 / 25

11/07: Biden wins election

DATE	CASES / DEATHS	WEEKLY INCREASE	DAILY AVERAGE
11/13	269,577 / 6,257	+14,813 / +148	2,116 / 21

11/15: IFR (infection fatality rate) = 2.28%
11/15: hospitalizations current = 1,506
11/15: hospitalizations cumulative = 23,049

11/20	291,696 / 6,427	+22,119 / +170	3,160 / 24

11/22: test positivity rate = 18.2%
11/26: Thanksgiving

11/27	318,638 / 6,588	+26,942 / +161	3,849 / 23

11/30: total tests = 2,654,075
12/01: deaths/million population = 926

12/04	352,101 / 6,885	+33,463 / +297	4,780 / 42
12/11	394,512 / 7,245	+42,411 / +360	6,059 / 51

12/14: first COVID-19 vaccinations given in the U.S.
12/15: IFR (infection fatality rate) = 1.75%
12/15: hospitalizations current = 3,702
12/15: hospitalizations cumulative = 31,266

12/18	442,671 / 7,819	+48,159 / +574	6,880 / 82

12/22: new U.K. variant identified in the U.S.
12/22: test positivity rate = 13.1%
12/25: Christmas

12/25	486,935 / 8,409	+44,264 / +590	6,323 / 84

12/31: total tests = 3,269,908
12/31: deaths/million population = 1,239
01/01: New Year's Day
01/01: CFR (case fatality rate) = 10.61% (106.1X more deadly than influenza at 0.1%)

01/01/2021	530,267 / 9,015	+43,332 / +606	6,190 / 87

BONUS: Enjoy additional week from upcoming book: PANDEMIC 2021: The U.S. Edition
01/06: right-wing mob insurrection at U.S. Capitol as Joe Biden confirmed president
01/08: Twitter permanently bans Trump's account

01/08	596,251 / 9,938	+65,984 / +923	9,426 / 132

*The daily average column is rounded to the nearest whole person. The infection fatality rate (IFR) is the number of deaths divided by the number of confirmed cases. The case fatality rate (CFR), shown only at the end of the year, is the number of deaths divided by the number of confirmed cases *which have had an outcome* (either recovery or death). The CFR excludes active cases.

CHAPTER 6

~ ARKANSAS *~*

POPULATION AS OF MARCH, 2020: 3,038,099
Republican Governor Asa Hutchinson
VOTED RED: Trump 62.4% / Biden 34.8%

DATE	CASES / DEATHS	WEEKLY INCREASE	DAILY AVERAGE
01/30: WHO declares Public Health Emergency of International Concern			
01/31: Trump issues a China "travel ban"			
03/11: Arkansas' first case			
03/11: Arkansas declares [State of] Emergency			
03/11: WHO declares COVID-19 a pandemic			
03/13	9 / 0	+8 / +0	+1 / +0
03/13: Trump issues a Europe "travel ban"			
03/17: schools close			
03/20	100 / 0	+91 / +0	13 / 0
03/24: Arkansas' first 2 deaths			
03/27	386 / 3	+352 / +3	50 / 0
03/31: total tests = 4,735			
04/03	738 / 12	+464 / +12	66 / 2
04/10	1,202 / 24	+519 / +12	74 / 2
04/12: Easter			
04/15: IFR (infection fatality rate) = 2.13%			
04/15: hospitalizations current = 83			
04/15: hospitalizations cumulative = 130			
04/17	1,700 / 37	+498 / +13	71 / 2
04/24	2,810 / 47	+1,110 / +10	159 / 1
04/30: total tests = 51,582			
05/01	3,321 / 64	+511 / +17	73 / 2
05/08	3,747 / 88	+426 / +24	61 / 3

DATE	CASES / DEATHS	WEEKLY INCREASE	DAILY AVERAGE
	05/10: Mother's Day		
	05/15: IFR (infection fatality rate) = 2.24%		
	05/15: hospitalizations current = 65		
	05/15: hospitalizations cumulative = 520		
05/15	4,463 / 98	+716 / +10	102 / 1
05/22	5,612 / 113	+1,149 / +15	164 / 2
	05/25: Memorial Day		
	05/26: George Floyd protests begin		
05/29	6,777 / 132	+1,165 / +19	166 / 3
	05/31: total tests = 126,497		
	NEW! 06/01: deaths/million population = 44		
06/05	8,651 / 152	+1,874 / +20	268 / 3
06/12	11,547 / 176	+2,896 / +24	414 / 3
	06/15: IFR (infection fatality rate) = 1.41%		
	06/15: hospitalizations current = 206		
	06/15: hospitalizations cumulative = 1,003		
06/19	14,631 / 214	+3,084 / +38	441 / 5
	06/21: Father's Day		
06/26	18,740 / 249	+4,109 / +35	587 / 5
	06/30: total tests = 311,203		
	07/01: deaths/million population = 92		
07/03	22,622 / 281	+3,882 / +32	555 / 5
	07/04: Independence Day		
07/10	26,803 / 313	+4,181 / +32	597 / 5
	07/15: IFR (infection fatality rate) = 1.11%		
	07/15: hospitalizations current = 458		
	07/15: hospitalizations cumulative = 1,948		
07/17	31,762 / 353	+4,959 / +40	708 / 6
	07/20: mask mandate		
07/24	37,249 / 394	+5,487 / +41	784 / 6
07/31	42,511 / 453	+5,262 / +59	752 / 8
	07/31: total tests = 509,028		
	08/01: deaths/million population = 152		
08/07	48,039 / 521	+5,528 / +68	790 / 10
08/14	52,392 / 587	+4,353 / +66	622 / 9
	08/15: IFR (infection fatality rate) = 1.13%		
	08/15: hospitalizations current = 464		
	08/15: hospitalizations cumulative = 3,562		

DATE	CASES / DEATHS	WEEKLY INCREASE	DAILY AVERAGE
08/21	55,652 / 663	+3,260 / +76	466 / 11
08/28	59,583 / 756	+3,931 / +93	562 / 13
	08/31: total tests = 765,411		
	09/01: deaths/million population = 292		
09/04	64,175 / 873	+4,592 / +117	656 / 17
	09/07: Labor Day		
09/11	67,911 / 953	+3,736 / +80	534 / 11
	09/15: IFR (infection fatality rate) = 1.42%		
	09/15: hospitalizations current = 389		
	09/15: hospitalizations cumulative = 4,802		
09/18	74,082 / 1,173	+6,171 / +220	882 / 31
	NEW! 09/22: test positivity rate = 21%		
09/25	79,946 / 1,266	+5,864 / +93	838 / 13
	09/30: total tests = 1,066,849		
	10/01: deaths/million population = 461		
10/02	85,779 / 1,391	+5,833 / +125	833 / 18
10/09	91,312 / 1,530	+5,533 / +139	790 / 20
	10/15: IFR (infection fatality rate) = 1.70%		
	10/15: hospitalizations current = 587		
	10/15: hospitalizations cumulative = 6,199		
10/16	97,539 / 1,655	+6,227 / +125	890 / 18
	10/22: test positivity rate = 9.0		
10/23	104,135 / 1,782	+6,596 / +127	942 / 18
10/30	110,874 / 1,900	+6,739 / +118	963 / 17
	10/31: total tests = 1,408,192		
	11/01: deaths/million population = 649		
	11/03: Election Day		
11/06	119,230 / 2,056	+8,356 / +156	1,194 / 22
	11/07: Biden wins election		
11/13	130,318 / 2,148	+11,088 / +92	1,584 / 13
	11/15: IFR (infection fatality rate) = 1.64%		
	11/15: hospitalizations = 830		
	11/15: hospitalizations cumulative = 7,876		
11/20	141,916 / 2,321	+11,598 / +173	1,657 / 25
	11/22: test positivity rate = 14.5%		
	11/26: Thanksgiving		
11/27	153,677 / 2,436	+11,761 / +115	1,680 / 16
	11/30: total tests = 1,848,132		

DATE	CASES / DEATHS	WEEKLY INCREASE	DAILY AVERAGE
	12/01: deaths/million population = 836		
12/04	**167,137 / 2,586**	**+13,460 / +150**	**1,923 / 21**
12/11	**181,524 / 2,875**	**+14,387 / +289**	**2,055 / 41**
	12/14: first COVID-19 vaccinations given in the U.S.		
	12/15: IFR (infection fatality rate) = 1.59%		
	12/15: hospitalizations current = 1,070		
	12/15: hospitalizations cumulative = 10,096		
12/18	**197,421 / 3,139**	**+15,897 / +264**	**2,271 / 38**
	12/22: new U.K. variant identified in the U.S.		
	12/22: test positivity rate = 18.7%		
	12/25: Christmas		
12/25	**213,267 / 3,438**	**+15,846 / +299**	**2,264 / 43**
	12/31: total tests = 2,297,510		
	12/31: deaths/million population = 1,218		
	01/01: New Year's Day		
	01/01: CFR (case fatality rate) = 1.81% (18.1X more deadly than influenza at 0.1%)		
01/01/2021	**229,442 / 3,711**	**+16,175 / +273**	**2,311 / 39**

BONUS: Enjoy additional week from upcoming book: PANDEMIC 2021: The U.S. Edition
01/06: right-wing mob insurrection at U.S. Capitol as Joe Biden confirmed president
01/08: Twitter permanently bans Trump's account

01/08	**248,860 / 3,966**	**+19,418 / +255**	**2,774 / 36**

*The daily average column is rounded to the nearest whole person. The infection fatality rate (IFR) is the number of deaths divided by the number of confirmed cases. The case fatality rate (CFR), shown only at the end of the year, is the number of deaths divided by the number of confirmed cases *which have had an outcome* (either recovery or death). The CFR excludes active cases.

CHAPTER 7

~ CALIFORNIA *~*

POPULATION AS OF MARCH, 2020: 39,937,489
Democratic Governor Gavin Newsom
VOTED BLUE: Biden 63.5% / Trump 34.3%

DATE	CASES / DEATHS	WEEKLY INCREASE	DAILY AVERAGE
	01/26: California's first 2 cases		
	01/30: WHO declares Public Health Emergency of International Concern		
	01/31: Trump issues a China "travel ban"		
02/29	**6 / 0**	**+4 / +0**	**1 / 0**
	03/04: California's first death		
	03/04: California declares State of Emergency		
03/06	**89 / 1**	**+83 / +1**	**12 / 0**
	03/11: WHO declares COVID-19 a pandemic		
	03/13: Trump declares a National Emergency		
	03/13: Trump issues a Europe "travel ban"		
03/13	**247 / 5**	**+158 / +4**	**23 / 1**
	03/15: IFR (infection fatality rate) = 1.53%		
	03/19: schools close / non-essential services close / stay-at-home order		
03/20	**1,224 / 23**	**+977 / +18**	**140 / 3**
03/27	**4,643 / 101**	**+3,419 / +78**	**488 / 11**
	03/31: total tests = 27,654		
04/03	**12,026 / 276**	**+7,383 / +175**	**1,055 / 25**
04/10	**21,073 / 584**	**+9,047 / +308**	**1,292 / 44**
	04/12: Easter		
	04/15: IFR (infection fatality rate) = 3.22%		
	04/15: hospitalizations current = 5,163		
	04/15: hospitalizations cumulative = not given for this state		
04/17	**29,175 / 1,041**	**+8,102 / +457**	**1,157 / 65**

DATE	CASES / DEATHS	WEEKLY INCREASE	DAILY AVERAGE
04/24	40,812 / 1,594	+11,637 / +553	1,662 / 79
04/30: total tests = 654,985			
05/01	51,775 / 2,111	+10,963 / +517	1,566 / 74
05/08	64,107 / 2,627	+12,332 / +516	1,762 / 74
05/10: Mother's Day			
05/15: IFR (infection fatality rate) = 4.08%			
05/15: hospitalizations current = 4,519			
05/15	76,819 / 3,153	+12,712 / +526	1,816 / 75
05/22	90,588 / 3,688	+13,769 / +535	1,967 / 76
05/25: Memorial Day			
05/26: George Floyd protests begin			
05/29	106,744 / 4,137	+16,156 / +449	2,308 / 64
05/31: total tests = 1,888,595			
NEW! 06/01: deaths/million population = 107			
06/05	126,408 / 4,558	+19,664 / +421	2,809 / 60
06/12	147,132 / 4,988	+20,724 / +430	2,961 / 61
06/15: IFR (infection fatality rate) = 3.29%			
06/15: hospitalizations current = 4,323			
06/18: mask mandate			
06/19	170,615 / 5,427	+23,483 / +439	3,355 / 63
06/21: Father's Day			
06/26	206,623 / 5,872	+36,008 / +445	5,144 / 64
06/30: total tests = 4,168,509			
07/01: deaths/million population = 156			
07/03	252,252 / 6,314	+45,629 / +442	6,518 / 63
07/04: Independence Day			
07/10	312,104 / 6,952	+59,852 / +638	8,550 / 91
07/15: IFR (infection fatality rate) =2.07%			
07/15: hospitalizations current = 8,353			
07/17	374,162 / 7,611	+62,058 / +659	8,865 / 94
07/24	442,938 / 8,337	+68,776 / +726	9,825 / 104
07/31	501,909 / 9,194	+58,971 / +857	8,424 / 122
07/31: total tests = 7,811,041			
08/01: deaths/million population = 237			
08/07	549,154 / 10,209	+47,245 / +1,015	6,749 / 145
08/14	613,000 / 11,148	+63,846 / +939	9,121 / 134
08/15: IFR (infection fatality rate) = 1.81%			
08/15: hospitalizations = 6,327			

44

DATE	CASES / DEATHS	WEEKLY INCREASE	DAILY AVERAGE
08/21	659,803 / 11,987	+46,803 / +839	6,686 / 120
08/28	698,186 / 12,836	+38,383 / +849	5,483 / 121
08/30: total tests = 11,916,323			
09/01: deaths/million population = 347			
09/04	731,453 / 13,643	+33,267 / +807	4,752 / 115
09/07: Labor Day			
09/11	755,714 / 14,262	+24,261 / +619	3,466 / 88
09/15: IFR (infection fatality rate) = 1.90%			
09/15: hospitalizations current = 3,735			
09/18	779,945 / 14,912	+24,231 / +650	3,462 / 93
NEW! 09/22: test positivity rate = 2.8%			
09/25	804,174 / 15,535	+24,229 / +623	3,461 / 89
09/30: total tests = 14,868,431			
10/01: deaths/million population = 407			
10/02	826,690 / 16,075	+22,516 / +540	3,217 / 77
10/09	849,552 / 16,509	+22,862 / +434	3,266 / 62
10/15: IFR (infection fatality rate) = 1.94%			
10/15: hospitalizations current = 3,078			
10/16	871,676 / 16,905	+22,124 / +396	3,161 / 57
10/18: Trump fundraiser			
10/22: test positivity rate = 2.7%			
10/23	900,483 / 17,317	+28,807 / +412	4,115 / 59
10/30	929,944 / 17,627	+29,461 / +310	4,209 / 44
10/31: total tests = 18,602,317			
11/01: deaths/million population = 447			
11/03: Election Day			
11/06	965,523 / 17,939	+35,579 / +312	5,083 / 45
11/07: Biden wins election			
11/13	1,017,123 / 18,221	+51,600 / +282	7,371 / 40
11/15: IFR (infection fatality rate) = 1.77%			
11/15: hospitalizations current = 4,454			
11/20	1,094,083 / 18,645	+76,960 / +424	10,994 / 61
11/22: test positivity rate = 6.0%			
11/26: Thanksgiving			
11/27	1,190,665 / 19,099	+96,582 / +454	13,797 / 65
11/30: total tests = 24,299,126			
12/01: deaths/million population = 492			
12/04	1,315,352 / 19,790	+124,687 / +691	17,812 / 99

DATE	CASES / DEATHS	WEEKLY INCREASE	DAILY AVERAGE
12/11	1,525,790 / 20,851	+210,438 / +1,061	30,063 / 152

12/14: first COVID-19 vaccinations given in the U.S.
12/15: IFR (infection fatality rate) = 1.30%
12/15: hospitalizations current = 15,198

12/18	1,809,469 / 22,437	+283,679 / +1,586	40,526 / 227

12/22: new U.K. variant identified in the U.S.
12/22: test positivity rate = 13.3%
12/25: Christmas

12/25	2,083,533 / 24,159	+274,064 / +1,722	39,152 / 246

12/31: total tests = 33,058,311
12/31: deaths/million population = 657
01/01: New Year's Day
01/01: CFR (case fatality rate) = 2.61% (26.1X more deadly than influenza at 0.1%)

01/01/2021	2,345,657 / 26,294	+262,124 / +2,135	37,446 / 305

BONUS: Enjoy additional week from upcoming book: PANDEMIC 2021: The U.S. Edition
01/06: right-wing mob insurrection at U.S. Capitol as Joe Biden confirmed president
01/08: Twitter permanently bans Trump's account

01/08	2,629,498 / 29,222	+283,841 / +2,928	40,549 / 418

*The daily average column is rounded to the nearest whole person. The infection fatality rate (IFR) is the number of deaths divided by the number of confirmed cases. The case fatality rate (CFR), shown only at the end of the year, is the number of deaths divided by the number of confirmed cases *which have had an outcome* (either recovery or death). The CFR excludes active cases.

CHAPTER 8

~ COLORADO *~*

POPULATION AS OF MARCH, 2020: 5,845,526
Democratic Governor Jared Polis
VOTED BLUE: Biden 55.4% / Trump 41.9%

DATE	CASES / DEATHS	WEEKLY INCREASE	DAILY AVERAGE
	01/30: WHO declares Public Health Emergency of International Concern		
	01/31: Trump issues a China "travel ban"		
	03/05: Colorado's first 2 cases		
03/06	**8 / 0**	**+6 / +0**	**1 / 0**
	03/10: Colorado declares Disaster Emergency		
	03/11: WHO declares COVID-19 a pandemic		
	03/13: Colorado's first death		
	03/13: Trump declares a National Emergency		
	03/13: Trump issues a Europe "travel ban"		
03/13	**77 / 1**	**+69 / +1**	**10 / 0**
	03/15: IFR (infection fatality rate) = 16%		
03/20	**363 / 4**	**+286 / +3**	**41 / 0**
	03/23: schools close		
	03/26: non-essential services close / stay-at-home order		
03/27	**1,734 / 31**	**+1,371 / +27**	**196 / 4**
	03/31: total tests = 7,701		
04/03	**4,173 / 111**	**+2,439 / +80**	**348 / 11**
04/10	**6,510 / 250**	**+2,337 / +139**	**334 / 20**
	04/12: Easter		
	04/15: IFR (infection fatality rate) = 4.31%		
	04/15: hospitalizations current = 859		
	04/15: hospitalizations cumulative = 1,636		
04/17	**9,047 / 391**	**+2,537 / +141**	**362 / 20**

DATE	CASES / DEATHS	WEEKLY INCREASE	DAILY AVERAGE
04/24	**12,256 / 674**	**+3,209 / +283**	**458 / 40**
04/30: total tests = 78,179			
05/01	**15,768 / 820**	**+3,512 / +146**	**502 / 21**
05/08	**18,827 / 960**	**+3,059 / +140**	**437 / 20**
05/10: Mother's Day			
05/15: IFR (infection fatality rate) = 5.24%			
05/15: hospitalizations current = 671			
05/15: hospitalizations cumulative = 3,842			
05/15	**21,232 / 1,150**	**+2,405 / +190**	**344 / 27**
05/22	**23,487 / 1,324**	**+2,255 / +174**	**322 / 25**
05/25: Memorial Day			
05/26: George Floyd Protests Begin			
05/29	**25,613 / 1,436**	**+2,126 / +112**	**304 / 16**
05/31: total tests = 178,196			
NEW! 06/01: deaths/million population = 249			
06/05	**27,615 / 1,524**	**+2,002 / +88**	**286 / 13**
06/12	**28,822 / 1,595**	**+1,207 / +71**	**172 / 10**
06/15: IFR (infection fatality rate) = 5.48%			
06/15: hospitalizations current = 276			
06/15: hospitalizations cumulative = 5,269			
06/19	**30,187 / 1,643**	**+1,365 / +48**	**195 / 7**
06/21: Father's Day			
06/26	**31,796 / 1,673**	**+1,609 / +30**	**230 / 4**
06/30: total tests = 324,632			
07/01: deaths/million population = 295			
07/03	**33,612 / 1,701**	**+1,816 / +28**	**259 / 4**
07/04: Independence Day			
07/10	**36,191 / 1,724**	**+2,579 / +23**	**368 / 3**
07/15: IFR (infection fatality rate) = 4.57%			
07/15: hospitalizations current = 389			
07/15: hospitalizations cumulative = 5,950			
07/17: mask mandate			
07/17	**39,344 / 1,751**	**+3,153 / +27**	**450 / 4**
07/24	**42,980 / 1,790**	**+3,636 / +39**	**519 / 6**
07/31	**46,809 / 1,838**	**+3,829 / +48**	**547 / 7**
07/31: total tests = 530,220			
08/01: deaths/million population = 320			
08/07	**49,893 / 1,857**	**+3,084 / +19**	**441 / 3**

DATE	CASES / DEATHS	WEEKLY INCREASE	DAILY AVERAGE
08/14	52,538 / 1,888	+2,645 / +31	378 / 4
08/15: IFR (infection fatality rate) = 3.59%			
08/15: hospitalizations current = 236			
08/15: hospitalizations cumulative = 6,727			
08/21	54,586 / 1,910	+2,048 / +22	293 / 3
08/28	56,773 / 1,937	+2,187 / +27	312 / 4
08/31: total tests = 738,563			
09/01: deaths/million population = 342			
09/04	58,655 / 1,966	+1,882 / +29	269 / 4
09/07: Labor Day			
09/11	60,492 / 1,985	+1,837 / +19	262 / 3
09/15: IFR (infection fatality rate) = 3.17%			
09/15: hospitalizations current = 273			
09/15: hospitalizations cumulative = 7,262			
09/18	63,750 / 2,009	+3,258 / +24	465 / 3
NEW! 09/22: test positivity rate = 4.4%			
09/25	67,926 / 2,037	+4,176 / +28	597 / 4
09/30: total tests = 932,914			
10/01: deaths/million population = 357			
10/02	71,898 / 2,057	+3,972 / +20	567 / 3
10/09	76,619 / 2,103	+4,721 / +46	674 / 7
10/15: IFR (infection fatality rate) = 2.64%			
10/15: hospitalizations current = 420			
10/15: hospitalizations cumulative = 8,127			
10/16	83,230 / 2,172	+6,611 / +69	944 / 10
10/22: test positivity rate = 5.8%			
10/23	91,572 / 2,211	+8,342 / +39	1,192 / 6
10/30	104,426 / 2,278	+12,854 / +67	1,836 / 10
10/31: total tests = 1, 222,226			
11/01: deaths/million population = 397			
11/03: Election Day			
11/06	124,469 / 2,376	+20,043 / +98	2,863 / 14
11/07: Biden wins election			
11/13	154,038 / 2,504	+29,569 / +128	4,224 / 18
11/15: IFR (infection fatality rate) = 1.56%			
11/15: hospitalizations current = 1,417			
11/15: hospitalizations cumulative = 11,124			
11/20	188,566 / 2,745	+34,528 / +241	4,933 / 34

DATE	CASES / DEATHS	WEEKLY INCREASE	DAILY AVERAGE
	11/22: test positivity rate = 11.2%		
	11/26: Thanksgiving		
11/27	**220,953 / 2,977**	**+32,387 / +232**	**4,627 / 33**
	11/30: total tests = 1,779,383		
	12/01: deaths/million population = 554		
12/04	**252,222 / 3,338**	**+31,269 / +361**	**4,467 / 52**
12/11	**281,673 / 3,846**	**+29,451 / +508**	**4,207 / 73**
	12/14: first COVID-19 vaccinations given in the U.S.		
	12/15: IFR (infection fatality rate) = 1.39%		
	12/15: hospitalizations current = 1,554		
	12/15: hospitalizations cumulative = 16,487		
12/18	**304,107 / 4,259**	**+22,434 / +413**	**3,205 / 59**
	12/22: new U.K. variant identified in the U.S.		
	12/22: test positivity rate = 7.5%		
	12/25: Christmas		
12/25	**322,189 / 4,586**	**+18,082 / +327**	**2,583 / 47**
	12/31: total tests = 2,135,590		
	12/31: deaths/million population = 836		
	01/01: New Year's Day		
	01/01: CFR (case fatality rate) = 6.46% (64.6X more deadly than influenza at 0.1%)		
01/01/2021	**337,161 / 4,873**	**+14,972 / +287**	**2,139 / 41**

BONUS: Enjoy additional week from upcoming book: PANDEMIC 2021: The U.S. Edition

	01/06: right-wing mob insurrection at U.S. Capitol as Joe Biden confirmed president		
	01/08: Twitter permanently bans Trump's account		
01/08	**356,110 / 5,138**	**+18,949 / +265**	**2,707 / 38**

*The daily average column is rounded to the nearest whole person. The infection fatality rate (IFR) is the number of deaths divided by the number of confirmed cases. The case fatality rate (CFR), shown only at the end of the year, is the number of deaths divided by the number of confirmed cases *which have had an outcome* (either recovery or death). The CFR excludes active cases.

CHAPTER 9

~ CONNECTICUT *~*

POPULATION AS OF MARCH, 2020: 3,563,077
Democratic Governor Ned Lamont
VOTED BLUE: Biden 59.2% / Trump 39.2%

DATE	CASES / DEATHS	WEEKLY INCREASE	DAILY AVERAGE
01/30: WHO declares Public Health Emergency of International Concern			
01/31: Trump issues a China "travel ban"			
03/08: Connecticut's first case			
03/10: Connecticut declares Public Health Emergency			
03/11: WHO declares COVID-19 a pandemic			
03/13: Trump declares a National Emergency			
03/13: Trump issues a Europe "travel ban"			
03/13:	**11 / 0**	**+10 / +0**	**1 / 0**
03/17: schools close			
03/20	**194 / 0**	**+183 / +0**	**26 / 0**
03/21: Connecticut's first 5 deaths			
03/27	**1,291 / 27**	**+1,097 / +27**	**157 / 4**
03/31: total tests = 14,300			
04/03	**4,915 / 132**	**+3,624 / +105**	**518 / 15**
04/10	**10,538 / 448**	**+5,623 / +316**	**803 / 45**
04/12: Easter			
04/15: IFR (infection fatality rate) = 5.88%			
04/15: hospitalizations current = 1,908			
04/15: hospitalizations cumulative = not given			
04/17: mask mandate			
04/17	**16,809 / 1,036**	**+6,271 / +588**	**896 / 84**
04/24	**23,921 / 1,764**	**+7,112 / +728**	**1,016 / 104**
04/30: total tests = 102,493			

DATE	CASES / DEATHS	WEEKLY INCREASE	DAILY AVERAGE
05/01	28,764 / 2,339	+4,843 / +575	692 / 82
05/08	32,411 / 2,874	+3,647 / +535	521 / 76

05/10: Mother's Day
05/15: IFR (infection fatality rate) = 9.08%
05/15: hospitalizations current = 1,033
05/15: hospitalizations cumulative = not given

05/15	36,085 / 3,285	+3,674 / +411	525 / 59
05/22	39,640 / 3,637	+3,555 / +352	508 / 50

05/25: Memorial Day
05/26: George Floyd protests begin

05/29	41,762 / 3,868	+2,122 / +231	303 / 33

05/31: total tests = 246,935
NEW! 06/01: deaths/million population = 1,113

06/05	43,460 / 4,038	+1,698 / +170	243 / 24
06/12	44,689 / 4,159	+1,229 / +121	176 / 17

06/15: IFR (infection fatality rate) = 9.31%
06/15: hospitalizations current = 203
06/15: hospitalizations cumulative = 9,912

06/19	45,557 / 4,238	+868 / +79	124 / 11

06/21: Father's Day

06/26	46,059 / 4,307	+502 / +69	72 / 10

06/30: total tests = 466,394
07/01: deaths/million population = 1,213

07/03	46,717 / 4,335	+658 / +28	94 / 4

07/04: Independence Day

07/10	47,287 / 4,348	+570 / +13	81 / 2

07/15: IFR (infection fatality rate) = 9.19%
07/15: hospitalizations current = 67
07/15: hospitalizations cumulative = 10,552

07/17	47,893 / 4,396	+606 / +48	87 / 7
07/24	48,776 / 4,413	+883 / +17	126 / 2
07/31	49,810 / 4,432	+1,034 / +19	148 / 3

07/31: total tests = 792,040
08/01: deaths/million population = 1,243

08/07	50,320 / 4,441	+510 / +9	73 / 1
08/14	50,897 / 4,453	+577 / +12	82 / 2

08/15: IFR (infection fatality rate) = 8.69%
08/15: hospitalizations current = 56

DATE	CASES / DEATHS	WEEKLY INCREASE	DAILY AVERAGE
08/15: hospitalizations cumulative = 11,015			
08/21	51,519 / 4,460	+622 / +7	89 / 1
08/28	52,495 / 4,465	+976 / +5	139 / 1
08/30: total tests = 1,235,514			
09/01: deaths/million population = 1,253			
09/04	53,365 / 4,468	+870 / +3	124 / 0
09/07: Labor Day			
09/11	54,326 / 4,480	+961 / +12	137 / 2
09/15: IFR (infection fatality rate) = 8.15%			
09/15: hospitalizations current = 71			
09/15: hospitalizations cumulative = 11,357			
09/18	55,527 / 4,492	+1,201 / +12	172 / 2
NEW! 09/22: test positivity rate = 1.3%			
09/25	56,587 / 4,501	+1,060 / +9	151 / 1
09/30: total tests = 1,673,975			
10/01: deaths/million population = 1,266			
10/02	58,297 / 4,513	+1,710 / +12	244 / 2
10/09	60,038 / 4,530	+1,741 / +17	249 / 2
10/15: IFR (infection fatality rate) = 7.32%			
10/15: hospitalizations current = 191			
10/15: hospitalizations cumulative = 12,043			
10/16	62,830 / 4,542	+2,792 / +12	399 / 2
10/22: test positivity rate = 2.1%			
10/23	66,052 / 4,577	+3,222 / +35	460 / 5
10/30	71,207 / 4,616	+5,155 / +39	736 / 6
10/31: total tests = 2,284,896			
11/01: deaths/million population = 1,295			
11/03: Election Day			
11/06	78,125 / 4,671	+6,918 / +55	988 / 8
11/07: Biden wins election			
11/13	88,645 / 4,737	+10,520 / +66	1,503 / 9
11/15: IFR (infection fatality rate) = 5.34%			
11/15: hospitalizations current = 659			
11/15: hospitalizations cumulative = 12,557			
11/20	101,469 / 4,828	+ 12,824 / +91	1,832 / 13
11/22: test positivity rate = 5.9%			
11/26: Thanksgiving			
11/27	112,581 / 4,961	+11,112 / +133	1,587 / 19

DATE	CASES / DEATHS	WEEKLY INCREASE	DAILY AVERAGE
11/30: total tests = 3,319,482			
12/01: deaths/million population = 1,428			
12/04	**127,715 / 5,146**	**+15,134 / +185**	**2,162 / 26**
12/11	**146,761 / 5,363**	**+19,046 / +217**	**2,721 / 31**
12/14: first COVID-19 vaccinations given in the U.S.			
12/15: IFR (infection fatality rate) = 3.52%			
12/15: hospitalizations current = 1,269			
12/15: hospitalizations cumulative = (no updated figure available)			
12/18	**162,782 / 5,581**	**+16,021 / +218**	**2,289 / 31**
12/22: new U.K. variant identified in the U.S.			
12/22: test positivity rate = 6.1%			
12/25: Christmas			
12/25	**172,743 / 5,791**	**+9,961 / +210**	**1,423 / 30**
12/31: total tests = 4,309,664			
12/31: deaths/million population = 1,681			
01/01: New Year's Day			
01/01: CFR (case fatality rate) = 10.33% (103.3X more deadly than influenza at 0.1%)			
01/01/2021	**185,708 / 5,995**	**+12,965 / +204**	**1,852 / 29**

BONUS: Enjoy additional week from upcoming book: PANDEMIC 2021: The U.S. Edition
01/06: right-wing mob insurrection at U.S. Capitol as Joe Biden confirmed president
01/08: Twitter permanently bans Trump's account

DATE	CASES / DEATHS	WEEKLY INCREASE	DAILY AVERAGE
01/08	**205,994 / 6,324**	**+20,286 / +329**	**2,898 / 47**

*The daily average column is rounded to the nearest whole person. The infection fatality rate (IFR) is the number of deaths divided by the number of confirmed cases. The case fatality rate (CFR), shown only at the end of the year, is the number of deaths divided by the number of confirmed cases *which have had an outcome* (either recovery or death). The CFR excludes active cases.

CHAPTER 10

~ DELAWARE *~*

POPULATION AS OF MARCH, 2020: 982,895
Democratic Governor John C. Carney Jr.
VOTED BLUE: Biden 58.8% / Trump 39.8%

DATE	CASES / DEATHS	WEEKLY INCREASE	DAILY AVERAGE
	01/30: WHO declares Public Health Emergency of International Concern		
	01/31: Trump issues a China "travel ban"		
	03/08: Delaware's first case		
	03/11: WHO declares COVID-19 a pandemic		
	03/12: Delaware declares State of Emergency		
	03/13: Trump declares a National Emergency		
	03/13: Trump issues a Europe "travel ban"		
03/13	6 / 0	+5 / +0	1 / 0
	03/16: schools close		
03/20	47 / 0	+41 / +0	6 / 0
	03/24: Delaware's first death		
	03/24: non-essential services close / stay-at-home order		
03/27	206 / 5	+159 / +5	23 / 1
	03/31: total tests = 3,959		
04/03	639 / 17	+433 / +12	62 / 2
04/10	1,326 / 36	+687 / +19	98 / 3
	04/12: Easter		
	04/15: IFR (infection fatality rate) = 3.33%		
	04/15: hospitalizations current = 208		
	04/15: hospitalizations current = not available for this state		
04/17	2,323 / 76	+997 / +40	142 / 6
04/24	3,442 / 147	+1,119 / +71	160 / 10
	04/30: total tests = 23,112		

DATE	CASES / DEATHS	WEEKLY INCREASE	DAILY AVERAGE
05/01: mask mandate			
05/01	4,918 / 222	+1,476 / +75	211 / 11
05/08	6,111 / 297	+1,193 / +75	170 / 11
05/10: Mother's Day			
05/15: IFR (infection fatality rate) = 5.01%			
05/15: hospitalizations current = 269			
05/15	7,373 / 373	+1,262 / +76	180 / 11
05/22	8,529 / 420	+1,156 / +47	165 / 7
05/25: Memorial Day			
05/26: George Floyd protests begin			
05/29	9,236 / 463	+707 / +43	101 / 6
05/31: total tests = 59,329			
NEW! 06/01: deaths/million population = 479			
06/05	9,773 / 483	+537 / +20	77 / 3
06/12	10,173 / 493	+400 / +10	57 / 1
06/15: IFR (infection fatality rate) = 4.79%			
06/15: hospitalizations current = 88			
06/19	10,611 / 502	+438 / +9	63 / 1
06/21: Father's Day			
06/26	11,017 / 507	+406 / +5	58 / 1
06/30: total tests = 110,881			
07/01: deaths/million population = 523			
07/03	11,923 / 512	+906 / +5	129 / 1
07/04: Independence Day			
07/10	12,652 / 517	+729 / +5	104 / 1
07/15: IFR (infection fatality rate) =3.99%			
07/15: hospitalizations current = 51			
07/17	13,337 / 521	+685 / +4	98 / 1
07/24	14,202 / 578	+865 / +57	124 / 8
07/31	14,788 / 585	+586 / +7	84 / 1
07/31: total tests = 181,047			
08/01: deaths/million population = 601			
08/07	15,445 / 588	+657 / +3	94 / 0
08/14	16,340 / 593	+895 / +5	128 / 1
08/15: IFR (infection fatality rate) = 3.62%			
08/15: hospitalizations current = 32			
08/21	16,770 / 600	+430 / +7	61 / 1
08/28	17,083 / 604	+313 / +4	45 / 1

DATE	CASES / DEATHS	WEEKLY INCREASE	DAILY AVERAGE
	08/31: total tests = 247,642		
	09/01: deaths/million population = 624		
09/04	17,752 / 606	+669 / +2	96 / 0
	09/07: Labor Day		
09/11	18,559 / 613	+807 / +7	115 / 1
	09/15: IFR (infection fatality rate) = 3.23%		
	09/15: hospitalizations current = 61		
09/18	19,366 / 620	+807 / +7	115 / 1
	NEW! 09/22: test positivity rate = 5.8%		
09/25	20,085 / 631	+719 / +11	103 / 2
	09/30: total tests = 289,185		
	10/01: deaths/million population = 659		
10/02	20,937 / 642	+852 / +11	122 / 2
10/09	21,827 / 651	+890 / +9	127 / 1
	10/15: IFR (infection fatality rate) = 2.93%		
	10/15: hospitalizations current = 111		
10/16	22,724 / 662	+897 / +11	128 / 2
	10/22: test positivity rate = 6.7%		
10/23	23,687 / 678	+963 / +16	138 / 2
10/30	24,751 / 704	+1,064 / +26	152 / 4
	10/31: total tests = 349,564		
	11/01: deaths/million population = 729		
	11/03: Election Day		
11/06	26,035 / 716	+1,284 / +12	183 / 2
	11/07: Biden wins election		
11/13	28,016 / 734	+1,981 / +18	283 / 3
	11/15: IFR (infection fatality rate) = 2.56%		
	11/15: hospitalizations current = 81		
11/20	30,816 / 746	+2,800 / +12	400 / 2
	11/22: test positivity rate = 9.2%		
	11/26: Thanksgiving		
11/27	34,170 / 763	+3,354 / +17	479 / 2
	11/30: total tests = 428,533		
	12/01: deaths/million population = 800		
12/04	38,398 / 782	+4,228 / +19	604 / 3
12/11	43,818 / 807	+5,420 / +25	774 / 4
	12/14: first COVID-19 vaccinations given in the U.S.		
	12/15: IFR (infection fatality rate) = 1.75%		

DATE	CASES / DEATHS	WEEKLY INCREASE	DAILY AVERAGE
12/15: hospitalizations current = 376			
12/18	**49,109 / 854**	**+5,291 / +47**	**756 / 7**
12/22: new U.K. variant identified in the U.S.			
12/22: test positivity rate = 7.7%			
12/25: Christmas			
12/25	**53,653 / 891**	**+4,544 / +37**	**649 / 5**
12/31: total tests = 510,085			
12/31: deaths/million population = 951			
01/01: New Year's Day			
01/01: CFR (case fatality rate) = N/A (active case counts are not available)			
01/01/2021	**58,064 / 930**	**+4,411 / +39**	**630 / 6**

BONUS: Enjoy additional week from upcoming book: PANDEMIC 2021: The U.S. Edition

01/06: right-wing mob insurrection at U.S. Capitol as Joe Biden confirmed president			
01/08: Twitter permanently bans Trump's account			
01/08	**65,503 / 957**	**+7,439 / +27**	**1,063 / 4**

*The daily average column is rounded to the nearest whole person. The infection fatality rate (IFR) is the number of deaths divided by the number of confirmed cases. The case fatality rate (CFR), shown only at the end of the year, is the number of deaths divided by the number of confirmed cases *which have had an outcome* (either recovery or death). The CFR excludes active cases.

CHAPTER 11

~ FLORIDA *~*

POPULATION AS OF MARCH, 2020: 21,992,985
Republican Governor Ron DeSantis
VOTED RED: Trump 51.2% / Biden 47.9%

DATE	CASES / DEATHS	WEEKLY INCREASE	DAILY AVERAGE
01/30: WHO declares Public Health Emergency of International Concern			
01/31: Trump issues a China "travel ban"			
03/01: Florida declares Public Health Emergency			
03/02: Florida's first 2 cases			
03/06	**3 / 0**	**+1 / +0**	**0 / 0**
03/07: Florida's first 2 deaths			
03/11: WHO declares COVID-19 a pandemic			
03/13: Trump declares a National Emergency			
03/13: Trump issues a Europe "travel ban"			
03/13	**77 / 3**	**+74 / +3**	**11 / 0**
03/15: IFR (infection fatality rate) = 2.68%			
03/17: schools close			
03/20	**563 / 11**	**+486 / +8**	**69 / 1**
03/27	**3,198 / 46**	**+2,635 / +35**	**376 / 5**
03/31: total tests = 48,289			
04/03: stay-at-home order			
04/03	**10,268 / 170**	**+7,070 / +124**	**1,010 / 18**
04/10	**17,968 / 419**	**+7,700 / +249**	**1,100 / 36**
04/12: Easter			
04/15: IFR (infection fatality rate) = 2.73%			
04/15: hospitalizations current = not given			
04/15: hospitalizations cumulative = 3,344			
04/17	**24,753 / 726**	**+6,785 / +307**	**929 / 44**

DATE	CASES / DEATHS	WEEKLY INCREASE	DAILY AVERAGE
04/24	30,533 / 1,046	+5,780 / +320	826 / 46
04/30: total tests = 417,762			
05/01	34,728 / 1,314	+4,195 / +268	599 / 38
05/08	39,199 / 1,669	+4,471 / +355	639 / 51
05/10: Mother's Day			
05/15: IFR (infection fatality rate) = 4.34%			
05/15: hospitalizations current = not given			
05/15: hospitalizations cumulative = 7,993			
05/15	44,138 / 1,918	+4,939 / +249	706 / 36
05/22	49,451 / 2,190	+5,313 / +272	759 / 39
05/25: Memorial Day			
05/26: George Floyd protests begin			
05/29	54,497 / 2,413	+5,046 / +223	721 / 32
05/31: total tests = 995,886			
NEW! 06/01: deaths/million population = 112			
06/05	61,488 / 2,660	+6,991 / +247	999 / 35
06/12	70,971 / 2,881	+9,483 / +221	1,355 / 32
06/15: IFR (infection fatality rate) = 3.80%			
06/15: hospitalizations current = not given			
06/15: hospitalizations cumulative = 12,298			
06/19	89,748 / 3,107	+18,777 / +226	2,682 / 32
06/21: Father's Day			
06/26	122,960 / 3,366	+33,212 / +259	4,745 / 37
06/30: total tests = 1,946,510			
07/01: deaths/million population = 165			
07/03	178,594 / 3,686	+55,634 / +320	7,948 / 46
07/04: Independence Day			
07/10	244,151 / 4,102	+65,557 / +416	9,365 / 59
07/15: IFR (infection fatality rate) = 1.50%			
07/15: hospitalizations current = 8,217			
07/15: hospitalizations cumulative = 19,659			
07/17	327,241 / 4,805	+83,090 / +703	11,870 / 100
07/24	402,312 / 5,653	+75,071 / +848	10,724 / 121
07/31	470,386 / 6,843	+68,074 / +1,190	9,725 / 170
07/31: total tests = 3,633,393			
08/01: deaths/million population = 327			
08/07	518,075 / 7,927	+47,689 / +1,084	6,813 / 155
08/14	563,285 / 9,146	+45,210 / +1,219	6,459 / 174

DATE	CASES / DEATHS	WEEKLY INCREASE	DAILY AVERAGE
	08/15: IFR (infection fatality rate) = 1.64%		
	08/15: hospitalizations current = 5,721		
	08/15: hospitalizations cumulative = 34,074		
08/21	593,286 / 10,177	+30,001 / +1,031	4,286 / 147
08/28	615,806 / 10,962	+22,520 / +785	3,217 / 112
	08/30: total tests = 4,763,807		
	09/01: deaths/million population = 550		
09/04	640,211 / 11,755	+24,405 / +793	3,486 / 113
	09/07: Labor Day		
	09/08: Trump rally		
09/11	658,381 / 12,507	+18,170 / +752	2,596 / 107
	09/15: IFR (infection fatality rate) = 1.91%		
	09/15: hospitalizations current = 2,574		
	09/15: hospitalizations cumulative = 42,127		
09/18	677,660 / 13,230	+19,279 / +723	2,754 / 103
	NEW! 09/22: test positivity rate = 11.7%		
	09/24: Trump rally		
09/25	695,887 / 13,915	+18,227 / +685	2,604 / 98
	09/30: total tests = 5,358,703		
	10/01: deaths/million population = 678		
10/02	711,804 / 14,557	+15,917 / +642	2,274 / 92
10/09	728,921 / 15,187	+17,117 / +630	2,445 / 90
	10/12: Trump rally		
	10/15: IFR (infection fatality rate) = 2.11%		
	10/15: hospitalizations current = 2,119		
	10/15: hospitalizations cumulative = 47,223		
	10/16: Trump visits seniors		
10/16	748,437 / 15,827	+19,516 / +640	2,788 / 91
	10/22: test positivity rate = 12.9%		
	10/23: 2 Trump rallies		
10/23	771,780 / 16,349	+23,343 / +522	3,335 / 75
10/30	800,216 / 16,720	+28,436 / +371	4,062 / 53
	10/31: total tests = 9,979,348		
	11/01: deaths/million population = 782		
	11/03: Election Day		
11/06	832,625 / 17,016	+32,409 / +296	4,630 / 42
	11/07: Biden wins election		
11/13	870,552 / 17,450	+37,927 / +434	5,418 / 62

DATE	CASES / DEATHS	WEEKLY INCREASE	DAILY AVERAGE
11/15: IFR (infection fatality rate) = 1.98%			
11/15: hospitalizations current = 3,118			
11/15: hospitalizations cumulative = 52,529			
11/20	**923,418 / 17,892**	**+52,866 / +442**	**7,552 / 63**
11/22: test positivity rate = 9.0%			
11/26: Thanksgiving			
11/27	**979,020 / 18,363**	**+55,602 / +471**	**7,943 / 67**
11/30: total tests = 12,615,881			
12/01: deaths/million population = 874			
12/04	**1,039,207 / 18,997**	**+60,187 / +634**	**8,598 / 91**
12/11	**1,106,396 / 19,714**	**+67,189 / +717**	**9,598 / 102**
12/14: first COVID-19 vaccinations given in the U.S.			
12/15: IFR (infection fatality rate) = 1.76%			
12/15: hospitalizations current = 5,103			
12/15: hospitalizations cumulative = 59,385			
12/18	**1,181,483 / 20,414**	**+75,087 / +700**	**10,727 / 100**
12/22: new U.K. variant identified in the U.S.			
12/22: test positivity rate = 9.7%			
12/25: Christmas			
12/25	**1,258,196 / 20,995**	**+76,713 / +581**	**10,959 / 83**
12/31: total tests = 15,703,599			
12/31: deaths/million population = 1,009			
01/01: New Year's Day			
01/01: CFR (case fatality rate) = 2.86% (28.6X more deadly than influenza at 0.1%)			
01/01/2021	**1,323,315 / 21,673**	**+65,119 / +678**	**9,303 / 97**

BONUS: Enjoy additional week from upcoming book: PANDEMIC 2021: The U.S. Edition
01/06: right-wing mob insurrection at U.S. Capitol as Joe Biden confirmed president
01/08: Twitter permanently bans Trump's account

01/08	**1,449,252 / 22,675**	**+125,937 / +1,002**	**17,991 / 143**

*The daily average column is rounded to the nearest whole person. The infection fatality rate (IFR) is the number of deaths divided by the number of confirmed cases. The case fatality rate (CFR), shown only at the end of the year, is the number of deaths divided by the number of confirmed cases *which have had an outcome* (either recovery or death). The CFR excludes active cases.

CHAPTER 12

~ GEORGIA *~*

POPULATION AS OF MARCH, 2020: 10,736,059
Republican Governor Brian Kemp
VOTED BLUE: Biden 49.5% / Trump 49.3%

DATE	CASES / DEATHS	WEEKLY INCREASE	DAILY AVERAGE
01/30: WHO declares Public Health Emergency of International Concern			
01/31: Trump issues a China "travel ban"			
03/02: Georgia's first 2 cases			
03/06	**3 / 0**	**N/A**	**N/A**
03/11: WHO declares COVID-19 a pandemic			
03/13: Georgia's first death			
03/13: Trump declares a National Emergency			
03/13: Trump issues a Europe "travel ban"			
03/13	**64 / 1**	**+61 / +1**	**9 / 0**
03/14: Georgia declares Public Health Emergency			
03/15: IFR (infection fatality rate) = 1.01%			
03/20	**420 / 13**	**+356 / +12**	**51 / 2**
03/27	**2,198 / 65**	**+1,778 / +52**	**254 / 7**
03/31: total tests = 13,053			
04/03	**5,967 / 198**	**+3,769 / +133**	**538 / 19**
04/10	**11,859 / 425**	**+5,892 / +227**	**842 / 32**
04/12: Easter			
04/15: IFR (infection fatality rate) = 3.77%			
04/15: hospitalizations current = not given			
04/15: hospitalizations cumulative = 2,922			
04/17	**17,432 / 668**	**+5,573 / +243**	**796 / 35**
04/24	**22,491 / 899**	**+5,059 / +231**	**723 / 33**
04/30: total tests = 194,616			

DATE	CASES / DEATHS	WEEKLY INCREASE	DAILY AVERAGE
05/01	27,496 / 1,166	+5,005 / +267	715 / 38
05/08	32,178 / 1,399	+4,682 / +233	669 / 33

05/10: Mother's Day
05/15: IFR (infection fatality rate) = 4.29%
05/15: hospitalizations current = 1,029
05/15: hospitalizations cumulative = 6,438

05/15	36,772 / 1,588	+4,594 / +189	656 / 27
05/22	41,482 / 1,808	+4,710 / +220	673 / 31

05/25: Memorial Day
05/26: George Floyd protests begin

05/29	45,863 / 1,984	+4,381 / +176	626 / 25

05/31: total tests = 539,641
NEW! 06/01: deaths/million population = 195

06/05	50,621 / 2,174	+4,758 / +190	680 / 27
06/12	55,783 / 2,418	+5,162 / +244	737 / 35

06/15: IFR (infection fatality rate) = 4.27%
06/15: hospitalizations current = 865
06/15: hospitalizations cumulative = 9,322

06/19	62,009 / 2,636	+6,226 / +218	889 / 31

06/21: Father's Day

06/26	72,995 / 2,770	+10,986 / +134	1,569 / 19

06/30: total tests = 991,501
07/01: deaths/million population = 266

07/03	90,493 / 2,856	+17,498 / +86	2,500 / 12

07/04: Independence Day

07/10	111,211 / 2,965	+20,718 / +109	2,960 / 16

07/15: IFR (infection fatality rate) = 2.42%
07/15: hospitalizations current = 2,786
07/15: hospitalizations cumulative = 14,102

07/17	135,183 / 3,132	+23,972 / +167	3,425 / 24
07/24	161,401 / 3,442	+26,218 / +310	3,745 / 44
07/31	186,352 / 3,752	+24,951 / +310	3,564 / 44

07/31: total tests = 1,896,900
08/01: deaths/million population = 360

08/07	209,004 / 4,117	+22,652 / +365	3,236 / 52
08/14	231,895 / 4,573	+22,891 / +456	3,270 / 55

08/15: IFR (infection fatality rate) = 1.99%
08/15: hospitalizations current = 2,586

DATE	CASES / DEATHS	WEEKLY INCREASE	DAILY AVERAGE
	08/15: hospitalizations cumulative = 22,028		
08/21	**249,630 / 4,998**	**+17,735 / +425**	**2,534 / 61**
08/28	**265,372 / 5,471**	**+15,742 / +473**	**2,249 / 68**
	08/31: total tests = 2,744,006		
	09/01: deaths/million population = 563		
09/04	**279,354 / 5,931**	**+13,982 / +460**	**1,997 / 66**
	09/07: Labor Day		
09/11	**290,781 / 6,246**	**+11,427 / +315**	**1,632 / 45**
	09/15: IFR (infection fatality rate) = 2.16%		
	09/15: hospitalizations current = 2,098		
	09/15: hospitalizations cumulative = 26,665		
09/18	**302,737 / 6,537**	**+11,956 / +291**	**1,708 / 42**
	NEW! 09/22: test positivity rate = 7.4%		
09/25	**312,514 / 6,874**	**+9,777 / +337**	**1,397 / 48**
	09/30: total tests = 3,274,564		
	10/01: deaths/million population = 669		
10/02	**320,634 / 7,106**	**+8,120 / +232**	**1,160 / 33**
10/09	**329,032 / 7,348**	**+8,398 / +242**	**1,200 / 35**
	10/15: IFR (infection fatality rate) = 2.23%		
	10/15: hospitalizations current = 1,682		
	10/15: hospitalizations cumulative = 30,081		
	10/16: Trump rally		
10/16	**337,850 / 7,556**	**+8,818 / +208**	**1,260 / 30**
	10/22: test positivity rate = 6.7%		
10/23	**347,759 / 7,766**	**+9,909 / +210**	**1,416 / 30**
10/30	**358,225 / 7,955**	**+10,466 / +189**	**1,495 / 27**
	10/31: total tests = 3,894,503		
	11/01: deaths/million population = 752		
	11/03: Election Day		
11/06	**402,427 / 8,608**	**+44,202 / +653**	**6,315 / 93**
	11/07: Biden wins election		
11/13	**419,870 / 8,905**	**+17,443 / +297**	**2,492 / 42**
	11/15: IFR (infection fatality rate) = 2.11%		
	11/15: hospitalizations current = 1,978		
	11/15: hospitalizations cumulative = 33,241		
11/20	**440,595 / 9,142**	**+20,725 / +237**	**2,961 / 34**
	11/22: test positivity rate = 8.6%		
	11/26: Thanksgiving		

DATE	CASES / DEATHS	WEEKLY INCREASE	DAILY AVERAGE
11/27	464,526 / 9,380	+23,931 / +238	3,419 / 34

    11/30: total tests = 4,728,290
    12/01: deaths/million population = 901

DATE	CASES / DEATHS	WEEKLY INCREASE	DAILY AVERAGE
12/04	494,354 / 9,725	+29,828 / +345	4,261 / 49
12/11	531,593 / 10,031	+37,239 / +306	5,320 / 44

    12/14: first COVID-19 vaccinations given in the U.S.
    12/15: IFR (infection fatality rate) = 1.83%
    12/15: hospitalizations current = 3,352
    12/15: hospitalizations cumulative = 38,111

DATE	CASES / DEATHS	WEEKLY INCREASE	DAILY AVERAGE
12/18	576,537 / 10,332	+44,944 / +301	6,241 / 43

    12/22: new U.K. variant identified in the U.S.
    12/22: test positivity rate = 13.7%
    12/25: Christmas

DATE	CASES / DEATHS	WEEKLY INCREASE	DAILY AVERAGE
12/25	624,630 / 10,631	+48,093 / +299	6,870 / 43

    12/31: total tests = 5,806,222
    12/31: deaths/million population = 1,032
    01/01: New Year's Day
    01/01: CFR (case fatality rate) = 3.07% (30.7X more deadly than influenza at 0.1%)

DATE	CASES / DEATHS	WEEKLY INCREASE	DAILY AVERAGE
01/01/2021	677,589 / 10,958	+52,959 / +327	7,566 / 47

BONUS: Enjoy additional week from upcoming book: PANDEMIC 2021: The U.S. Edition
    01/04-05: Trump rallies for runoff election
    01/06: right-wing mob insurrection at U.S. Capitol as Joe Biden confirmed president
    01/08: Twitter permanently bans Trump's account

DATE	CASES / DEATHS	WEEKLY INCREASE	DAILY AVERAGE
01/08	736,926 / 11,314	+59,337 / +356	8,477 / 51

*The daily average column is rounded to the nearest whole person. The infection fatality rate (IFR) is the number of deaths divided by the number of confirmed cases. The case fatality rate (CFR), shown only at the end of the year, is the number of deaths divided by the number of confirmed cases *which have had an outcome* (either recovery or death). The CFR excludes active cases.

CHAPTER 13

~ HAWAII *~*

POPULATION AS OF MARCH, 2020: 1,412,687
Democratic Governor David Ige
VOTED BLUE: Biden 63.7% / Trump 34.3%

DATE	CASES / DEATHS	WEEKLY INCREASE	DAILY AVERAGE
01/30: WHO declares Public Health Emergency of International Concern			
01/31: Trump issues a China "travel ban"			
03/04: Hawaii declares State of Emergency			
03/06: Hawaii's first case			
03/11: WHO declares COVID-19 a pandemic			
03/13: Trump declares a National Emergency			
03/13: Trump issues a Europe "travel ban"			
03/13	2 / 0	+1 / +0	0 / 0
03/20	37 / 0	+35 / +0	5 / 0
03/27	120 / 0	+83 / +0	12 / 0
03/31: Hawaii's first death			
03/31: total tests = 7,491			
04/03	319 / 3	+199 / +3	28 / 0
04/10	465 / 8	+146 / +5	21 / 1
04/12: Easter			
04/15: IFR (infection fatality rate) = 1.70%			
04/15: hospitalizations current = not given			
04/15: hospitalizations cumulative = 45			
04/17	553 / 9	+88 / +1	13 / 0
04/20: mask mandate			
04/24	601 / 13	+48 / +4	7 / 1
04/30: total tests = 32,432			
05/01	619 / 16	+18 / +3	3 / 0

DATE	CASES / DEATHS	WEEKLY INCREASE	DAILY AVERAGE
05/08	**629 / 17**	**+10 / +1**	**1 / 0**
05/10: Mother's Day			
05/15: IFR (infection fatality rate) = 2.66%			
05/15: hospitalizations current = not given			
05/15: hospitalizations cumulative = 81			
05/15	**638 / 17**	**+9 / +0**	**1 / 0**
05/22	**642 / 17**	**+4 / +0**	**1 / 0**
05/25: Memorial Day			
05/26: George Floyd protests begin			
05/29	**649 / 17**	**+7 / +0**	**1 / 0**
05/31: total tests = 54,620			
NEW! 06/01: deaths/million population = 12			
06/05	**656 / 17**	**+7 / +0**	**1 / 0**
06/12	**706 / 17**	**+50 / +0**	**7 / 0**
06/15: IFR (infection fatality rate) = 2.31%			
06/15: hospitalizations current = not given			
06/15: hospitalizations cumulative = 91			
06/19	**789 / 17**	**+83 / +0**	**12 / 0**
06/21: Father's Day			
06/26	**866 / 17**	**+77 / +0**	**11 / 0**
06/30: total tests = 92,225			
07/01: deaths/million population = 13			
07/03	**975 / 19**	**+109 / +2**	**16 / 0**
07/04: Independence Day			
07/10	**1,158 / 19**	**+183 / +0**	**26 / 0**
07/15: IFR (infection fatality rate) = 1.70%			
07/15: hospitalizations current = 31			
07/15: hospitalizations cumulative = 133			
07/17	**1,334 / 23**	**+176 / +4**	**25 / 1**
07/24	**1,549 / 26**	**+215 / +3**	**31 / 0**
07/31	**2,111 / 26**	**+562 / +0**	**80 / 0**
07/31: total tests = 152,976			
08/01: deaths/million population = 18			
08/07	**3,115 / 31**	**+1,004 / +5**	**143 / 1**
08/14	**4,543 / 40**	**+1,428 / +9**	**204 / 1**
08/15: IFR (infection fatality rate) = 0.83%			
08/15: hospitalizations current= 173			

DATE	CASES / DEATHS	WEEKLY INCREASE	DAILY AVERAGE
	08/15: hospitalizations cumulative = 277		
08/21	**6,072 / 46**	**+1,529 / +6**	**218 / 1**
08/28	**7,830 / 59**	**+1,758 / +13**	**251 / 2**
	08/31: total tests = 305,326		
	09/01: deaths/million population = 59		
09/04	**9,473 / 81**	**+1,643 / +22**	**235 / 3**
	09/07: Labor Day		
09/11	**10,459 / 96**	**+986 / +15**	**141 / 2**
	09/15: IFR (infection fatality rate) = 0.92%		
	09/15: hospitalizations current = 225		
	09/15: hospitalizations cumulative = 638		
09/18	**11,217 / 120**	**+758 / +24**	**108 / 3**
	NEW! 09/22: test positivity rate = 3.3%		
09/25	**11,891 / 127**	**+674 / +7**	**96 / 1**
	09/30: total tests = 427,746		
	10/01: deaths/million population = 100		
10/02	**12,601 / 142**	**+710 / +15**	**101 / 2**
10/09	**13,300 / 166**	**+699 / +24**	**100 / 3**
	10/15: IFR (infection fatality rate) = 1.34%		
	10/15: hospitalizations current = 105		
	10/15: hospitalizations cumulative = 961		
10/16	**13,853 / 185**	**+553 / +19**	**79 / 3**
	10/22: test positivity rate = 2.2%		
10/23	**14,335 / 206**	**+482 / +21**	**69 / 3**
10/30	**15,003 / 216**	**+668 / +10**	**95 / 1**
	10/31: total tests = 530,264		
	11/01: deaths/million population = 155		
	11/03: Election Day		
11/06	**15,691 / 219**	**+688 / +3**	**98 / 0**
	11/07: Biden wins election		
11/13	**16,412 / 222**	**+721 / +3**	**103 / 0**
	11/15: IFR (infection fatality rate) = 1.34%		
	11/15: hospitalizations current = 78		
	11/15: hospitalizations cumulative = 1,194		
11/20	**16,936 / 224**	**+524 / +2**	**75 / 0**
	11/22: test positivity rate = 2.0%		
	11/26: Thanksgiving		
11/27	**17,708 / 240**	**+772 / +16**	**110 / 2**

DATE	CASES / DEATHS	WEEKLY INCREASE	DAILY AVERAGE
11/30: total tests = 677,445			
12/01: deaths/million population = 172			
12/04	**18,290 / 256**	**+582 / +16**	**83 / 2**
12/11	**18,951 / 269**	**+661 / +13**	**94 / 2**
12/14: first COVID-19 vaccinations given in the U.S.			
12/15: IFR (infection fatality rate) = 1.41%			
12/15: hospitalizations current = 57			
12/15: hospitalizations cumulative = 1,364			
12/18	**19,859 / 281**	**+908 / +12**	**130 / 2**
12/22: new U.K. variant identified in the U.S.			
12/22: test positivity rate = 3.0%			
12/25: Christmas			
12/25	**20,769 / 285**	**+910 / +4**	**130 / 1**
12/31: total tests = 812,338			
12/31: deaths/million population = 203			
01/01: New Year's Day			
01/01: CFR (case fatality rate) = 2.14% (21.4X more deadly than influenza at 0.1%)			
01/01/2021	**21,638 / 289**	**+879 / +4**	**126 / 1**

BONUS: Enjoy additional week from upcoming book: PANDEMIC 2021: The U.S. Edition

01/06: right-wing mob insurrection at U.S. Capitol as Joe Biden confirmed president			
01/08: Twitter permanently bans Trump's account			
01/08	**22,895 / 303**	**+1,257 / +14**	**180 / 2**

---

*The daily average column is rounded to the nearest whole person. The infection fatality rate (IFR) is the number of deaths divided by the number of confirmed cases. The case fatality rate (CFR), shown only at the end of the year, is the number of deaths divided by the number of confirmed cases *which have had an outcome* (either recovery or death). The CFR excludes active cases.

CHAPTER 14

~ IDAHO *~*

POPULATION AS OF MARCH, 2020: 1,826,156
Republican Governor Brad Little
VOTED RED: Trump 63.8% / Biden 33.1%

DATE	CASES / DEATHS	WEEKLY INCREASE	DAILY AVERAGE
01/30: WHO declares Public Health Emergency of International Concern			
01/31: Trump issues a China "travel ban"			
03/11: WHO declares COVID-19 a pandemic			
03/13: Idaho's first case			
03/13: Idaho declares State of Emergency			
03/13: Trump declares a National Emergency			
03/13: Trump issues a Europe "travel ban"			
03/20	31 / 0	+30 / +0	4 / 0
03/26: Idaho's first 3 deaths			
03/27	230 / 4	+199 / +4	28 / 1
03/31: total tests = 1,960			
04/03	1,013 / 10	+783 / +6	112 / 1
04/10	1,396 / 25	+383 / +15	55 / 2
04/12: Easter			
04/15: IFR (infection fatality rate) = 2.58%			
04/15: hospitalizations current = 66			
04/15: hospitalizations cumulative = 141			
04/17	1,655 / 43	+259 / +18	37 / 3
04/24	1,870 / 54	+215 / +11	31 / 2
04/30: total tests = 24,361			
05/01	2,035 / 63	+165 / +9	24 / 1
05/08	2,205 / 67	+170 / +4	24 / 1

DATE	CASES / DEATHS	WEEKLY INCREASE	DAILY AVERAGE
05/10: Mother's Day			
05/15: IFR (infection fatality rate) = 3.06%			
05/15: hospitalizations current = 26			
05/15: hospitalizations cumulative = 212			
05/15	2,389 / 73	+184 / +6	26 / 1
05/22	2,595 / 79	+206 / +6	29 / 1
05/25: Memorial Day			
05/26: George Floyd protests begin			
05/29	2,803 / 82	+208 / +3	30 / 0
05/31: total tests = 46,436			
NEW! 06/01: deaths/million population = 45			
06/05	3,111 / 83	+308 / +1	44 / 0
06/12	3,353 / 87	+242 / +4	35 / 1
06/15: IFR (infection fatality rate) = 2.54%			
06/15: hospitalizations current = 23			
06/15: hospitalizations cumulative = 266			
06/19	3,871 / 89	+518 / +2	74 / 0
06/21: Father's Day			
06/26	5,148 / 90	+1,277 / +1	182 / 0
06/30: total tests = 90,476			
07/01: deaths/million population = 51			
07/03	6,994 / 93	+1,846 / +3	264 / 0
07/04: Independence Day			
07/10	9,928 / 101	+2,934 / +8	419 / 1
07/15: IFR (infection fatality rate) = 18%			
07/15: hospitalizations current = 153			
07/15: hospitalizations cumulative = 510			
07/17	13,752 / 118	+3,824 / +17	546 / 2
07/24	17,264 / 144	+3,512 / +26	502 / 4
07/31	20,721 / 189	+3,457 / +45	494 / 6
07/31: total tests = 180,615			
08/01: deaths/million population = 110			
08/07	23,922 / 229	+3,201 / +40	457 / 6
08/14	27,173 / 265	+3,251 / +36	464 / 5
08/15: IFR (infection fatality rate) = 18%			
08/15: hospitalizations current = 206			
08/15: hospitalizations cumulative = 1,091			
08/21	29,369 / 304	+2,196 / +39	314 / 6

DATE	CASES / DEATHS	WEEKLY INCREASE	DAILY AVERAGE
08/28	**31,384 / 353**	**+2,015 / +49**	**288 / 7**
08/31: total tests = 264,694			
09/01: deaths/million population = 215			
09/04	**33,196 / 382**	**+1,812 / +29**	**259 / 4**
09/07: Labor Day			
09/11	**34,950 / 412**	**+1,754 / +30**	**251 / 4**
09/15: IFR (infection fatality rate) = 1.18%			
09/15: hospitalizations current = 105			
09/15: hospitalizations cumulative = 1,612			
09/18	**36,959 / 438**	**+2,009 / +26**	**287 / 4**
NEW! 09/22: test positivity rate = 17.5%			
09/25	**39,757 / 458**	**+2,798 / +20**	**400 / 3**
09/30: total tests = 314,442			
10/01: deaths/million population = 265			
10/02	**43,238 / 474**	**+3,481 / +16**	**497 / 2**
10/09	**47,088 / 506**	**+3,850 / +32**	**550 / 5**
10/15: IFR (infection fatality rate) = 1.02%			
10/15: hospitalizations current = 219			
10/15: hospitalizations cumulative = 2,122			
10/16	**51,704 / 523**	**+4,616 / +17**	**659 / 2**
10/22: test positivity rate = 33.3%			
10/23	**57,673 / 562**	**+5,969 / +39**	**853 / 6**
10/30	**63,810 / 626**	**+6,137 / +64**	**877 / 9**
10/31: total tests = 523,318			
11/01: deaths/million population = 353			
11/03: Election Day			
11/06	**70,909 / 679**	**+7,099 / +53**	**1,014 / 8**
11/07: Biden wins election			
11/13	**79,798 / 752**	**+8,889 / +73**	**1,270 / 10**
11/15: IFR (infection fatality rate) = 0.92%			
11/15: hospitalizations current = 395			
11/15: hospitalizations cumulative = 3,148			
11/20	**89,764 / 845**	**+9,966 / +93**	**1,424 / 13**
11/22: test positivity rate = 42.2%			
11/26: Thanksgiving			
11/27	**98,500 / 909**	**+8,736 / +64**	**1,248 / 9**
11/30: total tests = 726,473			
12/01: deaths/million population = 555			

DATE	CASES / DEATHS	WEEKLY INCREASE	DAILY AVERAGE
12/04	108,366 / 1,032	+9,866 / +123	1,409 / 18
12/11	119,610 / 1,151	+11,244 / +119	1,606 / 17

12/14: first COVID-19 vaccinations given in the U.S.
12/15: IFR (infection fatality rate) = 0.98%
12/15: hospitalizations current = 444
12/15: hospitalizations cumulative = 4,827

12/18	128,218 / 1,275	+8,608 / +124	1,230 / 18

12/22: new U.K. variant identified in the U.S.
12/22: test positivity rate = 43.0%
12/25: Christmas

12/25	135,233 / 1,349	+7,015 / +74	1,002 / 11

12/31: total tests = 859,851
12/31: deaths/million population = 804
01/01: New Year's Day
01/01: CFR (case fatality rate) = 2.39% (23.9X more deadly than influenza at 0.1%)

01/01/2021	141,077 / 1,436	+5,844 / +87	835 / 12

BONUS: Enjoy additional week from upcoming book: PANDEMIC 2021: The U.S. Edition
01/06: right-wing mob insurrection at U.S. Capitol as Joe Biden confirmed president
01/08: Twitter permanently bans Trump's account

01/08	148,258 / 1,523	+7,181 / +87	1,026 / 12

*The daily average column is rounded to the nearest whole person. The infection fatality rate (IFR) is the number of deaths divided by the number of confirmed cases. The case fatality rate (CFR), shown only at the end of the year, is the number of deaths divided by the number of confirmed cases *which have had an outcome* (either recovery or death). The CFR excludes active cases.

CHAPTER 15

~ ILLINOIS *~*

POPULATION AS OF MARCH, 2020: 12,659,682
Democratic Governor J.B. Pritzker
VOTED BLUE: Biden 57.5% / Trump 40.5%

DATE	CASES / DEATHS	WEEKLY INCREASE	DAILY AVERAGE
01/24: Illinois' first case			
01/30: WHO declares Public Health Emergency of International Concern			
01/31: Trump issues a China "travel ban"			
02/29	3 / 0	+2 / +0	0 / 0
03/06	6 / 0	+3 / +0	0 / 0
03/09: Illinois declares Disaster [Emergency]			
03/11: WHO declares COVID-19 a pandemic			
03/13: Trump declares a National Emergency			
03/13: Trump issues a Europe "travel ban"			
03/13	46 / 0	+40 / +0	6 / 0
03/17: Illinois' first death			
03/20	585 / 5	+539 / +5	77 / 1
03/27	3,024 / 34	+2,439 / +29	348 / 4
03/31: total tests = 31,485			
04/03	8,904 / 210	+5,880 / +176	840 / 25
04/10	17,887 / 596	+8,983 / +386	1,283 / 55
04/12: Easter			
04/15: IFR (infection fatality rate) = 3.85%			
04/15: hospitalizations current = 4,283			
04/15: hospitalizations cumulative = data not available for this state			
04/17	27,575 / 1,134	+9,688 / +538	1,384 / 77
04/24	39,658 / 1,795	+12,083 / +661	1,726 / 94
04/30: total tests = 299,896			

DATE	CASES / DEATHS	WEEKLY INCREASE	DAILY AVERAGE
	05/01: mask mandate		
05/01	56,055 / 2,457	+16,397 / +662	2,342 / 95
05/08	73,760 / 3,241	+17,705 / +784	2,529 / 112
	05/10: Mother's Day		
	05/15: IFR (infection fatality rate) = 4.47%		
	05/15: hospitalizations current = 4,367		
05/15	90,369 / 4,058	+16,609 / +817	2,373 / 117
05/22	105,444 / 4,715	+15,075 / +657	2,154 / 94
	05/25: Memorial Day		
	05/26: George Floyd protests begin		
05/29	117,455 / 5,270	+12,011 / +555	1,716 / 79
	05/31: total tests = 877,105		
	NEW! 06/01: deaths/million population = 428		
06/05	125,915 / 5,795	+8,460 / +525	1,209 / 75
06/12	131,198 / 6,260	+5,283 / +465	755 / 66
	06/15: IFR (infection fatality rate) = 4.76%		
	06/15: hospitalizations current = 1,961		
06/19	135,470 / 6,580	+4,272 / +320	610 / 46
	06/21: Father's Day		
06/26	140,291 / 7,048	+4,821 / +468	689 / 67
	06/30: total tests = 1,604,018		
	07/01: deaths/million population = 564		
07/03	146,872 / 7,215	+6,581 / +167	940 / 24
	07/04: Independence Day		
07/10	152,899 / 7,345	+6,027 / +130	861 / 19
	07/15: IFR (infection fatality rate) = 4.71%		
	07/15: hospitalizations current = 1,454		
07/17	160,509 / 7,465	+7,610 / +120	1,087 / 17
07/24	169,699 / 7,577	+9,190 / +112	1,313 / 16
07/31	180,118 / 7,692	+10,419 / +115	1,488 / 16
	07/31: total tests = 2,699,568		
	08/01: deaths/million population = 608		
08/07	191,808 / 7,822	+11,690 / +130	1,670 / 19
08/14	204,023 / 7,932	+12,215 / +110	1,745 / 16
	08/15: IFR (infection fatality rate) = 3.86%		
	08/15: hospitalizations current = 1,538		
08/21	217,346 / 8,066	+13,323 / +133	1,903 / 19
08/28	231,185 / 8,206	+13,839 / +140	1,977 / 20

DATE	CASES / DEATHS	WEEKLY INCREASE	DAILY AVERAGE
	08/31: total tests = 4,371,876		
	09/01: deaths/million population = 662		
09/04	**247,299 / 8,362**	**+16,114 / +156**	**2,302 / 22**
	09/07: Labor Day		
09/11	**259,883 / 8,505**	**+12,584 / +143**	**1,798 / 20**
	09/15: IFR (infection fatality rate) = 3.22%		
	09/15: hospitalizations current = 1,584		
09/18	**272,525 / 8,647**	**+12,642 / +142**	**1,806 / 20**
	NEW! 09/22: test positivity rate = 3.5%		
09/25	**286,374 / 8,807**	**+13,849 / +160**	**1,978 / 23**
	09/30: total tests = 5,763,128		
	10/01: deaths/million population = 710		
10/02	**300,385 / 8,992**	**+14,011 / +185**	**2,002 / 26**
10/09	**316,556 / 9,191**	**+16,171 / +199**	**2,310 / 28**
	10/15: IFR (infection fatality rate) = 2.80%		
	10/15: hospitalizations = 1,932		
10/16	**339,761 / 9,425**	**+23,205 / +234**	**3,315 / 33**
	10/22: test positivity rate = 5.8%		
10/23	**368,746 / 9,688**	**+28,985 / +263**	**4,141 / 38**
10/30	**408,660 / 9,994**	**+39,914 / +306**	**5,702 / 44**
	10/31: total tests = 7,729,845		
	11/01: deaths/million population = 795		
	11/03: Election Day		
11/06	**465,540 / 10,397**	**+56,880 / +403**	**8,126 / 58**
	11/07: Biden wins election		
11/13	**551,957 / 10,891**	**+86,417 / +494**	**12,345 / 71**
	11/15: IFR (infection fatality rate) = 1.95%		
	11/15: hospitalizations current = 5,474		
11/20	**634,395 / 11,795**	**+82,438 / +904**	**11,777 / 129**
	11/22: test positivity rate = 11.6%		
	11/26: Thanksgiving		
11/27	**705,063 / 12,686**	**+70,668 / +891**	**10,095 / 127**
	11/30: total tests = 10,699,586		
	12/01: deaths/million population = 1,057		
12/04	**770,088 / 13,782**	**+65,025 / +1,096**	**9,289 / 157**
12/11	**832,951 / 15,067**	**+62,863 / +1,285**	**8,980 / 184**
	12/14: first COVID-19 vaccinations given in the U.S.		
	12/15: IFR (infection fatality rate) = 1.81%		

DATE	CASES / DEATHS	WEEKLY INCREASE	DAILY AVERAGE
	12/15: hospitalizations current = 4,965		
12/18	**886,805 / 16,206**	**+53,854 / +1,139**	**7,693 / 163**
	12/22: new U.K. variant identified in the U.S.		
	12/22: test positivity rate = 7.5%		
	12/25: Christmas		
12/25	**930,849 / 17,154**	**+44,044 / +948**	**6,292 / 135**
	12/31: total tests = 13,374,665		
	12/31: deaths/million population = 1,434		
	01/01: New Year's Day		
	01/01: CFR (case fatality rate) = 2.54% (25.4X more deadly than influenza at 0.1%)		
01/01/2021	**970,590 / 18,173**	**+39,741 / +1,019**	**5,677 / 146**

BONUS: Enjoy additional week from upcoming book: PANDEMIC 2021: The U.S. Edition

01/06: right-wing mob insurrection at U.S. Capitol as Joe Biden confirmed president
01/08: Twitter permanently bans Trump's account

01/08	**1,017,322 / 19,108**	**+46,732 / +935**	**6,676 / 134**

*The daily average column is rounded to the nearest whole person. The infection fatality rate (IFR) is the number of deaths divided by the number of confirmed cases. The case fatality rate (CFR), shown only at the end of the year, is the number of deaths divided by the number of confirmed cases *which have had an outcome* (either recovery or death). The CFR excludes active cases.

CHAPTER 16

~ INDIANA *~*

POPULATION AS OF MARCH, 2020: 6,745,354
Republican Governor Eric Holcomb
VOTED RED: Trump 57.0% / Biden 41.0%

DATE	CASES / DEATHS	WEEKLY INCREASE	DAILY AVERAGE
01/30: WHO declares Public Health Emergency of International Concern			
01/31: Trump issues a China "travel ban"			
03/06: Indiana's first case			
03/06: Indiana declares Public Health Emergency			
03/11: WHO declares COVID-19 a pandemic			
03/13: Trump declares a National Emergency			
03/13: Trump issues a Europe "travel ban"			
03/13	15 / 0	+14 / +0	2 / 0
03/15: Indiana's first death			
03/15: IFR (infection fatality rate) = 3.85%			
03/20	124 / 9	+109 / +9	16 / 1
03/27	1,221 / 47	+1,097 / +38	157 / 5
03/31: total tests = 39,215			
04/03	3,935 / 189	+2,714 / +142	388 / 20
04/10	7,395 / 400	+3,460 / +211	494 / 30
04/12: Easter			
04/15: IFR (infection fatality rate) = 5.99%			
04/15: hospitalizations current = not given			
04/15: hospitalizations cumulative = not given			
04/17	10,590 / 638	+3,195 / +238	456 / 34
04/24	13,680 / 814	+3,090 / +176	441 / 25
04/30: total tests = 99,784			
05/01	18,630 / 1,175	+4,950 / +361	707 / 52

DATE	CASES / DEATHS	WEEKLY INCREASE	DAILY AVERAGE
05/08	**23,146 / 1,447**	**+4,516 / +272**	**645 / 39**
05/10: Mother's Day			
05/15: IFR (infection fatality rate) = 6.32%			
05/15: hospitalizations current = 1,294			
05/15: hospitalizations cumulative = 4,389			
05/15	**26,655 / 1,691**	**+3,509 / +244**	**501 / 35**
05/22	**30,409 / 1,941**	**+3,754 / +250**	**536 / 36**
05/25: Memorial Day			
05/26: George Floyd protests begin			
05/29	**33,558 / 2,110**	**+3,149 / +169**	**450 / 24**
05/31: total tests = 256,395			
NEW! 06/01: deaths/million population = 318			
06/05	**36,578 / 2,258**	**+3,020 / +148**	**431 / 21**
06/12	**39,146 / 2,396**	**+2,568 / +138**	**367 / 20**
06/15: IFR (infection fatality rate) = 6.02%			
06/15: hospitalizations current = 882			
06/15: hospitalizations cumulative = 6,451			
06/19	**41,746 / 2,516**	**+2,600 / +120**	**371 / 17**
06/21: Father's Day			
06/26	**44,140 / 2,595**	**+2,394 / +79**	**342 / 11**
06/30: total tests = 484,196			
07/01: deaths/million population = 394			
07/03	**46,915 / 2,681**	**+2,775 / +86**	**396 / 12**
07/04: Independence Day			
07/10	**50,300 / 2,748**	**+3,385 / +67**	**484 / 10**
07/15: IFR (infection fatality rate) = 5.22%			
07/15: hospitalizations current = 881			
07/15: hospitalizations cumulative = 7,686			
07/17	**54,813 / 2,803**	**+4,513 / +55**	**645 / 8**
07/24	**60,598 / 2,884**	**+5,785 / +81**	**826 / 12**
*07/27: mask mandate			
07/31	**66,154 / 2,965**	**+5,556 / +81**	**794 / 12**
07/31: total tests = 747,383			
08/01: deaths/million population = 441			
08/07	**72,254 / 3,023**	**+6,100 / +58**	**871 / 8**
08/14	**78,632 / 3,113**	**+6,378 / +90**	**911 / 13**
08/15: IFR (infection fatality rate) = 3.93%			
08/15: hospitalizations current = 922			

DATE	CASES / DEATHS	WEEKLY INCREASE	DAILY AVERAGE
	08/15: hospitalizations cumulative = 9,872		
08/21	**84,317 / 3,208**	**+5,685 / +95**	**812 / 14**
08/28	**91,313 / 3,277**	**+6,996 / +69**	**999 / 10**
	08/31: total tests = 1,518,612		
	09/01: deaths/million population = 499		
09/04	**97,884 / 3,350**	**+6,571 / +73**	**939 / 10**
	09/07: Labor Day		
09/11	**103,505 / 3,420**	**+5,621 / +70**	**803 / 10**
	09/15: IFR (infection fatality rate) = 2.01%		
	09/15: hospitalizations current = 809		
	09/15: hospitalizations cumulative = 11,651		
09/18	**109,683 / 3,495**	**+6,178 / +75**	**883 / 11**
	NEW! 09/22: test positivity rate = 8.9%		
09/25	**115,407 / 3,566**	**+5,724 / +71**	**818 / 10**
	09/30: total tests = 2,114,835		
	10/01: deaths/million population = 543		
10/02	**122,640 / 3,656**	**+7,233 / +90**	**1,033 / 13**
10/09	**131,493 / 3,761**	**+8,853 / +105**	**1,265 / 15**
	10/15: IFR (infection fatality rate) = 2.74%		
	10/15: hospitalizations current = 1,355		
	10/15: hospitalizations cumulative = 14,353		
10/16	**143,495 / 3,887**	**+12,002 / +126**	**1,715 / 18**
	10/22: test positivity rate = 8.7%		
10/23	**157,713 / 4,092**	**+14,218 / +205**	**2,031 / 29**
10/30	**175,893 / 4,286**	**+18,180 / +194**	**2,597 / 28**
	10/31: total tests = 2,910,617		
	11/01: deaths/million population = 648		
	11/03: Election Day		
11/06	**200,823 / 4,547**	**+24,930 / +261**	**3,561 / 37**
	11/07: Biden wins election		
11/13	**236,565 / 4,863**	**+35,742 / +316**	**5,106 / 45**
	11/15: IFR (infection fatality rate) = 1.95%		
	11/15: hospitalizations current = 2,628		
	11/15: hospitalizations cumulative = 20,704		
11/20	**282,311 / 5,206**	**+45,746 / +343**	**6,535 / 49**
	11/22: test positivity rate = 12.5%		
	11/26: Thanksgiving		
11/27	**324,537 / 5,594**	**+42,226 / +388**	**6,032 / 55**

DATE	CASES / DEATHS	WEEKLY INCREASE	DAILY AVERAGE
	11/30: total tests = 4,342,486		
	12/01: deaths/million population = 887		
12/04	**367,329 / 6,122**	**+42,792 / +528**	**6,113 / 75**
12/11	**412,135 / 6,673**	**+44,806 / +551**	**6,401 / 79**
	12/14: first COVID-19 vaccinations given in the U.S.		
	12/15: IFR (infection fatality rate) = 1.60%		
	12/15: hospitalizations current = 3,229		
	12/15: hospitalizations cumulative = 31,324		
12/18	**453,139 / 7,265**	**+41,004 / +592**	**5,858 / 85**
	12/22: new U.K. variant identified in the U.S.		
	12/22: test positivity rate = 11.6%		
	12/25: Christmas		
12/25	**488,180 / 7,770**	**+35,041 / +505**	**5,006 / 72**
	12/31: total tests = 5,730,043		
	12/31: deaths/million population = 1,243		
	01/01: New Year's Day		
	01/01: CFR (case fatality rate) = 2.33% (23.3X more deadly than influenza at 0.1%)		
01/01/2021	**517,773 / 8,371**	**+29,593 / +601**	**4,228 / 86**

BONUS: Enjoy additional week from upcoming book: PANDEMIC 2021: The U.S. Edition

DATE	CASES / DEATHS	WEEKLY INCREASE	DAILY AVERAGE
	01/06: right-wing mob insurrection at U.S. Capitol as Joe Biden confirmed president		
	01/08: Twitter permanently bans Trump's account		
01/08	**552,594 / 8,892**	**+34,821 / +521**	**4,974 / 74**

*The daily average column is rounded to the nearest whole person. The infection fatality rate (IFR) is the number of deaths divided by the number of confirmed cases. The case fatality rate (CFR), shown only at the end of the year, is the number of deaths divided by the number of confirmed cases *which have had an outcome* (either recovery or death). The CFR excludes active cases.

CHAPTER 17

~ IOWA *~*

POPULATION AS OF MARCH, 2020: 3,179,849
Republican Governor Kim Reynolds
VOTED RED: Trump 53.1% / Biden 44.9%

DATE	CASES / DEATHS	WEEKLY INCREASE	DAILY AVERAGE
01/30: WHO declares Public Health Emergency of International Concern			
01/31: Trump issues a China "travel ban"			
03/07: Iowa's first 3 cases			
03/11: WHO declares COVID-19 a pandemic			
03/13: Trump declares a National Emergency			
03/13: Trump issues a Europe "travel ban"			
03/13	**17 / 0**	**N/A**	**N/A**
03/17: Iowa declares Disaster Emergency			
03/20	**84 / 0**	**+67 / +0**	**10 / 0**
03/24: Iowa's first death			
03/27	**380 / 3**	**+296 / +3**	**42 / 0**
03/31: total tests = 5,668			
04/03	**949 / 18**	**+569 / +15**	**81 / 2**
04/10	**1,388 / 31**	**+439 / +13**	**63 / 2**
04/12: Easter			
04/15: IFR (infection fatality rate) = 2.66%			
04/15: hospitalizations current = 171			
04/15: hospitalizations cumulative = not given for this state			
04/17	**2,332 / 64**	**+944 / +33**	**135 / 5**
04/24	**4,445 / 107**	**+2,113 / +43**	**302 / 6**
04/30: total tests = 49,727			
05/01	**7,884 / 170**	**+3,439 / +63**	**491 / 9**

DATE	CASES / DEATHS	WEEKLY INCREASE	DAILY AVERAGE
05/08	**11,457 / 243**	**+3,573 / +73**	**510 / 10**
05/10: Mother's Day			
05/15: IFR (infection fatality rate) = 2.33%			
05/15: hospitalizations current = 387			
05/15	**14,049 / 336**	**+2,592 / +93**	**370 / 13**
05/22	**16,508 / 433**	**+2,459 / +97**	**351 / 14**
05/25: Memorial Day			
05/26: George Floyd protests begin			
05/29	**18,956 / 524**	**+2,448 / +91**	**350 / 13**
05/31: total tests = 150,880			
NEW! 06/01: deaths/million population = 175			
06/05	**21,160 / 593**	**+2,204 / +69**	**315 / 10**
06/12	**23,350 / 644**	**+2,190 / +51**	**313 / 7**
06/15: IFR (infection fatality rate) = 2.73%			
06/15: hospitalizations current = 197			
06/19	**25,276 / 681**	**+1,926 / +37**	**275 / 5**
06/21: Father's Day			
06/26	**27,716 / 704**	**+2,440 / +23**	**349 / 3**
06/30: total tests = 304,607			
07/01: deaths/million population = 227			
07/03	**30,434 / 721**	**+2,718 / +17**	**388 / 2**
07/04: Independence Day			
07/10	**34,171 / 743**	**+3,737 / +22**	**534 / 3**
07/15: IFR (infection fatality rate) = 2.12%			
07/15: hospitalizations current = 190			
07/17	**37,777 / 784**	**+3,606 / +41**	**515 / 6**
07/24	**41,283 / 824**	**+3,506 / +40**	**501 / 6**
07/31	**44,582 / 867**	**+3,299 / +43**	**471 / 6**
07/31: total tests = 476,325			
08/01: deaths/million population = 276			
08/07	**47,888 / 915**	**+3,306 / +48**	**472 / 7**
08/14	**50,943 / 967**	**+3,055 / +52**	**436 / 7**
08/15: IFR (infection fatality rate) = 1.88%			
08/15: hospitalizations current = 261			
08/18: Trump rally			
08/21	**55,017 / 1,022**	**+4,074 / +55**	**582 / 8**
08/28	**62,375 / 1,097**	**+7,358 / +75**	**1,051 / 11**
08/31: total tests = 663,388			

DATE	CASES / DEATHS	WEEKLY INCREASE	DAILY AVERAGE
09/01: deaths/million population = 368			
09/04	68,412 / 1,153	+6,037 / +56	862 / 8
09/07: Labor Day			
09/11	73,085 / 1,213	+4,673 / +60	668 / 9
09/15: IFR (infection fatality rate) = 1.64%			
09/15: hospitalizations current = 284			
09/18	78,558 / 1,261	+5,473 / +48	782 / 7
NEW! 09/22: test positivity rate = 15.8%			
09/25	84,726 / 1,308	+6,168 / +47	881 / 7
09/30: total tests = 812,155			
10/01: deaths/million population = 436			
10/02	91,035 / 1,375	+6,309 / +67	901 / 10
10/09	97,475 / 1,441	+6,440 / +66	920 / 9
10/14: Trump rally			
10/15: IFR (infection fatality rate) = 1.45%			
10/15: hospitalizations current = 482			
10/16	105,432 / 1,523	+7,957 / +82	1,137 / 12
10/22: test positivity rate = 22.3%			
10/23	112,928 / 1,621	+7,496 / +98	1,071 / 14
10/30	125,177 / 1,706	+12,249 / +85	1,750 / 12
10/31: total tests = 973,502			
11/01: deaths/million population = 544			
11/03: Election Day			
11/06	145,071 / 1,819	+19,894 / +113	2,842 / 16
11/07: Biden wins election			
11/13	176,708 / 1,949	+31,637 / +130	4,520 / 19
11/15: IFR (infection fatality rate) = 1.07%			
11/15: hospitalizations = 1,279			
11/17: mask mandate			
11/20	203,975 / 2,135	+27,267 / +186	3,895 / 27
11/22: test positivity rate = 47.0%			
11/26: Thanksgiving			
11/27	224,258 / 2,352	+20,283 / +217	2,898 / 31
11/30: total tests = 1,224,362			
12/01: deaths/million population = 776			
12/04	240,323 / 2,605	+16,065 / +253	2,295 / 36
12/11	253,612 / 3,197	+13,289 / +592	1,898 / 85
12/14: first COVID-19 vaccinations given in the U.S.			

DATE	CASES / DEATHS	WEEKLY INCREASE	DAILY AVERAGE
	12/15: IFR (infection fatality rate) = 1.29%		
	12/15: hospitalizations current = 798		
12/18	**264,760 / 3,451**	**+11,148 / +254**	**1,593 / 36**
	12/22: new U.K. variant identified in the U.S.		
	12/22: test positivity rate = 32.3%		
	12/25: Christmas		
12/25	**274,016 / 3,744**	**+9,256 / +293**	**1,322 / 42**
	12/31: total tests = 1,360,191		
	12/31: deaths/million population = 1,235		
	01/01: New Year's Day		
	01/01: CFR (case fatality rate) = 1.59% (15.9X more deadly than influenza at 0.1%)		
01/01/2021	**282,663 / 3,898**	**+8,647 / +154**	**1,235 / 22**

BONUS: Enjoy additional week from upcoming book: PANDEMIC 2021: The U.S. Edition
01/06: right-wing mob insurrection at U.S. Capitol as Joe Biden confirmed president
01/08: Twitter permanently bans Trump's account

01/08	**294,009 / 4,124**	**+11,346 / +226**	**1,621 / 32**

*The daily average column is rounded to the nearest whole person. The infection fatality rate (IFR) is the number of deaths divided by the number of confirmed cases. The case fatality rate (CFR), shown only at the end of the year, is the number of deaths divided by the number of confirmed cases *which have had an outcome* (either recovery or death). The CFR excludes active cases.

CHAPTER 18

~ KANSAS *~*

POPULATION AS OF MARCH, 2020: 2,910,357
Democratic Governor Laura Kelly
VOTED RED: Trump 56.1% / Biden 41.5%

DATE	CASES / DEATHS	WEEKLY INCREASE	DAILY AVERAGE
	01/30: WHO declares Public Health Emergency of International Concern		
	01/31: Trump issues a China "travel ban"		
	03/07: Kansas' first case		
	03/11: WHO declares COVID-19 a pandemic		
	03/12: Kansas' first death		
	03/12: Kansas declares State of Disaster Emergency		
	03/13: Trump declares a National Emergency		
	03/13: Trump issues a Europe "travel ban"		
03/13	11 / 1	N/A	N/A
	03/15: IFR (infection fatality rate) = 7.14%		
03/20	75 / 1	+64 / +0	9 / 0
03/27	299 / 5	+224 / +4	32 / 1
	03/31: total tests = 4,184		
04/03	728 / 22	+429 / +17	61 / 2
04/10	1,228 / 56	+500 / +34	71 / 5
	04/12: Easter		
	04/15: IFR (infection fatality rate) = 5.09%		
	04/15: hospitalizations current = not given		
	04/15: hospitalizations cumulative = 342		
04/17	1,705 / 84	+477 / +28	68 / 4
04/24	2,955 / 118	+1,250 / +34	179 / 5
	04/30: total tests = 33,034		
05/01	4,536 / 138	+1,581 / +20	226 / 3

DATE	CASES / DEATHS	WEEKLY INCREASE	DAILY AVERAGE
05/08	**6,667 / 168**	**+2,131 / +30**	**304 / 4**
05/10: Mother's Day			
05/15: IFR (infection fatality rate) = 2.45%			
05/15: hospitalizations current = not given			
05/15: hospitalizations cumulative = 724			
05/15	**7,886 / 193**	**+1,219 / +25**	**174 / 4**
05/22	**9,024 / 207**	**+1,138 / +14**	**163 / 2**
05/25: Memorial Day			
05/26: George Floyd protests begin			
05/29	**9,764 / 216**	**+740 / +9**	**106 / 1**
05/31: total tests = 94,949			
NEW! 06/01: deaths/million population = 77			
06/05	**10,426 / 232**	**+662 / +16**	**95 / 2**
06/12	**11,124 / 245**	**+698 / +13**	**100 / 2**
06/15: IFR (infection fatality rate) = 2.15%			
06/15: hospitalizations current = not given			
06/15: hospitalizations cumulative = 988			
06/19	**12,125 / 254**	**+1,001 / +9**	**143 / 1**
06/21: Father's Day			
06/26	**13,613 / 266**	**+1,488 / +12**	**213 / 2**
06/30: total tests = 176,725			
07/01: deaths/million population = 95			
07/02: mask mandate			
07/03	**16,005 / 282**	**+2,392 / +16**	**342 / 2**
07/04: Independence Day			
07/10	**18,723 / 294**	**+2,718 / +12**	**388 / 2**
07/15: IFR (infection fatality rate) = 1.44%			
07/15: hospitalizations current = not given			
07/15: hospitalizations cumulative = 1,393			
07/17	**22,116 / 305**	**+3,393 / +11**	**485 / 2**
07/24	**25,348 / 328**	**+3,232 / +23**	**462 / 3**
07/31	**30,151 / 358**	**+4,803 / +30**	**686 / 4**
07/31: total tests = 292,507			
08/01: deaths/million population = 123			
08/07	**30,932 / 380**	**+781 / +22**	**112 / 3**
08/14	**34,177 / 405**	**+3,245 / +25**	**464 / 4**
08/15: IFR (infection fatality rate) = 1.18%			
08/15: hospitalizations current = 311			

DATE	CASES / DEATHS	WEEKLY INCREASE	DAILY AVERAGE
	08/15: hospitalizations cumulative = 2,020		
08/21	**37,225 / 422**	**+3,048 / +17**	**435 / 2**
08/28	**41,565 / 444**	**+4,340 / +22**	**620 / 3**
	08/31: total tests = 427,205		
	09/01: deaths/million population = 165		
09/04	**45,920 / 481**	**+4,355 / +37**	**622 / 5**
	09/07: Labor Day		
09/11	**49,188 / 515**	**+3,268 / +34**	**467 / 5**
	09/15: IFR (infection fatality rate) = 1.10%		
	09/15: hospitalizations current = 192		
	09/15: hospitalizations cumulative = 2,572		
09/18	**53,238 / 596**	**+4,050 / +81**	**579 / 12**
	NEW! 09/22: test positivity rate = 15.4%		
09/25	**57,613 / 634**	**+4,375 / +38**	**625 / 5**
	09/30: total tests = 531,117		
	10/01: deaths/million population = 240		
10/02	**61,111 / 698**	**+3,498 / +64**	**500 / 9**
10/09	**66,881 / 763**	**+5,770 / +65**	**824 / 9**
	10/15: IFR (infection fatality rate) = 1.19%		
	10/15: hospitalizations current = 488		
	10/15: hospitalizations cumulative = 3,309		
10/16	**72,084 / 859**	**+5,203 / +96**	**743 / 14**
	10/22: test positivity rate = 15.4%		
10/23	**76,230 / 975**	**+4,146 / +116**	**592 / 17**
10/30	**86,381 / 1,029**	**+10,151 / +54**	**1,450 / 8**
	10/31: total tests = 531,117		
	11/01: deaths/million population = 240		
	11/03: Election Day		
11/06	**98,755 / 1,166**	**+12,374 / +137**	**1,768 / 20**
	11/07: Biden wins election		
11/13	**116,858 / 1,256**	**+18,103 / +90**	**2,586 / 13**
	11/15: IFR (infection fatality rate) = 1.07%		
	11/15: hospitalizations current = 811		
	11/15: hospitalizations cumulative = 4,327		
11/20	**136,241 / 1,410**	**+19,383 / +154**	**2,769 / 22**
	11/22: test positivity rate = 35.1%		
	11/26: Thanksgiving		
11/27	**153,021 / 1,529**	**+16,780 / +119**	**2,397 / 17**

DATE	CASES / DEATHS	WEEKLY INCREASE	DAILY AVERAGE
11/30: total tests = 831,182			
12/01: deaths/million population = 576			
12/04	**170,469 / 1,786**	**+17,448 / +257**	**2,493 / 37**
12/11	**187,567 / 2,072**	**+17,098 / +286**	**2,443 / 41**
12/14: first COVID-19 vaccinations given in the U.S.			
12/15: IFR (infection fatality rate) = 1.09%			
12/15: hospitalizations current = 623			
12/15: hospitalizations cumulative = 5,895			
12/18	**202,596 / 2,341**	**+15,029 / +269**	**2,147 / 38**
12/22: new U.K. variant identified in the U.S.			
12/22: test positivity rate = 34.4%			
12/25: Christmas			
12/25	**212,214 / 2,507**	**+9,618 / +166**	**1,374 / 24**
12/31: total tests = 1,012,506			
12/31: deaths/million population = 988			
01/01: New Year's Day			
01/01: CFR (case fatality rate) = 1.91% (19.1X more deadly than influenza at 0.1%)			
01/01/2021	**229,556 / 2,879**	**+17,342 / +372**	**2,477 / 53**

BONUS: Enjoy additional week from upcoming book: PANDEMIC 2021: The U.S. Edition

01/06: right-wing mob insurrection at U.S. Capitol as Joe Biden confirmed president
01/08: Twitter permanently bans Trump's account

DATE	CASES / DEATHS	WEEKLY INCREASE	DAILY AVERAGE
01/08	**242,322 / 3,148**	**+12,766 / +272**	**1,824 / 39**

---

*The daily average column is rounded to the nearest whole person. The infection fatality rate (IFR) is the number of deaths divided by the number of confirmed cases. The case fatality rate (CFR), shown only at the end of the year, is the number of deaths divided by the number of confirmed cases *which have had an outcome* (either recovery or death). The CFR excludes active cases.

CHAPTER 19

~ KENTUCKY *~*

POPULATION AS OF MARCH, 2020: 4,499,692
Democratic Governor Andy Beshear
VOTED RED: Trump 62.1% / Biden 36.1%

DATE	CASES / DEATHS	WEEKLY INCREASE	DAILY AVERAGE
	01/30: WHO declares Public Health Emergency of International Concern		
	01/31: Trump issues a China "travel ban"		
	03/06: Kentucky declares State of Emergency		
	03/07: Kentucky's first case		
	03/11: WHO declares COVID-19 a pandemic		
	03/13: Breonna Taylor death		
	03/13: Trump declares a National Emergency		
	03/13: Trump issues a Europe "travel ban"		
03/13	14 / 0	N/A	N/A
	03/16: Kentucky's first death		
03/20	48 / 2	+34 / +2	5 / 0
03/27	302 / 8	+254 / +6	36 / 1
	03/31: total tests = 9,022		
04/03	831 / 37	+529 / +29	76 / 4
04/10	1,693 / 90	+862 / +53	123 / 8
	04/12: Easter		
	04/15: IFR (infection fatality rate) = 5.33%		
	04/15: hospitalizations current = 305		
	04/15: hospitalizations cumulative = 687		
04/17	2,522 / 137	+829 / +47	118 / 7
04/24	3,779 / 200	+1,257 / +63	180 / 9
	04/30: total tests = 57,648		
05/01	4,879 / 248	+1,100 / +48	157 / 7

DATE	CASES / DEATHS	WEEKLY INCREASE	DAILY AVERAGE
05/08	**6,288 / 298**	**+1,409 / +50**	**201 / 7**
05/10: Mother's Day			
05/15: IFR (infection fatality rate) = 4.54%			
05/15: hospitalizations current = 385			
05/15: hospitalizations cumulative = 1,887			
05/15	**7,444 / 332**	**+1,156 / +34**	**165 / 5**
05/22	**8,426 / 391**	**+982 / +59**	**140 / 8**
05/25: Memorial Day			
05/26: George Floyd protests begin			
05/29	**9,464 / 418**	**+1,038 / +27**	**148 / 4**
05/31: total tests = 234,142			
NEW! 06/01: deaths/million population = 128			
06/05	**10,977 / 466**	**+1,513 / +48**	**216 / 7**
06/12	**12,166 / 497**	**+1,189 / +31**	**170 / 4**
06/15: IFR (infection fatality rate) = 3.99%			
06/15: hospitalizations current = 383			
06/15: hospitalizations cumulative = 2,433			
06/19	**13,454 / 522**	**+1,288 / +25**	**184 / 4**
06/21: Father's Day			
06/26	**14,859 / 553**	**+1,405 / +31**	**201 / 4**
06/30: total tests = 404,781			
07/01: deaths/million population = 128			
07/03	**16,376 / 585**	**+1,517 / +32**	**217 / 5**
07/04: Independence Day			
07/10: mask mandate			
07/10	**18,670 / 620**	**+2,294 / +35**	**328 / 5**
07/15: IFR (infection fatality rate) = 3.12%			
07/15: hospitalizations current = 445			
07/15: hospitalizations cumulative = 2,823			
07/17	**21,605 / 658**	**+2,935 / +38**	**419 / 5**
07/24	**25,931 / 691**	**+4,326 / +33**	**618 / 5**
07/31	**30,151 / 736**	**+4,220 / +45**	**603 / 6**
07/31: total tests = 629,706			
08/01: deaths/million population = 166			
08/07	**33,796 / 764**	**+3,645 / +28**	**521 / 4**
08/14	**38,298 / 804**	**+4,502 / +40**	**643 / 6**
08/15: IFR (infection fatality rate) = 2.08%			
08/15: hospitalizations current = 618			

DATE	CASES / DEATHS	WEEKLY INCREASE	DAILY AVERAGE
	08/15: hospitalizations cumulative = 4,193		
08/21	**42,265 / 864**	**+3,967 / +60**	**567 / 9**
08/28	**46,747 / 918**	**+4,482 / +54**	**640 / 8**
	08/31: total tests = 930,374		
	09/01: deaths/million population = 222		
09/04	**51,677 / 987**	**+4,930 / +69**	**704 / 10**
	09/07: Labor Day		
09/11	**55,704 / 1,044**	**+4,027 / +57**	**575 / 8**
	09/15: IFR (infection fatality rate) = 1.85%		
	09/15: hospitalizations current = 533		
	09/15: hospitalizations cumulative = 4,924		
09/18	**60,128 / 1,101**	**+4,424 / +57**	**632 / 8**
	NEW! 09/22: test positivity rate = 6.9%		
09/25	**65,066 / 1,149**	**+4,938 / +48**	**705 / 7**
	09/30: total tests = 1,507,046		
	10/01: deaths/million population = 268		
10/02	**70,727 / 1,197**	**+5,661 / +48**	**809 / 7**
10/09	**78,456 / 1,242**	**+7,729 / +45**	**1,104 / 6**
	10/15: IFR (infection fatality rate) = 1,54%		
	10/15: hospitalizations current = 738		
	10/15: hospitalizations cumulative = 6,506		
10/16	**85,506 / 1,300**	**+7,050 / +58**	**1,007 / 8**
	10/22: test positivity rate = 7.3%		
10/23	**93,748 / 1,396**	**+8,242 / +96**	**1,177 / 14**
10/30	**105,242 / 1,476**	**+11,494 / +80**	**1,642 / 11**
	10/31: total tests = 2,044,583		
	11/01: deaths/million population = 333		
	11/03: Election Day		
11/06	**117,505 / 1,544**	**+12,263 / +68**	**1,752 / 10**
	11/07: Biden wins election		
11/13	**132,844 / 1,647**	**+15,339 / +103**	**2,191 / 15**
	11/15: IFR (infection fatality rate) = 1.21%		
	11/15: hospitalizations current = 1,378		
	11/15: hospitalizations cumulative = 8,783		
11/20	**152,206 / 1,762**	**+19,362 / +115**	**2,766 / +16**
	11/22: test positivity rate = 11.1%		
	11/26: Thanksgiving		
11/27	**171,755 / 1,871**	**+19,549 / +109**	**2,793 / 16**

DATE	CASES / DEATHS	WEEKLY INCREASE	DAILY AVERAGE
	11/30: total tests = 2,830,995		
	12/01: deaths/million population = 443		
12/04	**194,193 / 2,039**	**+22,438 / +168**	**3,205 / 24**
12/11	**217,120 / 2,168**	**+22,927 / +129**	**3,275 / 18**
	12/14: first COVID-19 vaccinations given in the U.S.		
	12/15: IFR (infection fatality rate) = 0.98%		
	12/15: hospitalizations current = 1,788		
	12/15: hospitalizations cumulative = 11,589		
12/18	**237,190 / 2,344**	**+20,070 / +176**	**2,867 / 25**
	12/22: new U.K. variant identified in the U.S.		
	12/22: test positivity rate = 17.1%		
	12/25: Christmas		
12/25	**254,801 / 2,530**	**+17,611 / +186**	**2,516 / 27**
	12/31: total tests = 3,414,879		
	12/31: deaths/million population = 587		
	01/01: New Year's Day		
	01/01: CFR (case fatality rate) = 6.66% (66.6X more deadly than influenza at 0.1%)		
01/01/2021	**265,262 / 2,623**	**+10,461 / +93**	**1,494 / 13**

BONUS: Enjoy additional week from upcoming book: PANDEMIC 2021: The U.S. Edition
01/06: right-wing mob insurrection at U.S. Capitol as Joe Biden confirmed president
01/08: Twitter permanently bans Trump's account

| **01/08** | **296,167 / 2,856** | **+30,905 / +233** | **4,415 / 33** |

*The daily average column is rounded to the nearest whole person. The infection fatality rate (IFR) is the number of deaths divided by the number of confirmed cases. The case fatality rate (CFR), shown only at the end of the year, is the number of deaths divided by the number of confirmed cases *which have had an outcome* (either recovery or death). The CFR excludes active cases.

CHAPTER 20

~ LOUISIANA *~*

POPULATION AS OF MARCH, 2020: 4,645,184
Republican Governor John Bel Edwards
VOTED RED: Trump 58.5% / Biden 39.9%

DATE	CASES / DEATHS	WEEKLY INCREASE	DAILY AVERAGE
01/30: WHO declares Public Health Emergency of International Concern			
01/31: Trump issues a China "travel ban"			
03/09: Louisiana's first case			
03/11: WHO declares COVID-19 a pandemic			
03/11: Louisiana declares Public Health Emergency			
03/13: Trump declares a National Emergency			
03/13: Trump issues a Europe "travel ban"			
03/13	36 / 0	N/A	N/A
03/14: Louisiana's first death			
03/16: schools close			
03/20	537 / 14	+501 / +14	72 / 2
03/22: non-essential services close			
03/27	2,746 / 119	+2,209 / +105	316 / 15
03/31: total tests = 31,086			
04/03	10,297 / 370	+7,551 / +251	1,079 / 36
04/10	19,253 / 755	+8,956 / +385	1,279 / 55
04/12: Easter			
04/15: IFR (infection fatality rate) = 5.02%			
04/15: hospitalizations current = 1,943			
04/15: hospitalizations cumulative = not given for this state			
04/17	23,118 / 1,213	+3,865 / +458	552 / 65
04/24	26,140 / 1,660	+3,022 / +447	432 / 64
04/30: total tests = 172,858			

DATE	CASES / DEATHS	WEEKLY INCREASE	DAILY AVERAGE
05/01	28,711 / 1,970	+2,571 / +310	367 / 44
05/08	30,855 / 2,227	+2,144 / +257	306 / 37

05/10: Mother's Day
05/15: IFR (infection fatality rate) = 7.22%
05/15: hospitalizations current = 1,091

| 05/15 | 33,837 / 2,448 | +2,982 / +221 | 426 / 32 |
| 05/22 | 36,925 / 2,668 | +3,088 / +220 | 441 / 31 |

05/25: Memorial Day
05/26: George Floyd protests begin

| 05/29 | 38,809 / 2,766 | +1,884 / +98 | 269 / 14 |

05/31: total tests = 368,819
NEW! 06/01: deaths/million population = 603

| 06/05 | 42,016 / 2,918 | +3,207 / +152 | 458 / 22 |
| 06/12 | 44,995 / 3,002 | +2,979 / +84 | 426 / 12 |

06/15: IFR (infection fatality rate) = 6.41%
06/15: hospitalizations current = 568

| 06/19 | 48,634 / 3,068 | +3,639 / +66 | 520 / 9 |

06/21: Father's Day

| 06/26 | 54,804 / 3,197 | +6,170 / +129 | 881 / 18 |

06/30: total tests = 752,081
07/01: deaths/million population = 697

| 07/03 | 63,289 / 3,283 | +8,485 / +86 | 1,212 / 12 |

07/04: Independence Day

| 07/10 | 74,636 / 3,385 | +11,347 / +102 | 1,621 / 15 |

07/13: mask mandate
07/15: IFR (infection fatality rate) = 4.12%
07/15: hospitalizations current = 1,369

07/17	88,590 / 3,511	+13,954 / +126	1,993 / 18
07/24	103,734 / 3,720	+15,144 / +209	2,163 / 30
07/31	116,280 / 3,953	+12,546 / +233	1,792 / 33

07/31: total tests = 1,342,243
08/01: deaths/million population = 850

| 08/07 | 128,746 / 4,207 | +12,466 / +254 | 1,781 / 36 |
| 08/14 | 136,737 / 4,433 | +7,991 / +226 | 1,142 / 32 |

08/15: IFR (infection fatality rate) = 3.24%
08/15: hospitalizations current = 1,243

| 08/21 | 141,720 / 4,687 | +4,983 / +254 | 712 / 36 |
| 08/28 | 146,243 / 4,904 | +4,523 / +217 | 646 / 31 |

DATE	CASES / DEATHS	WEEKLY INCREASE	DAILY AVERAGE
08/31: total tests = 1,931,748			
09/01: deaths/million population = 1,083			
09/04	**151,473 / 5,035**	**+5,230 / +131**	**747 / 19**
09/07: Labor Day			
09/11	**156,174 / 5,202**	**+4,701 / +167**	**672 / 24**
09/15: IFR (infection fatality rate) = 3.33%			
09/15: hospitalizations current = 667			
09/18	**160,283 / 5,340**	**+4,109 / +138**	**587 / 20**
NEW! 09/22: test positivity rate = 3.5%			
09/25	**163,928 / 5,444**	**+3,645 / +104**	**521 / 15**
09/30: total tests = 2,356,024			
10/01: deaths/million population = 1,193			
10/02	**167,401 / 5,545**	**+3,473 / +101**	**496 / 14**
10/09	**170,878 / 5,635**	**+3,477 / +90**	**497 / 13**
10/15: IFR (infection fatality rate) = 3.28%			
10/15: hospitalizations current = 566			
10/16	**174,638 / 5,727**	**+3,760 / +92**	**537 / 13**
10/22: test positivity rate = 4.7%			
10/23	**178,870 / 5,820**	**+4,232 / +93**	**605 / 13**
10/30	**182,270 / 5,919**	**+3,400 / +99**	**486 / 14**
10/31: total tests = 2,759,292			
11/01: deaths/million population = 1,275			
11/03: Election Day			
11/06	**186,695 / 6,016**	**+4,425 / +97**	**632 / 14**
11/07: Biden wins election			
11/13	**201,981 / 6,121**	**+15,286 / +105**	**2,184 / 15**
11/15: IFR (infection fatality rate) = 3.00%			
11/15: hospitalizations current = 753			
11/20	**216,709 / 6,233**	**+14,728 / +112**	**2,104 / 16**
11/22: test positivity rate = 8.0%			
11/26: Thanksgiving			
11/27	**230,602 / 6,391**	**+13,893 / +158**	**1,985 / 23**
11/30: total tests = 3,618,895			
12/01: deaths/million population = 1,398			
12/04	**247,177 / 6,548**	**+16,575 / +157**	**2,368 / 22**
12/11	**264,191 / 6,767**	**+17,014 / +219**	**2,431 / 31**
12/14: first COVID-19 vaccinations given in the U.S.			
12/15: IFR (infection fatality rate) = 2.53%			

DATE	CASES / DEATHS	WEEKLY INCREASE	DAILY AVERAGE
12/15: hospitalizations current = 1,597			
12/18	**282,434 / 6,994**	**+18,243 / +227**	**2,606 / 32**
12/22: new U.K. variant identified in the U.S.			
12/22: test positivity rate = 10.0%			
12/25: Christmas			
12/25	**296,499 / 7,272**	**+14,065 / +278**	**2,009 / 40**
12/31: total tests = 4,400,149			
12/31: deaths/million population = 1,611			
01/01: New Year's Day			
01/01: CFR (case fatality rate) = 2.76% (27.6X more deadly than influenza at 0.1%)			
01/01/2021	**315,275 / 7,488**	**+18,776 / +216**	**2,682 / 31**

BONUS: *Enjoy additional week from upcoming book: PANDEMIC 2021: The U.S. Edition*
01/06: right-wing mob insurrection at U.S. Capitol as Joe Biden confirmed president
01/08: Twitter permanently bans Trump's account

DATE	CASES / DEATHS	WEEKLY INCREASE	DAILY AVERAGE
01/08	**341,431 / 7,833**	**+26,156 / +345**	**3,737 / 49**

*The daily average column is rounded to the nearest whole person. The infection fatality rate (IFR) is the number of deaths divided by the number of confirmed cases. The case fatality rate (CFR), shown only at the end of the year, is the number of deaths divided by the number of confirmed cases *which have had an outcome* (either recovery or death). The CFR excludes active cases.

CHAPTER 21

~ MAINE *~*

POPULATION AS OF MARCH, 2020: 1,345,790
Democratic Governor Janet T. Mills
VOTED BLUE: Biden 53.1% / Trump 44.0%

DATE	CASES / DEATHS	WEEKLY INCREASE	DAILY AVERAGE
	01/30: WHO declares Public Health Emergency of International Concern		
	01/31: Trump issues a China "travel ban"		
	03/11: WHO declares COVID-19 a pandemic		
	03/12: Maine's first case		
	03/13: Trump declares a National Emergency		
	03/13: Trump issues a Europe "travel ban"		
03/13	3 / 0	N/A	N/A
	03/15: Maine declares State of Civil Emergency		
	03/16: schools close		
03/20	56 / 0	+53 / +0	8 / 0
	03/25: non-essential services close		
	03/27: Maine's first death		
03/27	168 / 1	+112 / +1	16 / 0
	03/31: total tests = 4,464		
04/03	432 / 9	+264 / +8	38 / 1
04/10	586 / 16	+154 / +7	22 / 1
	04/12: Easter		
	04/15: IFR (infection fatality rate) = 3.12%		
	04/15: hospitalizations current = 48		
	04/15: hospitalizations cumulative = 126		
04/17	827 / 29	+241 / +13	34 / 2
04/24	965 / 47	+138 / +18	20 / 3
	04/30: total tests = 20,641		

DATE	CASES / DEATHS	WEEKLY INCREASE	DAILY AVERAGE
05/01: mask mandate			
05/01	**1,123 / 55**	**+158 / +8**	**23 / 1**
05/08	**1,374 / 63**	**+251 / +8**	**36 / 1**
05/10: Mother's Day			
05/15: IFR (infection fatality rate) = 4.41%			
05/15: hospitalizations current = 35			
05/15: hospitalizations cumulative = 211			
05/15	**1,603 / 69**	**+229 / +6**	**33 / 1**
05/22	**1,948 / 76**	**+345 / +7**	**49 / 1**
05/25: Memorial Day			
05/26: George Floyd protests begin			
05/29	**2,226 / 85**	**+278 / +9**	**40 / 1**
05/31: total tests = 54,061			
NEW! 06/01: deaths/million population = 66			
06/05	**2,482 / 98**	**+256 / +13**	**37 / 2**
06/12	**2,721 / 100**	**+239 / +2**	**34 / 0**
06/15: IFR (infection fatality rate) = 3.59%			
06/15: hospitalizations current = 31			
06/15: hospitalizations cumulative = 317			
06/19	**2,913 / 102**	**+192 / +2**	**27 / 0**
06/21: Father's Day			
06/26	**3,102 / 103**	**+189 / +1**	**27 / 0**
06/30: total tests = 102,039			
07/01: deaths/million population = 78			
07/03	**3,373 / 105**	**+271 / +2**	**39 / 0**
07/04: Independence Day			
07/10	**3,499 / 111**	**+126 / +6**	**18 / 1**
07/15: IFR (infection fatality rate) = 3.19%			
07/15: hospitalizations current = 12			
07/15: hospitalizations cumulative = 373			
07/17	**3,636 / 115**	**+137 / +4**	**20 / 1**
07/24	**3,757 / 118**	**+121 / +3**	**17 / 0**
07/31	**3,912 / 123**	**+155 / +5**	**22 / 1**
07/31: total tests = 175,575			
08/01: deaths/million population = 92			
08/07	**4,014 / 124**	**+102 / +1**	**15 / 0**
08/14	**4,115 / 126**	**+101 / +2**	**14 / 0**
08/15: IFR (infection fatality rate) = 3.06%			

DATE	CASES / DEATHS	WEEKLY INCREASE	DAILY AVERAGE
	08/15: hospitalizations current = 5		
	08/15: hospitalizations cumulative = 399		
08/21	**4,285 / 129**	**+170 / +3**	**24 / 0**
08/28	**4,436 / 132**	**+151 / +3**	**22 / 0**
	08/31: total tests = 301,243		
	09/01: deaths/million population = 100		
09/04	**4,632 / 134**	**+196 / +2**	**28 / 0**
	09/07: Labor Day		
09/11	**4,792 / 134**	**+160 / +0**	**23 / 0**
	09/15: IFR (infection fatality rate) = 2.79%		
	09/15: hospitalizations current = 10		
	09/15: hospitalizations cumulative = 432		
09/18	**5,005 / 138**	**+213 / +4**	**30 / 1**
	NEW! 09/22: test positivity rate = 1%		
09/25	**5,235 / 140**	**+230 / +2**	**33 / 0**
	09/30: total tests = 459,167		
	10/01: deaths/million population = 106		
10/02	**5,468 / 142**	**+233 / +2**	**33 / 0**
10/09	**5,666 / 143**	**+198 / +1**	**28 / 0**
	10/15: IFR (infection fatality rate) = 2.47%		
	10/15: hospitalizations current = 11		
	10/15: hospitalizations cumulative = 464		
10/16	**5,865 / 145**	**+199 / +2**	**28 / 0**
	10/22: test positivity rate = 0.6%		
10/23	**6,095 / 146**	**+230 / +1**	**33 / 0**
10/30	**6,570 / 146**	**+475 / +0**	**68 / 0**
	10/31: total tests = 634,829		
	11/01: deaths/million population = 109		
	11/03: Election Day		
	11/04: mask mandate		
11/06	**7,444 / 150**	**+874 / +4**	**125 / 1**
	11/07: Biden wins election		
11/13	**8,639 / 162**	**+1,195 / +12**	**171 / 2**
	11/15: IFR (infection fatality rate) = 1.81%		
	11/15: hospitalizations current = 67		
	11/15: hospitalizations cumulative = 574		
11/20	**9,958 / 173**	**+1,319 / +11**	**188 / 2**
	11/22: test positivity rate = 30.0%		

PANDEMIC 2020: The U.S. Edition

DATE	CASES / DEATHS	WEEKLY INCREASE	DAILY AVERAGE
11/26: Thanksgiving			
11/27	11,265 / 190	+1,307 / +17	187 / 2
11/30: total tests = 927,793			
12/01: deaths/million population = 162			
12/04	12,844 / 224	+1,579 / +34	226 / 5
12/11	15,206 / 250	+2,362 / +26	337 / 4
12/14: first COVID-19 vaccinations given in the U.S.			
12/15: IFR (infection fatality rate) = 1.58%			
12/15: hospitalizations current = 195			
12/15: hospitalizations cumulative = 909			
12/18	18,337 / 281	+3,131 / +31	447 / 4
12/22: new U.K. variant identified in the U.S.			
12/22: test positivity rate = 5.8%			
12/25: Christmas			
12/25	21,547 / 319	+3,210 / +38	459 / 5
12/31: total tests = 1,207,730			
12/31: deaths/million population = 258			
01/01: New Year's Day			
01/01: CFR (case fatality rate) = 2.96% (29.6X more deadly than influenza at 0.1%)			
01/01/2021	24,201 / 347	+2,654 / +28	379 / 4

BONUS: Enjoy additional week from upcoming book: PANDEMIC 2021: The U.S. Edition
01/06: right-wing mob insurrection at U.S. Capitol as Joe Biden confirmed president
01/08: Twitter permanently bans Trump's account

| 01/08 | 28,407 / 426 | +4,206 / +79 | 601 / 11 |

*The daily average column is rounded to the nearest whole person. The infection fatality rate (IFR) is the number of deaths divided by the number of confirmed cases. The case fatality rate (CFR), shown only at the end of the year, is the number of deaths divided by the number of confirmed cases *which have had an outcome* (either recovery or death). The CFR excludes active cases.

CHAPTER 22

~ MARYLAND *~*

POPULATION AS OF MARCH, 2020: 6,083,116
Republican Governor Larry Hogan
VOTED BLUE: Biden 65.4% / Trump 32.1%

DATE	CASES / DEATHS	WEEKLY INCREASE	DAILY AVERAGE
01/30: WHO declares Public Health Emergency of International Concern			
01/31: Trump issues a China "travel ban"			
03/05: Maryland's first 3 cases			
03/05: State of Emergency declared			
03/11: WHO declares COVID-19 a pandemic			
03/13: Trump declares a National Emergency			
03/13: Trump issues a Europe "travel ban"			
03/13	**17 / 0**	**+14 / +0**	**2 / 0**
03/16: schools close			
03/18: Maryland's first death			
03/20	**150 / 2**	**+133 / +2**	**19 / 0**
03/23: non-essential services close			
03/27	**774 / 5**	**+624 / +3**	**89 / 0**
03/30: stay at home order			
03/31: total tests = 18,221			
04/03	**2,758 / 42**	**+1,984 / +37**	**283 / 5**
04/10	**6,968 / 171**	**+4,210 / +129**	**601 / 18**
04/12: Easter			
04/15: IFR (infection fatality rate) = 3.48%			
04/15: hospitalizations current = not given			
04/15: hospitalizations cumulative = 2,231			
04/17	**11,572 / 425**	**+4,604 / +254**	**658 / 36**
04/18: mask mandate			

DATE	CASES / DEATHS	WEEKLY INCREASE	DAILY AVERAGE
04/24	**16,616 / 798**	**+5,044 / +373**	**721 / 53**
04/30: total tests = 125,522			
05/01	**23,472 / 1,192**	**+6,856 / +394**	**979 / 56**
05/08	**30,485 / 1,560**	**+7,013 / +368**	**1,002 / 53**
05/10: Mother's Day			
05/15: IFR (infection fatality rate) = 5.17%			
05/15: hospitalizations current = 1,496			
05/15: hospitalizations cumulative = 6,679			
05/15	**36,986 / 1,911**	**+6,501 / +351**	**929 / 50**
05/22	**44,424 / 2,207**	**+7,438 / +296**	**1,063 / 42**
05/25: Memorial Day			
05/26: George Floyd protests begin			
05/29	**50,988 / 2,466**	**+6,564 / +259**	**938 / 37**
05/31: total tests = 339,361			
NEW! 06/01: deaths/million population = 420			
06/05	**56,770 / 2,702**	**+5,782 / +236**	**826 / 34**
06/12	**60,613 / 2,900**	**+3,843 / +198**	**549 / 28**
06/15: IFR (infection fatality rate) = 4.75%			
06/15: hospitalizations current = 745			
06/15: hospitalizations cumulative = 10,222			
06/19	**63,548 / 3,030**	**+2,935 / +130**	**419 / 19**
06/21: Father's Day			
06/26	**66,115 / 3,142**	**+2,567 / +112**	**367 / 16**
06/30: total tests = 652,701			
07/01: deaths/million population = 530			
07/03	**68,961 / 3,223**	**+2,846 / +81**	**407 / 12**
07/04: Independence Day			
07/10	**71,910 / 3,303**	**+2,949 / +80**	**421 / 11**
07/15: IFR (infection fatality rate) = 4.45%			
07/15: hospitalizations current = 447			
07/15: hospitalizations cumulative = 11,625			
07/17	**76,371 / 3,359**	**+4,461 / +56**	**637 / 8**
07/24	**81,766 / 3,422**	**+5,395 / +63**	**771 / 9**
07/31	**88,346 / 3,493**	**+6,580 / +71**	**940 / 10**
07/31: mask mandate			
07/31: total tests = 1,214,764			
08/01: deaths/million population = 580			
08/07	**93,806 / 3,565**	**+5,460 / +72**	**780 / 10**

DATE	CASES / DEATHS	WEEKLY INCREASE	DAILY AVERAGE
08/14	**98,875 / 3,631**	**+5,069 / +66**	**724 / 9**
08/15: IFR (infection fatality rate) = 3.65%			
08/15: hospitalizations current = 460			
08/15: hospitalizations cumulative = 13,556			
08/21	**102,899 / 3,674**	**+4,024 / +43**	**575 / 6**
08/28	**106,664 / 3,736**	**+3,765 / +62**	**538 / 9**
08/31: total tests = 2,047,516			
09/01: deaths/million population = 628			
09/04	**110,831 / 3,789**	**+4,167 / +53**	**595 / 8**
09/07: Labor Day			
09/11	**114,724 / 3,828**	**+3,893 / +39**	**556 / 6**
09/15: IFR (infection fatality rate) = 3.28%			
09/15: hospitalizations current = 371			
09/15: hospitalizations cumulative = 14,918			
09/18	**119,062 / 3,869**	**+4,338 / +41**	**620 / 6**
NEW! 09/22: test positivity rate = 5.1%			
09/25	**122,359 / 3,917**	**+3,297 / +48**	**471 / 7**
09/30: total tests = 2,660,800			
10/01: deaths/million population = 653			
10/02	**126,222 / 3,950**	**+3,863 / +33**	**552 / 5**
10/09	**130,159 / 3,990**	**+3,937 / +40**	**562 / 6**
10/15: IFR (infection fatality rate) = 3.02%			
10/15: hospitalizations current = 412			
10/15: hospitalizations cumulative = 16,255			
10/16	**134,329 / 4,032**	**+4,170 / +42**	**596 / 6**
10/22: test positivity rate = 2.4%			
10/23	**138,691 / 4,078**	**+4,362 / +46**	**623 / 7**
10/30	**144,314 / 4,137**	**+5,623 / +59**	**803 / 8**
10/31: total tests = 3,422,662			
11/01: deaths/million population = 887			
11/03: Election Day			
11/06	**151,505 / 4,194**	**+7,191 / +57**	**1,027 / 8**
11/07: Biden wins election			
11/13	**161,769 / 4,273**	**+10,264 / +79**	**1,466 / 11**
11/15: IFR (infection fatality rate) = 2.59%			
11/15: hospitalizations current = 938			
11/15: hospitalizations cumulative = 18,576			
11/20	**177,086 / 4,398**	**+15,317 / +125**	**2,188 / 18**

DATE	CASES / DEATHS	WEEKLY INCREASE	DAILY AVERAGE
11/22: test positivity rate = 6.3%			
11/26: Thanksgiving			
11/27	**192,858 / 4,569**	**+15,772 / +171**	**2,253 / 24**
11/30: total tests = 4,496,011			
12/01: deaths/million population = 780			
12/04	**209,191 / 4,790**	**+16,333 / +221**	**2,333 / 32**
12/11	**228,471 / 5,064**	**+19,280 / +274**	**2,754 / 39**
12/14: first COVID-19 vaccinations given in the U.S.			
12/15: IFR (infection fatality rate) = 2.17%			
12/15: hospitalizations current = 1,799			
12/15: hospitalizations cumulative = 23,711			
12/18	**246,553 / 5,358**	**+18,082 / +294**	**2,583 / 42**
12/22: new U.K. variant identified in the U.S.			
12/22: test positivity rate = 6.1%			
12/25: Christmas			
12/25	**263,160 / 5,659**	**+16,607 / +301**	**2,372 / 43**
12/31: total tests = 5,761,534			
12/31: deaths/million population = 983			
01/01: New Year's Day			
01/01: CFR (case fatality rate) = 38.84% (388.4X more deadly than influenza at 0.1%)			
01/01/2021	**280,219 / 5,942**	**+17,059 / +283**	**2,437 / 40**

BONUS: *Enjoy additional week from upcoming book: PANDEMIC 2021: The U.S. Edition*

01/06: right-wing mob insurrection at U.S. Capitol as Joe Biden confirmed president
01/08: Twitter permanently bans Trump's account

DATE	CASES / DEATHS	WEEKLY INCREASE	DAILY AVERAGE
01/08	**299,606 / 6,216**	**+19,387 / +274**	**2,770 / 39**

---

*The daily average column is rounded to the nearest whole person. The infection fatality rate (IFR) is the number of deaths divided by the number of confirmed cases. The case fatality rate (CFR), shown only at the end of the year, is the number of deaths divided by the number of confirmed cases *which have had an outcome* (either recovery or death). The CFR excludes active cases.

CHAPTER 23

~ MASSACHUSETTS *~*

POPULATION AS OF MARCH, 2020: 6,976,597
Republican Governor Charles D. Baker
VOTED BLUE: Biden 65.6% / Trump 32.1%

DATE	CASES / DEATHS	WEEKLY INCREASE	DAILY AVERAGE
01/30: WHO declares Public Health Emergency of International Concern			
01/31: Trump issues a China "travel ban"			
02/01: Massachusetts' first case			
03/06	8 / 0	+7 / +0	1 / 0
03/10: Massachusetts declares State of Emergency			
03/11: WHO declares COVID-19 a pandemic			
03/13: Trump declares a National Emergency			
03/13: Trump issues a Europe "travel ban"			
03/13	123 / 0	+115 / +0	16 / 0
03/17: schools close			
03/19: Massachusetts' first 2 deaths			
03/20	413 / 3	+290 / +3	41 / 0
03/27	3,240 / 42	+2,827 / +39	404 / 6
03/31: total tests = 43,749			
04/03	10,402 / 189	+7,162 / +147	1,023 / 21
04/10	20,974 / 599	+10,572 / +410	1,510 / 59
04/12: Easter			
04/15: IFR (infection fatality rate) = 3.70%			
04/15: hospitalizations current = 3,637			
04/15: hospitalizations cumulative = 3,637			
04/17	34,402 / 1,404	+13,428 / +805	1,918 / 115
04/24	50,969 / 2,556	+16,567 / +1,152	2,367 / 165
04/30: total tests = 298,994			

DATE	CASES / DEATHS	WEEKLY INCREASE	DAILY AVERAGE
05/01	64,311 / 3,716	+13,342 / +1,160	1,906 / 166
05/06: mask mandate			
05/08	75,333 / 4,702	+11,022 / +986	1,575 / 141
05/10: Mother's Day			
05/15: IFR (infection fatality rate) = 6.70%			
05/15: hospitalizations current = 2,767			
05/15: hospitalizations cumulative = 8,314			
05/15	83,421 / 5,592	+8,088 / +890	1,155 / 127
05/22	90,889 / 6,228	+7,468 / +636	1,067 / 91
05/25: Memorial Day			
05/26: George Floyd protests begin			
05/29	95,512 / 6,718	+4,623 / +490	660 / 70
05/31: total tests = 582,519			
NEW! 06/01: deaths/million population = 1,008			
06/05	102,557 / 7,235	+7,045 / +517	1,006 / 74
06/12	105,059 / 7,538	+2,502 / +303	357 / 43
06/15: IFR (infection fatality rate) = 7.24%			
06/15: hospitalizations current = 1,026			
06/15: hospitalizations cumulative = 10,817			
06/19	106,650 / 7,800	+1,591 / +262	227 / 37
06/21: Father's Day			
06/26	108,070 / 8,013	+1,420 / +213	203 / 30
06/30: total tests = 914,636			
07/01: deaths/million population = 1,172			
07/03	109,628 / 8,149	+1,558 / +136	223 / 19
07/04: Independence Day			
07/10	111,110 / 8,296	+1,482 / +147	212 / 21
07/15: IFR (infection fatality rate) = 7.45%			
07/15: hospitalizations current = 580			
07/15: hospitalizations cumulative = 11,651			
07/17	112,879 / 8,402	+1,769 / +106	253 / 15
07/24	114,985 / 8,498	+2,106 / +96	301 / 14
07/31	117,612 / 8,609	+2,627 / +111	375 / 16
07/31: total tests = 1,276,785			
08/01: deaths/million population = 1,252			
08/07	120,291 / 8,709	+2,679 / +100	383 / 14
08/14	122,728 / 8,810	+2,437 / +101	348 / 14
08/15: IFR (infection fatality rate) = 7.16%			

DATE	CASES / DEATHS	WEEKLY INCREASE	DAILY AVERAGE
08/15: hospitalizations current = 375			
08/15: hospitalizations cumulative = 12,170			
08/21	**125,216 / 8,901**	**+2,488 / +91**	**355 / 13**
08/28	**127,584 / 9,024**	**+2,368 / +123**	**338 / 18**
08/31: total tests = 2,047,135			
09/01: deaths/million population = 1,323			
09/04	**121,758 / 9,100**	***(-)5,826 / +76**	**(-) / 11**
09/07: Labor Day			
09/11	**123,986 / 9,180**	**+2,228 / +80**	**318 / 11**
09/15: IFR (infection fatality rate) = 7.36%			
09/15: hospitalizations current = 310			
09/15: hospitalizations cumulative = 12,462			
09/18	**126,582 / 9,269**	**+2,596 / +89**	**371 / 13**
NEW! 09/22: test positivity rate = 0.6%			
09/25	**129,481 / 9,373**	**+2,899 / +104**	**414 / 15**
09/30: total tests = 2,528,986			
10/01: deaths/million population = 1,377			
10/02	**133,631 / 9,490**	**+4,150 / +117**	**593 / 17**
10/09	**137,701 / 9,577**	**+4,070 / +87**	**581 / 12**
10/15: IFR (infection fatality rate) = 6.83%			
10/15: hospitalizations current = 503			
10/15: hospitalizations cumulative = 12,946			
10/16	**142,346 / 9,702**	**+4,645 / +125**	**664 / 18**
10/22: test positivity rate = 1.2%			
10/23	**148,285 / 9,830**	**+5,939 / +128**	**848 / 18**
10/30	**157,146 / 9,975**	**+8,861 / +145**	**1,266 / 21**
10/31: total tests = 3,056,025			
11/01: deaths/million population = 1,453			
11/03: Election Day			
11/06: mask mandate			
11/06	**167,274 / 10,106**	**+10,128 / +131**	**1,447 / 19**
11/07: Biden wins election			
11/13	**183,095 / 10,265**	**+15,821 / +159**	**2,260 / 23**
11/15: IFR (infection fatality rate) = 5.49%			
11/15: hospitalizations current = 737			
11/15: hospitalizations cumulative = 13,588			
11/20	**200,949 / 10,469**	**+17,854 / +204**	**2,551 / 29**
11/22: test positivity rate = 3.3%			

DATE	CASES / DEATHS	WEEKLY INCREASE	DAILY AVERAGE
11/26: Thanksgiving			
11/27	219,252 / 10,635	+18,303 / +166	2,615 / 24
11/30: total tests = 8,566,262			
12/01: deaths/million population = 1,570			
12/04	246,398 / 10,910	+27,146 / +275	3,878 / 39
12/11	280,436 / 11,257	+34,038 / +347	4,863 / 50
12/14: first COVID-19 vaccinations given in the U.S.			
12/15: IFR (infection fatality rate) = 3.84%			
12/15: hospitalizations current = 1,834			
12/15: hospitalizations cumulative = 14,823			
12/18	314,926 / 11,610	+34,490 / +353	4,927 / 50
12/22: new U.K. variant identified in the U.S.			
12/22: test positivity rate = 5.4%			
12/25: Christmas			
12/25	341,925 / 11,963	+26,999 / +353	3,857 / 50
12/31: total tests = 10,944,699			
12/31: deaths/million population = 1,802			
01/01: New Year's Day			
01/01: CFR (case fatality rate) = 4.21% (42.1X more deadly than influenza at 0.1%)			
01/01/2021	375,178 / 12,423	+33,253 / +460	4,750 / 66

BONUS: Enjoy additional week from upcoming book: PANDEMIC 2021: The U.S. Edition
 01/06: right-wing mob insurrection at U.S. Capitol as Joe Biden confirmed president
 01/08: Twitter permanently bans Trump's account

01/08	419,721 / 12,985	+44,543 / +562	6,363 / 80

*authorities occasionally make a case/death correction, resulting in a subtraction

*The daily average column is rounded to the nearest whole person. The infection fatality rate (IFR) is the number of deaths divided by the number of confirmed cases. The case fatality rate (CFR), shown only at the end of the year, is the number of deaths divided by the number of confirmed cases *which have had an outcome* (either recovery or death). The CFR excludes active cases.

CHAPTER 24

~ MICHIGAN *~*

POPULATION AS OF MARCH, 2020: 10,045,029
Democratic Governor Gretchen Whitmer
VOTED BLUE: Biden 50.6% / Trump 47.8%

DATE	CASES / DEATHS	WEEKLY INCREASE	DAILY AVERAGE
01/30: WHO declares Public Health Emergency of International Concern			
01/31: Trump issues a China "travel ban"			
03/10: Michigan's first 2 cases			
03/10: Michigan declares State of Emergency			
03/11: WHO declares COVID-19 a pandemic			
03/13: Trump declares a National Emergency			
03/13: Trump issues a Europe "travel ban"			
03/13	25 / 0	N/A	N/A
03/16: schools close			
03/18: Michigan's first death			
03/20	549 / 3	+524 / +3	75 / 0
03/23: non-essential services close			
03/24: stay at home order			
03/27	3,657 / 92	+3,108 / +89	444 / 13
03/31: total tests = 73,014			
04/03	12,744 / 479	+9,087 / +387	1,298 / 55
04/10	22,783 / 1,281	+10,039 / +802	1,434 / 115
04/12: Easter			
04/15: IFR (infection fatality rate) = 6.85%			
04/15: hospitalizations current = 3,918			
04/15: hospitalizations cumulative = not given for this state			
04/17: Trump tweets LIBERATE MICHIGAN			
04/17	30,023 / 2,227	+7,240 / +946	1,034 / 135

DATE	CASES / DEATHS	WEEKLY INCREASE	DAILY AVERAGE
04/24	**36,641 / 3,085**	**+6,618 / +858**	**945 / 123**
04/26: mask mandate			
04/30: total tests = 207,184			
05/01	**42,356 / 3,866**	**+5,715 / +781**	**816 / 112**
05/08	**46,326 / 4,393**	**+3,970 / +527**	**567 / 75**
05/10: Mother's Day			
05/15: IFR (infection fatality rate) = 9.63%			
05/15: hospitalizations current = 1,256			
05/15	**50,079 / 4,825**	**+3,753 / +432**	**536 / 62**
05/22	**53,913 / 5,158**	**+3,834 / +333**	**548 / 48**
05/25: Memorial Day			
05/26: George Floyd protests begin			
05/29	**56,621 / 5,406**	**+2,708 / +248**	**387 / 35**
05/31: total tests = 538,812			
NEW! 06/01: deaths/million population = 549			
06/05	**63,539 / 5,855**	**+6,918 / +449**	**988 / 64**
06/12	**65,672 / 5,990**	**+2,133 / +135**	**305 / 19**
06/15: IFR (infection fatality rate) = 9.10%			
06/15: hospitalizations current = 562			
06/19	**67,097 / 6,067**	**+1,425 / +77**	**204 / 11**
06/21: Father's Day			
06/26	**69,329 / 6,134**	**+2,232 / +67**	**319 / 10**
06/30: total tests = 1,222,547			
07/01: deaths/million population = 621			
07/03	**72,175 / 6,215**	**+2,846 / +81**	**407 / 12**
07/04: Independence Day			
07/10	**75,685 / 6,285**	**+3,510 / +70**	**501 / 10**
07/15: IFR (infection fatality rate) = 8.02%			
07/15: hospitalizations current = 543			
07/17	**80,593 / 6,355**	**+4,908 / +70**	**701 / 10**
07/24	**85,072 / 6,400**	**+4,479 / +45**	**640 / 6**
07/31	**90,574 / 6,450**	**+5,502 / +50**	**786 / 7**
07/31: total tests = 20,083,079			
08/01: deaths/million population = 647			
08/07	**95,470 / 6,524**	**+4,896 / +74**	**699 / 11**
08/14	**100,724 / 6,566**	**+5,254 / +42**	**751 / 6**
08/15: IFR (infection fatality rate) = 6.54%			
08/15: hospitalizations current = 713			

DATE	CASES / DEATHS	WEEKLY INCREASE	DAILY AVERAGE
08/21	104,618 / 6,634	+3,894 / +68	556 / 10
08/28	111,136 / 6,712	+6,518 / +78	931 / 11
08/31: total tests = 3,215,536			
09/01: deaths/million population = 681			
09/04	116,295 / 6,798	+5,159 / +86	737 / 12
09/07: Labor Day			
09/10: Trump rally			
09/11	122,251 / 6,900	+5,956 / +102	851 / 15
09/15: IFR (infection fatality rate) = 5.74%			
09/15: hospitalizations current = 590			
09/18	127,500 / 6,955	+5,249 / +55	750 / 8
NEW! 09/22: test positivity rate = 2.7%			
09/25	133,377 / 7,027	+5,877 / +72	840 / 10
09/30: total tests = 4,056,442			
10/01: deaths/million population = 712			
10/02	139,996 / 7,110	+6,619 / +83	946 / 12
10/05: mask mandate			
10/09	147,816 / 7,200	+7,820 / +90	1,117 / 13
10/15: IFR (infection fatality rate) = 4.65%			
10/15: hospitalizations current = 1,000			
10/16	159,119 / 7,317	+11,303 / +117	1,615 / 17
10/17: Trump rally			
10/22: test positivity rate = 4.4%			
10/23	172,122 / 7,484	+13,003 / +167	1,858 / 24
10/27: Trump rally			
10/30	193,388 / 7,665	+21,266 / +181	3,038 / 26
10/31: total tests = 5,282,297			
11/01: deaths/million population = 771			
11/03: Election Day			
11/06	222,509 / 7,880	+29,121 / +215	4,160 / 31
11/07: Biden wins election			
11/13	268,362 / 8,308	+45,853 / +428	6,550 / 61
11/15: IFR (infection fatality rate) = 3.04%			
11/15: hospitalizations current = 3,241			
11/20	321,181 / 8,774	+52,819 / +466	7,546 / 67
11/22: test positivity rate = 11.7%			
11/26: Thanksgiving			
11/27	369,801 / 9,357	+48,620 / +583	6,946 / 83

DATE	CASES / DEATHS	WEEKLY INCREASE	DAILY AVERAGE
	11/30: total tests = 7,201,724		
	12/01: deaths/million population = 985		
12/04	**420,268 / 10,118**	**+50,467 / +761**	**7,210 / 109**
12/11	**460,346 / 10,965**	**+40,078 / +847**	**5,725 / 121**
	12/14: first COVID-19 vaccinations given in the U.S.		
	12/15: IFR (infection fatality rate) = 2.40%		
	12/15: hospitalizations current = 3,674		
12/18	**491,875 / 11,868**	**+31,529 / +903**	**4,504 / 129**
	12/22: new U.K. variant identified in the U.S.		
	12/22: test positivity rate = 8.1%		
	12/25: Christmas		
12/25	**513,343 / 12,415**	**+21,468 / +547**	**3,067 / 78**
	12/31: total tests = 8,630,181		
	12/31: deaths/million population = 1,304		
	01/01: New Year's Day		
	01/01: CFR (case fatality rate) = 3.93% (39.3X more deadly than influenza at 0.1%)		
01/01/2021	**528,621 / 13,018**	**+15,278 / +603**	**2,183 / 86**

BONUS: Enjoy additional week from upcoming book: PANDEMIC 2021: The U.S. Edition
01/06: right-wing mob insurrection at U.S. Capitol as Joe Biden confirmed president
01/08: Twitter permanently bans Trump's account

01/08	**559,655 / 13,913**	**+31,034 / +895**	**4,433 / 128**

---

*The daily average column is rounded to the nearest whole person. The infection fatality rate (IFR) is the number of deaths divided by the number of confirmed cases. The case fatality rate (CFR), shown only at the end of the year, is the number of deaths divided by the number of confirmed cases *which have had an outcome* (either recovery or death). The CFR excludes active cases.

CHAPTER 25

~ MINNESOTA *~*

POPULATION AS OF MARCH, 2020: 5,700,671
Democratic Governor Tim Walz
VOTED BLUE: Biden 52.4% / Trump 45.3%

DATE	CASES / DEATHS	WEEKLY INCREASE	DAILY AVERAGE
01/30: WHO declares Public Health Emergency of International Concern			
01/31: Trump issues a China "travel ban"			
03/05: Minnesota's first case			
03/11: WHO declares COVID-19 a pandemic			
03/13: Minnesota declares Peacetime Emergency			
03/13: Trump declares a National Emergency			
03/13: Trump issues a Europe "travel ban"			
03/13	62 / 0	+61 / +0	9 / 0
03/18: schools close			
03/20	303 / 0	+241 / +0	34 / 0
03/21: Minnesota's first death			
03/27: stay at home order			
03/27	640 / 4	+337 / +4	48 / 1
03/31: total tests = 11,475			
04/03	1,119 / 22	+479 / +18	68 / 3
04/10	1,598 / 54	+479 / +32	68 / 5
04/12: Easter			
04/15: IFR (infection fatality rate) = 4.81%			
04/15: hospitalizations current = 197			
04/15: hospitalizations cumulative = 445			
04/17: Trump tweets LIBERATE MINNESOTA			
04/17	2,071 / 111	+473 / +57	68 / 8
04/24	3,185 / 221	+1,114 / +110	159 / 16

DATE	CASES / DEATHS	WEEKLY INCREASE	DAILY AVERAGE
04/30: total tests = 79,007			
05/01	**5,730 / 371**	**+2,545 / +150**	**364 / 21**
05/08	**10,088 / 534**	**+4,358 / +163**	**623 / 23**
05/10: Mother's Day			
05/15: IFR (infection fatality rate) = 4.86%			
05/15: hospitalizations current = 498			
05/15: hospitalizations cumulative = 1,985			
05/15	**14,240 / 692**	**+4,152 / +158**	**593 / 23**
05/22	**19,005 / 851**	**+4,765 / +159**	**681 / 23**
05/25: Memorial Day			
05/26: George Floyd protests begin			
05/29	**23,531 / 1,006**	**+4,526 / +155**	**647 / 22**
05/31: total tests = 242,508			
NEW! 06/01: deaths/million population = 186			
06/05	**26,980 / 1,159**	**+3,449 / +153**	**493 / 22**
06/12	**29,795 / 1,305**	**+2,815 / +146**	**402 / 21**
06/15: IFR (infection fatality rate) = 4.35%			
06/15: hospitalizations current = 353			
06/15: hospitalizations cumulative = 3,630			
06/19	**32,031 / 1,393**	**+2,236 / +88**	**319 / 13**
06/21: Father's Day			
06/26	**34,616 / 1,446**	**+2,585 / +53**	**369 / 8**
06/30: total tests = 605,316			
07/01: deaths/million population = 263			
07/03	**37,624 / 1,503**	**+3,008 / +57**	**430 / 8**
07/04: Independence Day			
07/10	**40,767 / 1,533**	**+3,143 / +30**	**449 / 4**
07/15: IFR (infection fatality rate) = 3.56%			
07/15: hospitalizations current = 254			
07/15: hospitalizations cumulative = 4,495			
07/17	**45,013 / 1,573**	**+4,246 / +40**	**607 / 6**
07/24	**49,488 / 1,606**	**+4,475 / +33**	**639 / 5**
07/25: mask mandate			
07/31	**54,463 / 1,640**	**+4,975 / +34**	**711 / 5**
07/31: total tests = 1,024,916			
08/01: deaths/million population = 292			
08/07	**59,185 / 1,681**	**+4,722 / +41**	**675 / 6**
08/14	**63,723 / 1,739**	**+4,538 / +58**	**648 / 8**

DATE	CASES / DEATHS	WEEKLY INCREASE	DAILY AVERAGE
08/15: IFR (infection fatality rate) = 2.71%			
08/15: hospitalizations current = 307			
08/15: hospitalizations cumulative = 5,822			
08/17: Trump rally			
08/21	68,133 / 1,799	+4,410 / +60	630 / 9
08/28	73,240 / 1,859	+5,107 / +60	730 / 9
08/31: total tests = 1,577,466			
09/01: deaths/million population = 337			
09/04	78,966 / 1,899	+5,726 / +40	818 / 6
09/07: Labor Day			
09/11	82,716 / 1,949	+3,750 / +50	536 / 7
09/15: IFR (infection fatality rate) = 2.32%			
09/15: hospitalizations current = 238			
09/15: hospitalizations cumulative = 6,979			
09/18: Trump rally			
09/18	87,807 / 2,002	+5,091 / +53	727 / 8
NEW! 09/22: test positivity rate = 4.7%			
09/25	94,189 / 2,046	+6,382 / +44	912 / 6
09/30: Trump rally			
09/30: total tests = 2,086,963			
10/01: deaths/million population = 374			
10/02	101,366 / 2,112	+7,177 / +66	1,025 / 9
10/09	109,312 / 2,174	+7,946 / +62	1,135 / 9
10/15: IFR (infection fatality rate) = 1.92%			
10/15: hospitalizations current = 445			
10/15: hospitalizations cumulative = 8,652			
10/16	119,396 / 2,265	+10,084 / +91	1,441 / 13
10/22: test positivity rate = 6.2%			
10/23	129,863 / 2,367	+10,467 / +102	1,495 / 15
10/30	145,465 / 2,491	+15,602 / +124	2,229 / 18
10/31: total tests = 2,839,304			
11/01: deaths/million population = 448			
11/03: Election Day			
11/06	170,307 / 2,645	+24,842 / +154	3,549 / 22
11/07: Biden wins election			
11/13	207,339 / 2,895	+37,032 / +250	5,290 / 36
11/15: IFR (infection fatality rate) = 1.32%			
11/15: hospitalizations current = 1,424			

DATE	CASES / DEATHS	WEEKLY INCREASE	DAILY AVERAGE
11/15: hospitalizations cumulative = 13,074			
11/20	**256,700 / 3,206**	**+49,361 / +311**	**7,052 / 44**
11/22: test positivity rate = 15.0%			
11/26: Thanksgiving			
11/27	**295,001 / 3,535**	**+38,301 / +329**	**5,472 / 47**
11/30: total tests = 4,326,347			
12/01: deaths/million population = 665			
12/04	**338,973 / 3,904**	**+43,972 / +369**	**6,282 / 53**
12/11	**370,968 / 4,351**	**+31,995 / +447**	**4,571 / 64**
12/14: first COVID-19 vaccinations given in the U.S.			
12/15: IFR (infection fatality rate) = 1.18%			
12/15: hospitalizations current = 1,309			
12/15: hospitalizations cumulative = 19,785			
12/18	**391,889 / 4,782**	**+20,921 / +431**	**2,989 / 62**
12/22: new U.K. variant identified in the U.S.			
12/22: test positivity rate = 6.5%			
12/25: Christmas			
12/25	**404,403 / 5,109**	**+12,514 / +327**	**1,788 / 47**
12/31: total tests = 5,574,962			
12/31: deaths/million population = 954			
01/01: New Year's Day			
01/01: CFR (case fatality rate) = 1.34% (13.4X more deadly than influenza at 0.1%)			
01/01/2021	**415,302 / 5,382**	**+10,889 / +273**	**1,556 / 39**

BONUS: Enjoy additional week from upcoming book: PANDEMIC 2021: The U.S. Edition
01/06: right-wing mob insurrection at U.S. Capitol as Joe Biden confirmed president
01/08: Twitter permanently bans Trump's account

| **01/08** | **431,944 / 5,688** | **+16,642 / +306** | **2,377 / 44** |

*The daily average column is rounded to the nearest whole person. The infection fatality rate (IFR) is the number of deaths divided by the number of confirmed cases. The case fatality rate (CFR), shown only at the end of the year, is the number of deaths divided by the number of confirmed cases *which have had an outcome* (either recovery or death). The CFR excludes active cases.

CHAPTER 26

~ MISSISSIPPI *~*

POPULATION AS OF MARCH, 2020: 2,989,260
Republican Governor Tate Reeves
VOTED RED: Trump 57.5% / Biden 41.0%

DATE	CASES / DEATHS	WEEKLY INCREASE	DAILY AVERAGE
01/30: WHO declares Public Health Emergency of International Concern			
01/31: Trump issues a China "travel ban"			
03/11: WHO declares COVID-19 a pandemic			
03/11: Mississippi's first case			
03/13: Trump declares a National Emergency			
03/13: Trump issues a Europe "travel ban"			
03/13	6 / 0	N/A	N/A
03/14: Mississippi declares State of Emergency			
03/19: Mississippi's first death			
03/19: schools close			
03/20	80 / 1	+74 / +1	11 / 0
03/27	579 / 8	+499 / +7	71 / 1
03/31: total tests = 3,943			
04/03: non-essential services close			
04/03: stay at home order			
04/03	1,358 / 29	+779 / +21	111 / 3
04/10	2,469 / 82	+1,111 / +53	159 / 8
04/12: Easter			
04/15: IFR (infection fatality rate) = 3.63%			
04/15: hospitalizations current = not given			
04/15: hospitalizations cumulative = 645			
04/17	3,793 / 140	+1,324 / +58	189 / 8
04/24	5,434 / 209	+1,641 / +69	234 / 10

DATE	CASES / DEATHS	WEEKLY INCREASE	DAILY AVERAGE
04/30: total tests = 74,475			
05/01	**7,212 / 281**	**+1,778 / +72**	**254 / 10**
05/08	**9,090 / 409**	**+1,878 / +128**	**268 / 18**
05/10: Mother's Day			
05/15: IFR (infection fatality rate) = 4.56%			
05/15: hospitalizations current = 573			
05/15: hospitalizations cumulative = 1,712			
05/15	**10,801 / 493**	**+1,711 / +84**	**244 / 12**
05/22	**12,624 / 596**	**+1,823 / +103**	**260 / 15**
05/25: Memorial Day			
05/26: George Floyd protests begin			
05/29	**14,790 / 710**	**+2,166 / +114**	**309 / 16**
05/31: total tests = 173,468			
NEW! 06/01: deaths/million population = 247			
06/05	**16,769 / 803**	**+1,979 / +93**	**283 / 13**
06/12	**19,091 / 881**	**+2,322 / +78**	**332 / 11**
06/15: IFR (infection fatality rate) = 4.52%			
06/15: hospitalizations current = 661			
06/15: hospitalizations cumulative = 2,680			
06/19	**21,022 / 943**	**+1,931 / +62**	**276 / 9**
06/21: Father's Day			
06/26	**25,066 / 1,022**	**+4,044 / +79**	**578 / 11**
06/30: total tests = 299,691			
07/01: deaths/million population = 364			
07/03	**29,684 / 1,103**	**+4,618 / +81**	**660 / 12**
07/04: Independence Day			
07/10	**34,622 / 1,215**	**+4,938 / +112**	**705 / 16**
07/15: IFR (infection fatality rate) = 3.34%			
07/15: hospitalizations current = 1,099			
07/15: hospitalizations cumulative = 3,629			
07/17	**40,829 / 1,332**	**+6.207 / +117**	**887 / 17**
07/24	**49,663 / 1,463**	**+8,834 / +131**	**1,262 / 19**
07/31	**58,747 / 1,663**	**+9,084 / +200**	**1,298 / 29**
07/31: total tests = 470,048			
08/01: deaths/million population = 569			
08/07	**65,436 / 1,848**	**+6,689 / +185**	**956 / 26**
08/14	**70,830 / 2,043**	**+5,394 / +195**	**771 / 28**
08/15: IFR (infection fatality rate) = 2.94%			

DATE	CASES / DEATHS	WEEKLY INCREASE	DAILY AVERAGE
08/15: hospitalizations current = 1,126			
08/15: hospitalizations cumulative = 4,916			
08/21	**76,323 / 2,214**	**+5,493 / +171**	**785 / 24**
08/28	**81,294 / 2,413**	**+4,971 / +199**	**710 / 28**
08/31: total tests = 653,779			
09/01: deaths/million population = 863			
09/04	**85,939 / 2,558**	**+4,645 / +145**	**664 / 21**
09/07: Labor Day			
09/11	**89,175 / 2,670**	**+3,236 / +112**	**462 / 16**
09/15: IFR (infection fatality rate) = 3.02%			
09/15: hospitalizations current = 667			
09/15: hospitalizations cumulative = 5,499			
09/18	**92,432 / 2,792**	**+3,257 / +122**	**465 / 17**
NEW! 09/22: test positivity rate = 4.1%			
09/25	**96,032 / 2,894**	**+3,600 / +102**	**514 / 15**
09/30: total tests = 823,185			
10/01: deaths/million population = 1,008			
10/02	**99,558 / 2,999**	**+3,526 / +105**	**504 / 15**
10/09	**103,681 / 3,080**	**+4,123 / +81**	**589 / 12**
10/15: IFR (infection fatality rate) = 2.91%			
10/15: hospitalizations current = 598			
10/15: hospitalizations cumulative = 6,237			
10/16	**109,255 / 3,160**	**+5,574 / +80**	**796 / 11**
10/22: test positivity rate = 16.6%			
10/23	**113,876 / 3,238**	**+4,621 / +78**	**660 / 11**
10/30	**119,336 / 3,328**	**+5,460 / +90**	**780 / 13**
10/31: total tests = 1,046,565			
11/01: deaths/million population = 1,125			
11/03: Election Day			
11/06	**124,854 / 3,419**	**+5,518 / +91**	**788 / 13**
11/07: Biden wins election			
11/13	**131,970 / 3,519**	**+7,116 / +100**	**1,017 / 14**
11/15: IFR (infection fatality rate) = 2.64%			
11/15: hospitalizations current = 756			
11/15: hospitalizations cumulative = 6,914			
11/20	**140,429 / 3,642**	**+8,459 / +123**	**1,208 / 18**
11/22: test positivity rate = 86.0%			
11/26: Thanksgiving			

DATE	CASES / DEATHS	WEEKLY INCREASE	DAILY AVERAGE
11/27	148,387 / 3,769	+7,958 / +127	1,137 / 18
11/30: total tests = 1,366,833			
12/01: deaths/million population = 1,294			
12/04	161,516 / 3,916	+13,129 / +147	1,876 / 21
12/11	175,282 / 4,124	+13,766 / +208	1,967 / 30
12/14: first COVID-19 vaccinations given in the U.S.			
12/15: IFR (infection fatality rate) = 2.32%			
12/15: hospitalizations current = 1,316			
12/15: hospitalizations cumulative = 7,901			
12/18	190,411 / 4,354	+15,129 / +230	2,161 / 33
12/22: new U.K. variant identified in the U.S.			
12/22: test positivity rate = 23.1%			
12/25: Christmas			
12/25	204,178 / 4,562	+13,767 / +208	1,967 / 30
12/31: total tests = 1,730,435			
12/31: deaths/million population = 1,618			
01/01: New Year's Day			
01/01: CFR (case fatality rate) = 2.80% (28.0X more deadly than influenza at 0.1%)			
01/01/2021	218,386 / 4,816	+14,208 / +234	2,030 / 33

BONUS: Enjoy additional week from upcoming book: PANDEMIC 2021: The U.S. Edition
  01/06: right-wing mob insurrection at U.S. Capitol as Joe Biden confirmed president
  01/08: Twitter permanently bans Trump's account

01/08	233,665 / 5,101	+15,279 / +285	2,183 / 41

---

*The daily average column is rounded to the nearest whole person. The infection fatality rate (IFR) is the number of deaths divided by the number of confirmed cases. The case fatality rate (CFR), shown only at the end of the year, is the number of deaths divided by the number of confirmed cases *which have had an outcome* (either recovery or death). The CFR excludes active cases.

CHAPTER 27

~ MISSOURI *~*

POPULATION AS OF MARCH, 2020: 6,169,270
Republican Governor Mike Parson
VOTED RED: Trump 56.8% / Biden 41.4%

DATE	CASES / DEATHS	WEEKLY INCREASE	DAILY AVERAGE
01/30: WHO declares Public Health Emergency of International Concern			
01/31: Trump issues a China "travel ban"			
03/07: Missouri's first case			
03/11: WHO declares COVID-19 a pandemic			
03/13: Missouri declares State of Emergency			
03/13: Trump declares a National Emergency			
03/13: Trump issues a Europe "travel ban"			
03/13	4 / 0	N/A	N/A
03/18: first death			
03/20	47 / 1	+43 / +1	6 / 0
03/23: schools close			
03/27	670 / 9	+623 / +8	89 / 1
03/31: total tests = 17,935			
04/03	2,113 / 19	+1,443 / +10	206 / 1
04/06: stay at home order			
04/10	3,799 / 96	+1,686 / +77	241 / 11
04/12: Easter			
04/15: IFR (infection fatality rate) = 3.25%			
04/15: hospitalizations current = 1,024			
04/15: hospitalizations cumulative = not given for this state			
04/17	5,283 / 182	+1,484 / +86	212 / 12
04/24	6,694 / 267	+1,411 / +85	202 / 12
04/30: total tests = 82,152			

DATE	CASES / DEATHS	WEEKLY INCREASE	DAILY AVERAGE
05/01	8,018 / 358	+1,324 / +91	189 / 13
05/08	9,692 / 479	+1,674 / +121	239 / 17
05/10: Mother's Day			
05/15: IFR (infection fatality rate) = 5.41%			
05/15: hospitalizations current = 812			
05/15	10,734 / 581	+1,042 / +102	149 / 15
05/22	11,852 / 681	+1,118 / +100	160 / 14
05/25: Memorial Day			
05/26: George Floyd protests begin			
05/29	13,147 / 741	+1,295 / +60	185 / 9
05/31: total tests = 208,686			
NEW! 06/01: deaths/million population = 128			
06/05	14,691 / 817	+1,544 / +76	221 / 11
06/12	16,141 / 887	+1,450 / +70	207 / 10
06/15: IFR (infection fatality rate) = 5.36%			
06/15: hospitalizations current = 612			
06/19	17,898 / 970	+1,757 / +83	251 / 12
06/21: Father's Day			
06/26	20,432 / 1,016	+2,534 / +46	362 / 7
06/30: total tests = 415,991			
07/01: deaths/million population = 171			
07/03	23,717 / 1,071	+3,285 / +55	469 / 8
07/04: Independence Day			
07/10	27,856 / 1,103	+4,139 / +32	591 / 5
07/15: IFR (infection fatality rate) = 3.67%			
07/15: hospitalizations current = 875			
07/17	33,586 / 1,158	+5,730 / +55	819 / 8
07/24	41,103 / 1,224	+7,517 / +66	1,074 / 9
07/31	50,911 / 1,305	+9,808 / +81	1,401 / 12
07/31: total tests = 746,383			
08/01: deaths/million population = 214			
08/07	58,070 / 1,378	+7,159 / +73	1,023 / 10
08/14	66,077 / 1,443	+8,007 / +65	1,144 / 9
08/15: IFR (infection fatality rate) = 2.17%			
08/15: hospitalizations current = 871			
08/21	73,990 / 1,532	+7,913 / +89	1,130 / 13
08/28	82,263 / 1,620	+8,273 / +88	1,182 / 13
08/31: total tests = 1,108,148			

DATE	CASES / DEATHS	WEEKLY INCREASE	DAILY AVERAGE
	09/01: deaths/million population = 282		
09/04	**91,980 / 1,728**	**+9,717 / +108**	**1,388 / 15**
	09/07: Labor Day		
09/11	**101,138 / 1,812**	**+9,158 / +84**	**1,308 / 12**
	09/15: IFR (infection fatality rate) = 1.73%		
	09/15: hospitalizations current = 1,021		
09/18	**112,836 / 1,930**	**+11,698 / +118**	**1,671 / 17**
	NEW! 09/22: test positivity rate = 11.6%		
09/25	**123,853 / 2,124**	**+11,017 / +194**	**1,574 / 28**
	09/30: total tests = 1,968,138		
	10/01: deaths/million population = 370		
10/02	**133,439 / 2,268**	**+9,586 / +144**	**1,369 / 21**
10/09	**146,754 / 2,485**	**+13,315 / +217**	**1,902 / 31**
	10/15: IFR (infection fatality rate) = 1.63%		
	10/15: hospitalizations current = 1,443		
10/16	**158,349 / 2,582**	**+11,595 / +97**	**1,656 / 14**
	10/22: test positivity rate = 9.8%		
10/23	**171,085 / 2,789**	**+12,736 / +207**	**1,819 / 30**
10/30	**188,988 / 3,077**	**+17,903 / +288**	**2,558 / 41**
	10/31: total tests = 2,647,874		
	11/01: deaths/million population = 514		
	11/03: Election Day		
11/06	**211,479 / 3,297**	**+22,491 / +220**	**3,213 / 31**
	11/07: Biden wins election		
11/13	**241,830 / 3,524**	**+30,351 / +227**	**4,336 / 32**
	11/15: IFR (infection fatality rate) = 1.41%		
	11/15: hospitalizations current = 2,462		
11/20	**276,775 / 3,742**	**+34,945 / +218**	**4,992 / 31**
	11/22: test positivity rate = 22.5%		
	11/26: Thanksgiving		
11/27	**303,186 / 4,033**	**+26,411 / +291**	**3,773 / 42**
	11/30: total tests = 3,329,825		
	12/01: deaths/million population = 697		
12/04	**332,082 / 4,466**	**+28,896 / +433**	**4,128 / 62**
12/11	**361,369 / 4,877**	**+29,287 / +411**	**4,184 / 59**
	12/14: first COVID-19 vaccinations given in the U.S.		
	12/15: IFR (infection fatality rate) = 1.36%		
	12/15: hospitalizations current = 2,543		

DATE	CASES / DEATHS	WEEKLY INCREASE	DAILY AVERAGE
12/18	385,101 / 5,291	+23,732 / +414	3,390 / 59

12/22: new U.K. variant identified in the U.S.
12/22: test positivity rate = 15.6%
12/25: Christmas

12/25	404,563 / 5,804	+19,462 / +513	2,780 / 73

12/31: total tests = 4,080,302
12/31: deaths/million population = 988
01/01: New Year's Day
01/01: CFR (case fatality rate) = 4.50% (45.0X more deadly than influenza at 0.1%)

01/01/2021	424,972 / 6,081	+20,409 / +277	2,916 / 40

BONUS: Enjoy additional week from upcoming book: PANDEMIC 2021: The U.S. Edition
01/06: right-wing mob insurrection at U.S. Capitol as Joe Biden confirmed president
01/08: Twitter permanently bans Trump's account

01/08	449,868 / 6,466	+24,896 / +385	3,557 / 55

*The daily average column is rounded to the nearest whole person. The infection fatality rate (IFR) is the number of deaths divided by the number of confirmed cases. The case fatality rate (CFR), shown only at the end of the year, is the number of deaths divided by the number of confirmed cases *which have had an outcome* (either recovery or death). The CFR excludes active cases.

CHAPTER 28

~ MONTANA *~*

POPULATION AS OF MARCH, 2020: 1,086,759
Democratic Governor Steve Bullock
VOTED RED: Trump 56.7% / Biden 40.4%

DATE	CASES / DEATHS	WEEKLY INCREASE	DAILY AVERAGE
01/30: WHO declares Public Health Emergency of International Concern			
01/31: Trump issues a China "travel ban"			
03/11: Montana's first case			
03/11: WHO declares COVID-19 a pandemic			
03/13: Trump declares a National Emergency			
03/13: Trump issues a Europe "travel ban"			
03/13	5 / 0	N/A	N/A
03/12: Montana declares State of Emergency			
03/20	24 / 0	+19 / +0	3 / 0
03/26: Montana's first death			
03/26: non-essential services close			
03/26: stay at home order			
03/27	131 / 1	+107 / +1	15 / 0
03/31: total tests = 3,098			
04/03	266 / 5	+135 / +4	19 / 1
04/10	365 / 6	+99 / +1	14 / 0
04/12: Easter			
04/15: IFR (infection fatality rate) = 1.73%			
04/15: hospitalizations current = 21			
04/15: hospitalizations cumulative = 51			
04/17	422 / 8	+57 / +2	8 / 0
04/24	444 / 14	+22 / +6	3 / 1
04/30: total tests = 8,581			

DATE	CASES / DEATHS	WEEKLY INCREASE	DAILY AVERAGE
05/01	453 / 16	+9 / +2	1 / 0
05/08	458 / 16	+5 / +0	1 / 0
05/10: Mother's Day			
05/15: IFR (infection fatality rate) = 3.43%			
05/15: hospitalizations current = 3			
05/15: hospitalizations cumulative = 63			
05/15	466 / 16	+8 / +0	1 / 0
05/22	479 / 16	+13 / +0	2 / 0
05/25: Memorial Day			
05/26: George Floyd protests begin			
05/29	493 / 17	+14 / +1	2 / 0
05/31: total tests = 39,284			
NEW! 06/01: deaths/million population = 16			
06/05	541 / 18	+48 / +1	7 / 0
06/12	573 / 18	+32 / +0	5 / 0
06/15: IFR (infection fatality rate) = 3.12%			
06/15: hospitalizations current = 7			
06/15: hospitalizations cumulative = 78			
06/19	666 / 20	+93 / +2	13 / 0
06/21: Father's Day			
06/26	829 / 22	+163 / +2	23 / 0
06/30: total tests = 90,861			
07/01: deaths/million population = 21			
07/03	1,128 / 23	+299 / +1	43 / 0
07/04: Independence Day			
07/10	1,593 / 28	+465 / +5	66 / 1
07/15: IFR (infection fatality rate) = 1.62%			
07/15: hospitalizations current = 37			
07/15: hospitalizations cumulative = 145			
07/15: mask mandate			
07/17	2,366 / 37	+773 / +9	110 / 1
07/24	3,039 / 46	+673 / +9	96 / 1
07/31	3,965 / 60	+926 / +14	132 / 2
07/31: total tests = 169,970			
08/01: deaths/million population = 57			
08/07	4,757 / 70	+792 / +10	113 / 1
08/14	5,541 / 81	+784 / +11	112 / 2
08/15: IFR (infection fatality rate) = 1.45%			

DATE	CASES / DEATHS	WEEKLY INCREASE	DAILY AVERAGE
	08/15: hospitalizations current = 90		
	08/15: hospitalizations cumulative = 324		
08/21	6,216 / 89	+675 / +8	96 / 1
08/28	7,063 / 100	+847 / +11	121 / 2
	08/31: total tests = 261,050		
	09/01: deaths/million population = 109		
09/04	8,019 / 114	+956 / +14	137 / 2
	09/07: Labor Day		
09/11	8,785 / 131	+766 / +17	109 / 2
	09/15: IFR (infection fatality rate) = 1.51%		
	09/15: hospitalizations current = 109		
	09/15: hospitalizations cumulative = 539		
09/18	9,871 / 146	+1,086 / +15	155 / 2
	NEW! 09/22: test positivity rate = 5.9%		
09/25	11,564 / 170	+1,693 / +24	242 / 3
	09/30: total tests = 353,362		
	10/01: deaths/million population = 174		
10/02	13,855 / 186	+2,291 / +16	327 / 2
10/09	17,399 / 206	+3,544 / +20	506 / 3
	10/15: IFR (infection fatality rate) = 1.10%		
	10/15: hospitalizations current = 301		
	10/15: hospitalizations cumulative = 959		
10/16	21,595 / 235	+4,196 / +29	599 / 4
	10/22: test positivity rate = 14.3%		
10/23	26,503 / 282	+4,908 / +47	701 / 7
10/30	31,916 / 364	+5,413 / +82	773 / 12
	10/31: total tests = 498,915		
	11/01: deaths/million population = 352		
	11/03: Election Day		
11/06	37,947 / 419	+6,031 / +55	862 / 8
	11/07: Biden wins election		
11/13	44,244 / 477	+6,297 / +58	900 / 8
	11/15: IFR (infection fatality rate) = 1.10%		
	11/15: hospitalizations current = 435		
	11/15: hospitalizations cumulative = 2,047		
11/20	53,293 / 567	+9,049 / +90	1,293 / 13
	11/22: test positivity rate = 41.5%		
	11/26: Thanksgiving		

DATE	CASES / DEATHS	WEEKLY INCREASE	DAILY AVERAGE
11/27	**59,796 / 658**	**+6,503 / +91**	**929 / 13**
	11/30: total tests = 663,581		
	12/01: deaths/million population = 667		
12/04	**66,436 / 727**	**+6,640 / +69**	**949 / 10**
12/11	**71,870 / 805**	**+5,434 / +78**	**776 / 11**
	12/14: first COVID-19 vaccinations given in the U.S.		
	12/15: IFR (infection fatality rate) = 1.12%		
	12/15: hospitalizations current = 338		
	12/15: hospitalizations cumulative = 3,119		
12/18	**75,992 / 854**	**+4,122 / +49**	**589 / 7**
	12/22: new U.K. variant identified in the U.S.		
	12/22: test positivity rate = 11.0%		
	12/25: Christmas		
12/25	**78,929 / 916**	**+2,937 / +62**	**420 / 9**
	12/31: total tests = 791,589		
	12/31: deaths/million population = 899		
	01/01: New Year's Day		
	01/01: CFR (case fatality rate) = 1.27% (12.7X more deadly than influenza at 0.1%)		
01/01/2021	**81,555 / 961**	**+2,626 / +45**	**375 / 6**

BONUS: Enjoy additional week from upcoming book: PANDEMIC 2021: The U.S. Edition
01/06: right-wing mob insurrection at U.S. Capitol as Joe Biden confirmed president
01/08: Twitter permanently bans Trump's account

01/08	**85,568 / 1,049**	**+4,013 / +88**	**573 / 13**

*The daily average column is rounded to the nearest whole person. The infection fatality rate (IFR) is the number of deaths divided by the number of confirmed cases. The case fatality rate (CFR), shown only at the end of the year, is the number of deaths divided by the number of confirmed cases *which have had an outcome* (either recovery or death). The CFR excludes active cases.

CHAPTER 29

~ NEBRASKA *~*

POPULATION AS OF MARCH, 2020: 1,952,570
Republican Governor Pete Ricketts
VOTED RED: Trump 58.2% / Biden 39.2%

DATE	CASES / DEATHS	WEEKLY INCREASE	DAILY AVERAGE
01/30: WHO declares Public Health Emergency of International Concern			
01/31: Trump issues a China "travel ban"			
02/13: Nebraska's first case??			
03/11: WHO declares COVID-19 a pandemic			
03/13: Nebraska declares State of Emergency			
03/13: Trump declares a National Emergency			
03/13: Trump issues a Europe "travel ban"			
03/13	14 / 0	+13 / +0	2 / 0
03/20	38 / 0	+24 / +0	3 / 0
03/27: first 2 deaths			
03/27	89 / 2	+51 / +2	7 / 0
03/31: total tests = 3,365			
04/03	293 / 6	+204 / +4	29 / 1
04/10	648 / 17	+355 / +11	51 / 2
04/12: Easter			
04/15: IFR (infection fatality rate) = 2.21%			
04/15: hospitalizations current = not given			
04/15: hospitalizations cumulative = not given			
04/17	1,138 / 24	+490 / +7	70 / 1
04/24	2,421 / 50	+1,283 / +26	183 / 4
04/30: total tests = 31,332			
05/01	4,838 / 73	+2,417 / +23	345 / 3
05/08	7,831 / 92	+2,993 / +19	428 / 3

DATE	CASES / DEATHS	WEEKLY INCREASE	DAILY AVERAGE
05/10: Mother's Day			
05/15: IFR (infection fatality rate) = 1.22%			
05/15: hospitalizations current = 192			
05/15: hospitalizations cumulative = not given			
05/15	**9,772 / 119**	**+1,941 / +27**	**277 / 4**
05/22	**11,662 / 147**	**+1,890 / +28**	**270 / 4**
05/25: Memorial Day			
05/26: George Floyd protests begin			
05/29	**13,654 / 170**	**+1,992 / +23**	**285 / 3**
05/31: total tests = 101,290			
NEW! 06/01: deaths/million population = 91			
06/05	**15,379 / 189**	**+1,725 / +19**	**246 / 3**
06/12	**16,513 / 216**	**+1,134 / +27**	**162 / 4**
06/15: IFR (infection fatality rate) = 1.31%			
06/15: hospitalizations current = 160			
06/15: hospitalizations cumulative = 1,088			
06/19	**17,591 / 244**	**+1,078 / +28**	**154 / 4**
06/21: Father's Day			
06/26	**18,524 / 266**	**+933 / +22**	**133 / 3**
06/30: total tests = 180,826			
07/01: deaths/million population = 143			
07/03	**19,660 / 284**	**+1,136 / +18**	**162 / 3**
07/04: Independence Day			
07/10	**20,777 / 286**	**+1,117 / +2**	**160 / 0**
07/15: IFR (infection fatality rate) = 1.32%			
07/15: hospitalizations current = 110			
07/15: hospitalizations cumulative = 1,442			
07/17	**22,361 / 301**	**+1,584 / +15**	**226 / 2**
07/24	**24,174 / 316**	**+1,813 / +15**	**259 / 2**
07/31	**26,211 / 332**	**+2,037 / +16**	**291 / 2**
07/31: total tests = 275,544			
08/01: deaths/million population = 172			
08/07	**28,104 / 345**	**+1,893 / +13**	**270 / 2**
08/14	**29,988 / 361**	**+1,884 / +16**	**269 / 2**
08/15: IFR (infection fatality rate) = 1.19%			
08/15: hospitalizations current = 145			
08/15: hospitalizations cumulative = 1,880			
08/21	**31,626 / 376**	**+1,638 / +15**	**234 / 2**

DATE	CASES / DEATHS	WEEKLY INCREASE	DAILY AVERAGE
08/28	**33,436 / 392**	**+1,810 / +16**	**259 / 2**
08/31: total tests = 377,290			
09/01: deaths/million population = 209			
09/04	**35,661 / 404**	**+2,225 / +12**	**318 / 2**
09/07: Labor Day			
09/11	**37,841 / 434**	**+2,180 / +30**	**311 / 4**
09/15: IFR (infection fatality rate) = 1.12%			
09/15: hospitalizations current = 176			
09/15: hospitalizations cumulative = 2,154			
09/18	**40,387 / 442**	**+2,546 / +8**	**364 / 1**
NEW! 09/22: test positivity rate = 12.8%			
09/25	**43,162 / 468**	**+2,775 / +26**	**396 / 4**
09/30: total tests = 470,281			
10/01: deaths/million population = 255			
10/02	**46,977 / 493**	**+3,815 / +25**	**545 / 4**
10/09	**50,059 / 514**	**+3,082 / +21**	**440 / 3**
10/15: IFR (infection fatality rate) = %			
10/15: hospitalizations current = 311			
10/15: hospitalizations cumulative = 2,593			
10/16	**56,714 / 547**	**+6,655 / +33**	**951 / 5**
10/22: test positivity rate = 19.0%			
10/23	**62,510 / 591**	**+5,796 / +44**	**828 / 6**
10/27: Trump rally			
10/30	**69,645 / 646**	**+7,135 / +55**	**1,019 / 8**
10/31: total tests = 594,749			
11/01: deaths/million population = 337			
11/03: Election Day			
11/06	**80,693 / 701**	**+11,048 / +55**	**1,578 / 8**
11/07: Biden wins election			
11/13	**92,553 / 756**	**+11,860 / +55**	**1,694 / 8**
11/15: IFR (infection fatality rate) = 0.79%			
11/15: hospitalizations current = 889			
11/15: hospitalizations cumulative = 3,551			
11/20	**109,280 / 854**	**+16,727 / +98**	**2,390 / 14**
11/22: test positivity rate = 14.8%			
11/26: Thanksgiving			
11/27	**122,952 / 982**	**+13,672 / +128**	**1,953 / 18**
11/30: total tests = 748,721			

DATE	CASES / DEATHS	WEEKLY INCREASE	DAILY AVERAGE
12/01: deaths/million population = 558			
12/04	136,325 / 1,186	+13,373 / +204	1,910 / 29
12/11	146,877 / 1,343	+10,552 / +157	1,507 / 22
12/14: first COVID-19 vaccinations given in the U.S.			
12/15: IFR (infection fatality rate) = 0.95%			
12/15: hospitalizations current = 693			
12/15: hospitalizations cumulative = 4,831			
12/18	154,745 / 1,470	+7,868 / +127	1,124 / 18
12/22: new U.K. variant identified in the U.S.			
12/22: test positivity rate = 9.0%			
12/25: Christmas			
12/25	161,162 / 1,568	+6,417 / +98	917 / 14
12/31: total tests = 848,067			
12/31: deaths/million population = 853			
01/01: New Year's Day			
01/01: CFR (case fatality rate) = 1.51% (15.1X more deadly than influenza at 0.1%)			
01/01/2021	167,716 / 1,668	+6,554 / +100	936 / 14

BONUS: Enjoy additional week from upcoming book: PANDEMIC 2021: The U.S. Edition

01/06: right-wing mob insurrection at U.S. Capitol as Joe Biden confirmed president			
01/08: Twitter permanently bans Trump's account			
01/08	174,614 / 1,811	+6,898 / +143	985 / 20

*The daily average column is rounded to the nearest whole person. The infection fatality rate (IFR) is the number of deaths divided by the number of confirmed cases. The case fatality rate (CFR), shown only at the end of the year, is the number of deaths divided by the number of confirmed cases *which have had an outcome* (either recovery or death). The CFR excludes active cases.

CHAPTER 30

~ NEVADA *~*

POPULATION AS OF MARCH, 2020: 3,139,658
Democratic Governor Steve Sisolak
VOTED BLUE: Biden 50.1% / Trump 47.7%

DATE	CASES / DEATHS	WEEKLY INCREASE	DAILY AVERAGE
01/30: WHO declares Public Health Emergency of International Concern			
01/31: Trump issues a China "travel ban"			
03/04: Nevada's first case			
03/06	4 / 0	N/A	N/A
03/11: WHO declares COVID-19 a pandemic			
03/12: Nevada declares State of Emergency			
03/13: Trump declares a National Emergency			
03/13: Trump issues a Europe "travel ban"			
03/13	34 / 0	+30 / +0	4 / 0
03/15: Nevada's first death			
03/16: schools close			
03/20: non-essential services close			
03/20	124 / 3	+90 / +3	13 / 0
03/27	621 / 21	+497 / +18	71 / 3
03/31: total tests = 12,988			
04/01: stay at home order			
04/03	1,742 / 59	+1,121 / +38	160 / 5
04/10	2,700 / 120	+958 / +61	137 / 9
04/12: Easter			
04/15: IFR (infection fatality rate) = 4.24%			
04/15: hospitalizations current = not given			
04/15: hospitalizations cumulative = not given for this state			
04/17	3,524 / 142	+824 / +22	118 / 3

DATE	CASES / DEATHS	WEEKLY INCREASE	DAILY AVERAGE
04/24	4,398 / 197	+874 / +55	125 / 8
04/30: total tests = 54,918			
05/01	5,227 / 254	+829 / +57	118 / 8
05/08	5,884 / 301	+657 / +47	94 / 7
05/10: Mother's Day			
05/15: IFR (infection fatality rate) = 5.22%			
05/15: hospitalizations current = 425			
05/15	6,614 / 345	+730 / +44	104 / 6
05/22	7,401 / 387	+787 / +42	112 / 6
05/25: Memorial Day			
05/26: George Floyd protests begin			
05/29	8,350 / 415	+949 / +28	136 / 4
05/31: total tests = 160,499			
NEW! 06/01: deaths/million population = 134			
06/05	9,266 / 433	+916 / +18	131 / 3
06/12	10,678 / 462	+1,412 / +29	202 / 4
06/15: IFR (infection fatality rate) = 4.12%			
06/15: hospitalizations current = 346			
06/19	12,486 / 478	+1,808 / +16	258 / 2
06/21: Father's Day			
06/25: mask mandate			
06/26	15,240 / 498	+2,754 / +20	393 / 3
06/30: total tests = 322,944			
07/01: deaths/million population = 166			
07/03	20,718 / 528	+5,478 / +30	783 / 4
07/04: Independence Day			
07/10	25,908 / 579	+5,190 / +51	741 / 7
07/15: IFR (infection fatality rate) = 2.03%			
07/15: hospitalizations current = 1,051			
07/17	33,295 / 637	+7,387 / +58	1,055 / 8
07/24	40,885 / 722	+7,590 / +85	1,084 / 12
07/31	48,088 / 830	+7,203 / +108	1,029 / 15
07/31: total tests = 616,731			
08/01: deaths/million population = 271			
08/07	54,533 / 920	+6,445 / +90	921 / 13
08/14	59,749 / 1,045	+5,216 / +125	745 / 18
08/15: IFR (infection fatality rate) = 1.76%			
08/15: hospitalizations current = 941			

DATE	CASES / DEATHS	WEEKLY INCREASE	DAILY AVERAGE
08/21	64,433 / 1,185	+4,684 / +140	669 / 20
08/28	67,852 / 1,287	+3,419 / +102	488 / 15

08/31: total tests = 885,384
09/01: deaths/million population = 451

09/04	70,712 / 1,375	+2,860 / +88	409 / 13

09/07: Labor Day

09/11	72,806 / 1,439	+2,094 / +64	299 / 9

09/12 & 09/13: Trump rallies
09/15: IFR (infection fatality rate) = 2.00%
09/15: hospitalizations current = 483

09/18	75,096 / 1,524	+2,290 / +85	327 / 12

NEW! 09/22: test positivity rate = 10.0%

09/25	77,753 / 1,573	+2,657 / +49	380 / 7

09/30: total tests = 1,068,802
10/01: deaths/million population = 522

10/02	81,182 / 1,609	+3,429 / +36	490 / 5
10/09	84,593 / 1,657	+3,411 / +48	487 / 7

10/15: IFR (infection fatality rate) = 1.93%
10/15: hospitalizations current = 486

10/16	88,685 / 1,707	+4,092 / +50	585 / 7

10/18: Trump rally
10/22: test positivity rate = 17.0%

10/23	93,666 / 1,738	+4,981 / +31	712 / 4
10/30	99,786 / 1,777	+6,120 / +39	874 / 6

10/31: total tests = 1,253,083
11/01: deaths/million population = 578
11/03: Election Day

11/06	106,922 / 1,845	+7,136 / +68	1,019 / 10

11/07: Biden wins election

11/13	116,737 / 1,893	+9,815 / +48	1,402 / 7

11/15: IFR (infection fatality rate) = 1.59%
11/15: hospitalizations current = 1,025

11/20	129,714 / 1,982	+12,977 / +89	1,854 / 13

11/22: test positivity rate = 17.0%
11/26: Thanksgiving

11/27	146,317 / 2,095	+16,603 / +113	2,372 / 16

11/30: total tests = 1,664,999
12/01: deaths/million population = 715

DATE	CASES / DEATHS	WEEKLY INCREASE	DAILY AVERAGE
12/04	162,434 / 2,272	+16,117 / +177	2,302 / 25
12/11	180,218 / 2,479	+17,784 / +207	2,541 / 30

12/14: first COVID-19 vaccinations given in the U.S.
12/15: IFR (infection fatality rate) = 1.35%
12/15: hospitalizations current = 1,979

12/18	199,257 / 2,708	+19,039 / +229	2,720 / 33

12/22: new U.K. variant identified in the U.S.
12/22: test positivity rate = 14.4%
12/25: Christmas

12/25	214,064 / 2,943	+14,807 / +235	2,115 / 34

12/31: total tests = 2,095,778
12/31: deaths/million population = 1,021
01/01: New Year's Day
01/01: CFR (case fatality rate) = 2.71% (27.1X more deadly than influenza at 0.1%)

01/01/2021	227,046 / 3,146	+12,982 / +203	1,855 / 29

BONUS: Enjoy additional week from upcoming book: PANDEMIC 2021: The U.S. Edition
01/06: right-wing mob insurrection at U.S. Capitol as Joe Biden confirmed president
01/08: Twitter permanently bans Trump's account

01/08	243,661 / 3,394	+16,615 / +248	2,374 / 35

*The daily average column is rounded to the nearest whole person. The infection fatality rate (IFR) is the number of deaths divided by the number of confirmed cases. The case fatality rate (CFR), shown only at the end of the year, is the number of deaths divided by the number of confirmed cases *which have had an outcome* (either recovery or death). The CFR excludes active cases.

CHAPTER 31

~ NEW HAMPSHIRE *~*

POPULATION AS OF MARCH, 2020: 1,371,246
Republican Governor Steve Sununu
VOTED BLUE: Biden 52.8% / Trump 45.5%

DATE	CASES / DEATHS	WEEKLY INCREASE	DAILY AVERAGE
01/30: WHO declares Public Health Emergency of International Concern			
01/31: Trump issues a China "travel ban"			
03/02: New Hampshire's first case			
03/06	2 / 0	N/A	N/A
03/11: WHO declares COVID-19 a pandemic			
03/13: New Hampshire declares State of Emergency			
03/13: Trump declares a National Emergency			
03/13: Trump issues a Europe "travel ban"			
03/13	6 / 0	+4 / +0	1 / 0
03/16: schools close			
03/20	55 / 0	+49 / +0	7 / 0
03/23: New Hampshire's first death			
03/27: non-essential services close			
03/27: stay at home order			
03/27	187 / 2	+132 / +2	19 / 0
03/31: total tests = (not given)			
04/03	540 / 7	+353 / +5	50 / 1
04/10	885 / 22	+345 / +15	49 / 2
04/12: Easter			
04/15: IFR (infection fatality rate) = 2.81%			
04/15: hospitalizations current = 70			
04/15: hospitalizations cumulative = 178			
04/17	1,287 / 37	+402 / +15	57 / 2

DATE	CASES / DEATHS	WEEKLY INCREASE	DAILY AVERAGE
04/24	**1,720 / 53**	**+433 / +16**	**62 / 2**
04/30: total tests = 23,393			
05/01	**2,310 / 81**	**+590 / +28**	**84 / 4**
05/08	**2,947 / 121**	**+637 / +40**	**91 / 6**
05/10: Mother's Day			
05/15: IFR (infection fatality rate) = 4.59%			
05/15: hospitalizations current = 115			
05/15: hospitalizations cumulative = 335			
05/15	**3,464 / 159**	**+517 / +38**	**74 / 5**
05/22	**4,014 / 204**	**+550 / +45**	**79 / 6**
05/25: Memorial Day			
05/26: George Floyd protests begin			
05/29	**4,492 / 238**	**+478 / +34**	**68 / 5**
05/31: total tests = 80,129			
NEW! 06/01: deaths/million population = 179			
06/05	**4,953 / 278**	**+461 / +40**	**66 / 6**
06/12	**5,251 / 315**	**+298 / +37**	**43 / 5**
06/15: IFR (infection fatality rate) = 5.99%			
06/15: hospitalizations current = 69			
06/15: hospitalizations cumulative = 519			
06/19	**5,486 / 337**	**+235 / +22**	**34 / 3**
06/21: Father's Day			
06/26	**5,671 / 365**	**+185 / +28**	**26 / 4**
06/30: total tests = 138,433			
07/01: deaths/million population = 274			
07/03	**5,857 / 376**	**+186 / +11**	**27 / 2**
07/04: Independence Day			
07/10	**5,991 / 390**	**+134 / +14**	**19 / 2**
07/15: IFR (infection fatality rate) = 6.45%			
07/15: hospitalizations current = 23			
07/15: hospitalizations cumulative = 665			
07/17	**6,165 / 395**	**+174 / +5**	**25 / 1**
07/24	**6,375 / 407**	**+210 / +12**	**30 / 2**
07/31	**6,583 / 415**	**+208 / +8**	**30 / 1**
07/31: total tests = 186,721			
08/01: deaths/million population = 306			
08/07	**6,779 / 419**	**+196 / +4**	**28 / 1**
08/14	**6,964 / 423**	**+185 / +4**	**26 / 1**

DATE	CASES / DEATHS	WEEKLY INCREASE	DAILY AVERAGE
	08/15: IFR (infection fatality rate) = 6.06%		
	08/15: hospitalizations current = 15		
	08/15: hospitalizations cumulative = 706		
08/21	**7,071 / 428**	**+107 / +5**	**15 / 1**
	08/28: Trump rally		
08/28	**7,216 / 432**	**+145 / +4**	**21 / 1**
	08/31: total tests = 248,850		
	09/01: deaths/million population = 318		
09/04	**7,368 / 432**	**+152 / +0**	**22 / 0**
	09/07: Labor Day		
	09/10: Trump rally		
09/11	**7,620 / 434**	**+252 / +2**	**36 / 0**
	09/15: IFR (infection fatality rate) = 5.65%		
	09/15: hospitalizations current = 9		
	09/15: hospitalizations cumulative = 722		
09/18	**7,861 / 438**	**+241 / +4**	**34 / 1**
	NEW! 09/22: test positivity rate = 1%		
09/25	**8,085 / 438**	**+224 / +0**	**32 / 0**
	09/30: total tests = 309,061		
	10/01: deaths/million population = 325		
10/02	**8,534 / 442**	**+449 / +4**	**64 / 1**
10/09	**8,970 / 450**	**+436 / +8**	**62 / 1**
	10/15: IFR (infection fatality rate) = 4.91%		
	10/15: hospitalizations current = 18		
	10/15: hospitalizations cumulative = 761		
10/16	**9,514 / 465**	**+544 / +15**	**78 / 2**
	10/22: test positivity rate = 1.3%		
10/23	**10,112 / 471**	**+598 / +6**	**85 / 1**
	10/25: Trump rally		
10/30	**10,884 / 482**	**+772 / +11**	**110 / 2**
	10/31: total tests = 377,255		
	11/01: deaths/million population = 355		
	11/03: Election Day		
11/06	**12,012 / 488**	**+1,128 / +6**	**161 / 1**
	11/07: Biden wins election		
11/13	**13,929 / 498**	**+1,917 / +10**	**274 / 1**
	11/15: IFR (infection fatality rate) = 3.40%		
	11/15: hospitalizations current = 69		

DATE	CASES / DEATHS	WEEKLY INCREASE	DAILY AVERAGE
	11/15: hospitalizations cumulative = 804		
11/20	**16,797 / 507**	**+2,868 / +9**	**410 / 1**
	11/20: mask mandate		
	11/22: test positivity rate = 5.1%		
	11/26: Thanksgiving		
11/27	**19,313 / 517**	**+2,516 / +10**	**359 / 1**
	11/30: total tests = 831,649		
	12/01: deaths/million population = 395		
12/04	**23,690 / 552**	**+4,377 / +35**	**625 / 5**
12/11	**29,460 / 590**	**+5,770 / +38**	**824 / 5**
	12/14: first COVID-19 vaccinations given in the U.S.		
	12/15: IFR (infection fatality rate) = 1.86%		
	12/15: hospitalizations current = 252		
	12/15: hospitalizations cumulative = 863		
12/18	**34,960 / 638**	**+5,500 / +48**	**786 / 7**
	12/22: new U.K. variant identified in the U.S.		
	12/22: test positivity rate = 11.5%		
	12/25: Christmas		
12/25	**38,902 / 690**	**+3,942 / +52**	**563 / 7**
	12/31: total tests = 1,032,929		
	12/31: deaths/million population = 558		
	01/01: New Year's Day		
	01/01: CFR (case fatality rate) = 1.99% (19.9X more deadly than influenza at 0.1%)		
01/01/2021	**44,028 / 759**	**+5,126 / +69**	**732 / 10**

BONUS: *Enjoy additional week from upcoming book: PANDEMIC 2021: The U.S. Edition*

01/06: right-wing mob insurrection at U.S. Capitol as Joe Biden confirmed president
01/08: Twitter permanently bans Trump's account

DATE	CASES / DEATHS	WEEKLY INCREASE	DAILY AVERAGE
01/08	**50,152 / 846**	**+6,124 / +87**	**875 / 12**

*The daily average column is rounded to the nearest whole person. The infection fatality rate (IFR) is the number of deaths divided by the number of confirmed cases. The case fatality rate (CFR), shown only at the end of the year, is the number of deaths divided by the number of confirmed cases *which have had an outcome* (either recovery or death). The CFR excludes active cases.

CHAPTER 32

~ NEW JERSEY *~*

POPULATION AS OF MARCH, 2020: 8,936,574
Democratic Governor Phil Murphy
VOTED BLUE: Biden 57.1% / Trump 41.3%

DATE	CASES / DEATHS	WEEKLY INCREASE	DAILY AVERAGE
01/30: WHO declares Public Health Emergency of International Concern			
01/31: Trump issues a China "travel ban"			
03/04: New Jersey's first case			
03/06	4 / 0	N/A	N/A
03/09: Public Health Emergency declared			
03/11: WHO declares COVID-19 a pandemic			
03/10: New Jersey's first death			
03/13: Trump declares a National Emergency			
03/13: Trump issues a Europe "travel ban"			
03/13	67 / 1	+63 / +1	9 / 0
03/18: schools close			
03/20	1,336 / 11	+1,269 / +10	181 / 1
03/21: non-essential services close			
03/21: stay at home order			
03/27	11,124 / 108	+9,788 / +97	1,398 / 14
03/31: total tests = 41,860			
04/03	34,124 / 646	+23,000 / +538	3,286 / 77
04/10: mask mandate			
04/10	54,588 / 1,932	+20,464 / +1,286	2,923 / 184
04/12: Easter			
04/15: IFR (infection fatality rate) = 4.08%			
04/15: hospitalizations current = 8,270			
04/15: hospitalizations cumulative = not given			

DATE	CASES / DEATHS	WEEKLY INCREASE	DAILY AVERAGE
04/17	78,467 / 3,840	+23,879 / +1,908	3,411 / 273
04/24	102,196 / 5,617	+23,729 / +1,777	3,390 / 254
04/30: total tests = 223,125			
05/01	121,190 / 7,538	+18,994 / +1,921	2,713 / 274
05/08	137,212 / 8,986	+16,022 / +1,448	2,289 / 207
05/10: Mother's Day			
05/15: IFR (infection fatality rate) = 6.98%			
05/15: hospitalizations current = 3,823			
05/15: hospitalizations cumulative = not given			
05/15	145,490 / 10,150	+8,278 / +1,164	1,183 / 166
05/22	154,349 / 10,986	+8,859 / +836	1,266 / 119
05/25: Memorial Day			
05/26: George Floyd protests begin			
05/29	160,391 / 11,536	+6,042 / +550	863 / 79
05/31: total tests = 745,308			
NEW! 06/01: deaths/million population = 1,313			
06/05	165,162 / 12,082	+4,771 / +546	682 / 78
06/12	168,846 / 12,601	+3,684 / +519	526 / 74
06/15: IFR (infection fatality rate) = 7.53%			
06/15: hospitalizations current = 1,342			
06/15: hospitalizations cumulative = 18,755			
06/19	171,442 / 12,960	+2,596 / +359	371 / 51
06/21: Father's Day			
06/26	175,759 / 15,057	+4,317 / +2,097	617 / 300
06/30: total tests = 1,422,374			
07/01: deaths/million population = 1,713			
07/03	176,455 / 15,270	+696 / +213	99 / 30
07/04: Independence Day			
07/08: mask mandate			
07/10	178,218 / 15,553	+1,763 / +283	252 / 40
07/15: IFR (infection fatality rate) = 8.62%			
07/15: hospitalizations current = 923			
07/15: hospitalizations cumulative = 20,774			
07/17	182,804 / 15,756	+4,586 / +203	655 / 29
07/24	184,394 / 15,841	+1,590 / +85	227 / 12
07/31	187,534 / 15,897	+3,140 / +56	449 / 8
07/31: total tests = 2,096,329			
08/01: deaths/million population = 1,791			

DATE	CASES / DEATHS	WEEKLY INCREASE	DAILY AVERAGE
08/07	189,855 / 15,925	+2,321 / +28	332 / 4
08/14	192,397 / 15,973	+2,542 / +48	363 / 7

08/15: IFR (infection fatality rate) = 8.29%
08/15: hospitalizations current = 520
08/15: hospitalizations cumulative = 22,197

08/21	194,795 / 16,046	+2,398 / +73	343 / 10
08/28	196,705 / 16,034	+1,910 / (-12)	273 / (-2)

08/31: total tests = 2,964,722
09/01: deaths/million population = 1,811

09/04	198,987 / 16,083	+2,282 / +49	326 / 7

09/07: Labor Day

09/11	199,435 / 16,145	+448 / +622	64 / 9

09/15: IFR (infection fatality rate) = 8.04%
09/15: hospitalizations current = 406
09/15: hospitalizations cumulative = 23,003

09/18	202,489 / 16,184	+3,054 / +39	436 / 6

NEW! 09/22: test positivity rate = 1.7%

09/25	205,892 / 16,216	+3,403 / +32	486 / 5

09/30: total tests = 3,672,127
10/01: deaths/million population = 1,830

10/02	210,411 / 16,251	+4,519 / +35	646 / 5
10/09	215,943 / 16,283	+5,532 / +32	790 / 5

10/15: IFR (infection fatality rate) = 7.38%
10/15: hospitalizations current = 733
10/15: hospitalizations cumulative = 24,092

10/16	222,087 / 16,330	+6,144 / +47	878 / 7

10/22: test positivity rate = 3.3%

10/23	229,825 / 16,398	+7,738 / +68	1,105 / 10
10/30	241,411 / 16,470	+11,586 / +72	1,655 / 10

10/31: total tests = 4,656,106
11/01: deaths/million population = 1,856
11/03: Election Day

11/06	254,924 / 16,547	+13,513 / +77	1,930 / 11

11/07: Biden wins election

11/13	276,366 / 16,651	+21,442 / +104	3,063 / 15

11/15: IFR (infection fatality rate) = 5.87%
11/15: hospitalizations current = 2,004
11/15: hospitalizations cumulative = 39,018

DATE	CASES / DEATHS	WEEKLY INCREASE	DAILY AVERAGE
11/20	**304,538 / 16,842**	**+28,172 / +191**	**4,025 / 27**
	11/22: test positivity rate = 34.0%		
	11/26: Thanksgiving		
11/27	**333,766 / 17,078**	**+29,228 / +236**	**4,175 / 34**
	11/30: total tests = 6,133,587		
	12/01: deaths/million population = 1,946		
12/04	**365,182 / 17,391**	**+31,416 / +313**	**4,488 / 45**
12/11	**400,584 / 17,805**	**+35,402 / +414**	**5,057 / 59**
	12/14: first COVID-19 vaccinations given in the U.S.		
	12/15: IFR (infection fatality rate) = 4.29%		
	12/15: hospitalizations current = 3,660		
	12/15: hospitalizations cumulative = 44,136		
12/18	**433,843 / 18,247**	**+33,259 / +442**	**4,751 / 63**
	12/22: new U.K. variant identified in the U.S.		
	12/22: test positivity rate = 6.0%		
	12/25: Christmas		
12/25	**464,723 / 18,724**	**+30,880 / +477**	**4,411 / 68**
	12/31: total tests = 7,792,714		
	12/31: deaths/million population = 2,173		
	01/01: New Year's Day		
	01/01: CFR (case fatality rate) = 6.65% (66.5X more deadly than influenza at 0.1%)		
01/01/2021	**491,951 / 19,297**	**+27,228 / +573**	**3,890 / 82**

BONUS: *Enjoy additional week from upcoming book: PANDEMIC 2021: The U.S. Edition*
 01/06: right-wing mob insurrection at U.S. Capitol as Joe Biden confirmed president
 01/08: Twitter permanently bans Trump's account

DATE	CASES / DEATHS	WEEKLY INCREASE	DAILY AVERAGE
01/08	**588,731 / 19,847**	**+96,780 / +550**	**13,826 / 79**

*The daily average column is rounded to the nearest whole person. The infection fatality rate (IFR) is the number of deaths divided by the number of confirmed cases. The case fatality rate (CFR), shown only at the end of the year, is the number of deaths divided by the number of confirmed cases *which have had an outcome* (either recovery or death). The CFR excludes active cases.

CHAPTER 33

~ NEW MEXICO *~*

POPULATION AS OF MARCH, 2020: 2,096,640
Democratic Governor Michelle Lujan Grisham
VOTED BLUE: Biden 54.3% / Trump 43.5%

DATE	CASES / DEATHS	WEEKLY INCREASE	DAILY AVERAGE
01/30: WHO declares Public Health Emergency of International Concern			
01/31: Trump issues a China "travel ban"			
03/11: WHO declares COVID-19 a pandemic			
03/11: New Mexico's first 4 cases			
03/11: New Mexico declares Public Health Emergency			
03/13: schools close			
03/13: Trump declares a National Emergency			
03/13: Trump issues a Europe "travel ban"			
03/13	10 / 0	N/A	N/A
03/20	43 / 0	+33 / +0	5 / 0
03/24: non-essential services close			
03/25: New Mexico's first death			
03/27	191 / 1	+148 / +1	21 / 0
03/31: total tests = 11,179			
04/03	495 / 10	+304 / +9	43 / 1
04/10	1,091 / 19	+596 / +9	85 / 1
04/12: Easter			
04/15: IFR (infection fatality rate) = 2.43%			
04/15: hospitalizations current = 90			
04/15: hospitalizations cumulative = 215			
04/17	1,711 / 51	+620 / +32	89 / 5
04/24	2,521 / 84	+810 / +33	116 / 5
04/30: total tests = 63,179			

DATE	CASES / DEATHS	WEEKLY INCREASE	DAILY AVERAGE
05/01	3,513 / 131	+992 / +47	142 / 7
05/08	4,673 / 181	+1,160 / +50	166 / 7

05/10: Mother's Day
05/15: IFR (infection fatality rate) = 4.47%
05/15: hospitalizations current = 223
05/15: hospitalizations cumulative = 886

05/15	5,662 / 253	+989 / +72	141 / 10

05/16: mask mandate

05/22	6,625 / 302	+963 / +49	138 / 7

05/25: Memorial Day
05/26: George Floyd protests begin

05/29	7,493 / 344	+868 / +42	124 / 6

05/31: total tests = 194,447
NEW! 06/01: deaths/million population = 173

06/05	8,672 / 387	+1,179 / +43	168 / 6
06/12	9,526 / 426	+854 / +39	122 / 6

06/15: IFR (infection fatality rate) = 4.47%
06/15: hospitalizations current = 161
06/15: hospitalizations cumulative = 1,686

06/19	10,260 / 464	+734 / +38	105 / 5

06/21: Father's Day

06/26	11,408 / 489	+1,148 / +25	164 / 4

06/30: total tests = 344,181
07/01: deaths/million population = 238

07/03	12,776 / 511	+1,368 / +22	195 / 3

07/04: Independence Day

07/10	14,549 / 539	+1,773 / +28	253 / 4

07/15: IFR (infection fatality rate) = 3.52%
07/15: hospitalizations current = 174
07/15: hospitalizations cumulative = 2,284

07/17	16,456 / 565	+1,907 / +26	272 / 4
07/24	18,475 / 601	+2,019 / +36	288 / 5
07/31	20,600 / 642	+2,125 / +41	304 / 6

07/31: total tests = 558,012
08/01: deaths/million population = 310

08/07	21,965 / 675	+1,365 / +33	195 / 5
08/14	23,160 / 703	+1,195 / +28	171 / 4

08/15: IFR (infection fatality rate) = 3.05%

DATE	CASES / DEATHS	WEEKLY INCREASE	DAILY AVERAGE
	08/15: hospitalizations current = 113		
	08/15: hospitalizations cumulative = 2,957		
08/21	**24,095 / 739**	**+935 / +36**	**134 / 5**
08/28	**25,042 / 767**	**+947 / +28**	**135 / 4**
	08/31: total tests = 787,811		
	09/01: deaths/million population = 382		
09/04	**25,902 / 794**	**+860 / +27**	**123 / 4**
	09/07: Labor Day		
09/11	**26,563 / 818**	**+661 / +24**	**94 / 3**
	09/15: IFR (infection fatality rate) = 3.08%		
	09/15: hospitalizations current = 59		
	09/15: hospitalizations cumulative = 3,284		
09/18	**27,350 / 841**	**+787 / +23**	**112 / 3**
	NEW! 09/22: test positivity rate = 2.1%		
09/25	**28,487 / 865**	**+1,137 / +24**	**162 / 3**
	09/30: total tests = 935,401		
	10/01: deaths/million population = 423		
10/02	**30,000 / 887**	**+1,513 / +22**	**216 / 3**
10/09	**32,241 / 902**	**+2,241 / +15**	**320 / 2**
	10/15: IFR (infection fatality rate) = 2.64%		
	10/15: hospitalizations current = 150		
	10/15: hospitalizations cumulative = 3,819		
10/16	**35,770 / 928**	**+3,529 / +26**	**504 / 4**
	10/22: test positivity rate = 7.5%		
10/23	**40,168 / 960**	**+4,398 / +32**	**628 / 5**
10/30	**45,909 / 1,007**	**+5,741 / +47**	**820 / 7**
	10/31: total tests = 1,172,720		
	11/01: deaths/million population = 489		
	11/03: Election Day		
11/06	**52,394 / 1,088**	**+6,485 / +81**	**926 / 12**
	11/07: Biden wins election		
11/13	**62,006 / 1,198**	**+9,612 / +110**	**1,373 / 16**
	11/15: IFR (infection fatality rate) = 1.89%		
	11/15: hospitalizations current = 506		
	11/15: hospitalizations cumulative = 5,570		
11/20	**77,098 / 1,325**	**+15,092 / +127**	**2,156 / 18**
	11/22: test positivity rate = 18.0%		
	11/26: Thanksgiving		

DATE	CASES / DEATHS	WEEKLY INCREASE	DAILY AVERAGE
11/27	91,852 / 1,504	+14,754 / +179	2,108 / 26
	11/30: total tests = 1,592,222		
	12/01: deaths/million population = 777		
12/04	104,935 / 1,706	+13,083 / +202	1,869 / 29
12/11	116,565 / 1,889	+11,630 / +183	1,661 / 26
	12/14: first COVID-19 vaccinations given in the U.S.		
	12/15: IFR (infection fatality rate) = 1.64%		
	12/15: hospitalizations current = 865		
	12/15: hospitalizations cumulative = 8,139		
12/18	127,500 / 2,128	+10,935 / +239	1,562 / 34
	12/22: new U.K. variant identified in the U.S.		
	12/22: test positivity rate = 9.5%		
	12/25: Christmas		
12/25	136,622 / 2,307	+9,122 / +179	1,303 / 26
	12/31: total tests = 1,970,212		
	12/31: deaths/million population = 1,181		
	01/01: New Year's Day		
	01/01: CFR (case fatality rate) = 3.64% (36.4X more deadly than influenza at 0.1%)		
01/01/2021	144,142 / 2,502	+7,520 / +195	1,074 / 28

BONUS: Enjoy additional week from upcoming book: PANDEMIC 2021: The U.S. Edition
01/06: right-wing mob insurrection at U.S. Capitol as Joe Biden confirmed president
01/08: Twitter permanently bans Trump's account

| 01/08 | 153,456 / 2,710 | +9,314 / +208 | 1,331 / 30 |

*The daily average column is rounded to the nearest whole person. The infection fatality rate (IFR) is the number of deaths divided by the number of confirmed cases. The case fatality rate (CFR), shown only at the end of the year, is the number of deaths divided by the number of confirmed cases *which have had an outcome* (either recovery or death). The CFR excludes active cases.

CHAPTER 34

~ NEW YORK *~*

POPULATION AS OF MARCH, 2020: 19,440,469
Democratic Governor Andrew Cuomo
VOTED BLUE: Biden 60.9% / Trump 37.7%

DATE	CASES / DEATHS	WEEKLY INCREASE	DAILY AVERAGE
01/30: WHO declares Public Health Emergency of International Concern			
01/31: Trump issues a China "travel ban"			
03/01: New York's first case			
03/06	**76 / 0**	**N/A**	**N/A**
03/07: New York declares Disaster Emergency			
03/11: WHO declares COVID-19 a pandemic			
03/13: New York's first 2 deaths			
03/13: Trump declares a National Emergency			
03/13: Trump issues a Europe "travel ban"			
03/13	**613 / 2**	**+537 / +2**	**77 / 0**
03/18: schools close			
03/20: non-essential services close			
03/20	**10,356 / 58**	**+9,743 / +56**	**1,392 / 8**
03/22: stay at home order			
03/27	**52,318 / 728**	**+41,962 / +670**	**5,995 / 96**
03/31: total tests = 186,468			
04/03	**113,704 / 3,565**	**+61,386 / +2,837**	**8,769 / 405**
04/10	**172,358 / 7,884**	**+58,654 / +4,319**	**8,379 / 617**
04/12: Easter			
04/15: IFR (infection fatality rate) = 5.40%			
04/15: hospitalizations current = 18,335			
04/15: hospitalizations cumulative = not reliable for this state			
04/17: mask mandate			

DATE	CASES / DEATHS	WEEKLY INCREASE	DAILY AVERAGE
04/17	233,951 / 17,131	+61,593 / +9,247	8,799 / 1,321
04/24	277,445 / 21,291	+43,494 / +4,160	6,213 / 594
04/30: total tests = 859,017			
05/01	315,222 / 24,069	+37,777 / +2,778	5,397 / 397
05/08	340,705 / 26,585	+25,483 / +2,516	3,640 / 359
05/10: Mother's Day			
05/15: IFR (infection fatality rate) = 7.75%			
05/15: hospitalizations current = 6,294			
05/15	356,016 / 27,574	+15,311 / +989	2,187 / 141
05/22	367,936 / 29,009	+11,920 / +1,435	1,703 / 205
05/25: Memorial Day			
05/26: George Floyd protests begin			
05/29	377,714 / 29,751	+9,778 / +742	1,397 / 106
05/31: total tests = 2,005,381			
NEW! 06/01: deaths/million population = 1,543			
06/05	396,699 / 30,372	+18,985 / +621	2,712 / 89
06/12	402,914 / 30,824	+6,215 / +452	888 / 65
06/15: IFR (infection fatality rate) = 7.64%			
06/15: hospitalizations current = 1,608			
06/19	409,593 / 31,159	+6,679 / +335	954 / 48
06/21: Father's Day			
06/26	415,207 / 31,421	+5,614 / +262	802 / 37
06/30: total tests = 3,914,938			
07/01: deaths/million population = 1,652			
07/03	420,774 / 32,191	+5,567 / +770	795 / 110
07/04: Independence Day			
07/10	426,016 / 32,375	+5,242 / +184	749 / 26
07/15: IFR (infection fatality rate) = 7.55%			
07/15: hospitalizations current = 831			
07/17	432,412 / 32,535	+6,396 / +160	914 / 23
07/24	438,435 / 32,665	+6,023 / +130	860 / 19
07/31	443,745 / 32,765	+5,310 / +100	759 / 14
07/31: total tests = 5,889,237			
08/01: deaths/million population = 1,685			
08/07	448,991 / 32,822	+5,246 / +57	749 / 8
08/14	454,148 / 32,895	+5,157 / +73	737 / 10
08/15: IFR (infection fatality rate) = 7.23%			
08/15: hospitalizations current = 523			

DATE	CASES / DEATHS	WEEKLY INCREASE	DAILY AVERAGE
08/21	459,096 / 32,937	+4,948 / +42	707 / 6
08/28	463,915 / 33,005	+4,819 / +68	688 / 10
08/31: total tests = 8,710,614			
09/01: deaths/million population = 1,700			
09/04	470,460 / 33,065	+6,545 / +60	935 / 9
09/07: Labor Day			
09/11	476,021 / 33,109	+5,561 / +44	794 / 6
09/15: IFR (infection fatality rate) = 6.92%			
09/15: hospitalizations current = 481			
09/18	481,788 / 33,172	+5,767 / +63	824 / 9
NEW! 09/22: test positivity rate = 1%			
09/25	487,963 / 33,202	+6,175 / +30	882 / 4
09/30: total tests = 10,976,024			
10/01: deaths/million population = 1,711			
10/02	496,314 / 33,289	+8,351 / +87	1,193 / 12
10/09	506,890 / 33,372	+10,576 / +83	1,511 / 12
10/15: IFR (infection fatality rate) = 6.49%			
10/15: hospitalizations current = 897			
10/16	516,752 / 33,451	+9,862 / +79	1,409 / 11
10/22: test positivity rate = 1.3%			
10/23	528,066 / 33,549	+11,314 / +98	1,616 / 14
10/30	542,094 / 33,655	+14,028 / +106	2,004 / 15
10/31: total tests = 14,527,718			
11/01: deaths/million population = 1,732			
11/03: Election Day			
11/06	558,950 / 33,786	+16,856 / +131	2,408 / 19
11/07: Biden wins election			
11/13	588,381 / 33,955	+29,431 / +169	4,204 / 24
11/15: IFR (infection fatality rate) = 5.69%			
11/15: hospitalizations current = 1,845			
11/20	623,242 / 34,186	+34,861 / +231	4,980 / 33
11/22: test positivity rate = 2.9%			
11/26: Thanksgiving			
11/27	666,642 / 34,437	+43,400 / +251	6,200 / 36
11/30: total tests = 19,761,724			
12/01: deaths/million population = 1,795			
12/04	724,437 / 34,886	+57,795 / +449	8,256 / 64
12/11	793,396 / 35,421	+68,959 / +535	9,851 / 76

DATE	CASES / DEATHS	WEEKLY INCREASE	DAILY AVERAGE

12/14: first COVID-19 vaccinations given in the U.S.
12/15: IFR (infection fatality rate) = 4.30%
12/15: hospitalizations current = 5,982

| **12/18** | **868,068 / 36,222** | **+74,672 / +801** | **10,667 / 114** |

12/22: new U.K. variant identified in the U.S.
12/22: test positivity rate = 5.4%
12/25: Christmas

| **12/25** | **943,264 / 37,129** | **+75,196 / +907** | **10,742 / 130** |

12/31: total tests = 25,504,313
12/31: deaths/million population = 1,961
01/01: New Year's Day
01/01: CFR (case fatality rate) = 7.38% (73.8X more deadly than influenza at 0.1%)

| **01/01/2021** | **1,031,053 / 38,145** | **+87,789 / +1,016** | **12,541 / 145** |

BONUS: Enjoy additional week from upcoming book: PANDEMIC 2021: The U.S. Edition
01/06: right-wing mob insurrection at U.S. Capitol as Joe Biden confirmed president
01/08: Twitter permanently bans Trump's account

| **01/08** | **1,135,593 / 39,298** | **+104,540 / +1,153** | **14,934 / 165** |

*The daily average column is rounded to the nearest whole person. The infection fatality rate (IFR) is the number of deaths divided by the number of confirmed cases. The case fatality rate (CFR), shown only at the end of the year, is the number of deaths divided by the number of confirmed cases *which have had an outcome* (either recovery or death). The CFR excludes active cases.

CHAPTER 35

~ NORTH CAROLINA *~*

POPULATION AS OF MARCH, 2020: 10,611,862
Democratic Governor Roy Cooper
VOTED RED: Trump 49.9% / Biden 48.6%

DATE	CASES / DEATHS	WEEKLY INCREASE	DAILY AVERAGE
01/30: WHO declares Public Health Emergency of International Concern			
01/31: Trump issues a China "travel ban"			
03/08: North Carolina's first 2 cases			
03/10: North Carolina declares State of Emergency			
03/11: WHO declares COVID-19 a pandemic			
03/13: Trump declares a National Emergency			
03/13: Trump issues a Europe "travel ban"			
03/13	15 / 0	N/A	N/A
03/14: schools close			
03/20	137 / 0	+122 / +0	17 / 0
03/25: North Carolina's first death			
03/27	763 / 3	+626 / +3	89 / 0
03/30: non-essential services close			
03/30: stay at home order			
03/31: total tests = 20,864			
04/03	2,093 / 19	+1,330 / +16	190 / 2
04/10	4,088 / 84	+1,995 / +65	285 / 9
04/12: Easter			
04/15: IFR (infection fatality rate) = 2.45%			
04/15: hospitalizations current = 431			
04/15: hospitalizations cumulative = not given for this state			
04/17	6,031 / 172	+1,943 / +88	278 / 13
04/24	8,250 / 293	+2,219 / +121	317 / 17

DATE	CASES / DEATHS	WEEKLY INCREASE	DAILY AVERAGE
	04/30: total tests = 125,265		
05/01	**11,071 / 419**	**+2,821 / +126**	**403 / 18**
05/08	**14,007 / 530**	**+2,936 / +111**	**419 / 16**
	05/10: Mother's Day		
	05/15: IFR (infection fatality rate) = 3.81%		
	05/15: hospitalizations current = 492		
05/15	**17,494 / 667**	**+3,487 / +137**	**498 / 20**
05/22	**22,110 / 775**	**+4,616 / +108**	**659 / 15**
	05/25: Memorial Day		
	05/26: George Floyd protests begin		
05/29	**26,849 / 919**	**+4,739 / +144**	**677 / 21**
	05/31: total tests = 404,157		
	NEW! 06/01: deaths/million population = 89		
06/05	**33,294 / 1,015**	**+6,445 / +96**	**921 / 14**
06/12	**41,416 / 1,121**	**+8,122 / +106**	**1,160 / 15**
	06/15: IFR (infection fatality rate) = 2.53%		
	06/15: hospitalizations current = 797		
06/19	**49,840 / 1,250**	**+8,424 / +129**	**1,203 / 18**
	06/21: Father's Day		
	06/26: mask mandate		
06/26	**59,080 / 1,347**	**+9,240 / +97**	**1,320 / 14**
	06/30: total tests = 910,033		
	07/01: deaths/million population = 133		
07/03	**70,562 / 1,420**	**+11,482 / +73**	**1,640 / 10**
	07/04: Independence Day		
07/10	**81,499 / 1,507**	**+10,937 / +87**	**1,562 / 12**
	07/15: IFR (infection fatality rate) = 1.75%		
	07/15: hospitalizations current = 1,142		
07/17	**95,572 / 1,634**	**+14,073 / +127**	**2,010 / 18**
07/24	**109,271 / 1,778**	**+13,699 / +144**	**1,957 / 21**
07/31	**122,612 / 1,952**	**+13,341 / +174**	**1,906 / 25**
	07/31: total tests = 1,757,102		
	08/01: deaths/million population = 189		
08/07	**133,353 / 2,158**	**+10,741 / +206**	**1,534 / 29**
08/14	**142,170 / 2,321**	**+8,817 / +163**	**1,260 / 23**
	08/15: IFR (infection fatality rate) = 1.64%		
	08/15: hospitalizations current = 1,032		
08/21	**152,889 / 2,531**	**+10,719 / +210**	**1,531 / 30**

DATE	CASES / DEATHS	WEEKLY INCREASE	DAILY AVERAGE
08/24: Trump rally			
08/28	**163,402 / 2,683**	**+10,513 / +152**	**1,502 / 22**
08/31: total tests = 2,410,871			
09/01: deaths/million population = 278			
09/02: Trump rally			
09/04	**175,559 / 2,879**	**+12,157 / +196**	**1,737 / 28**
09/07: Labor Day			
09/08: Trump rally			
09/11	**182,286 / 3,023**	**+6,727 / +144**	**961 / 21**
09/15: IFR (infection fatality rate) = 1.66%			
09/15: hospitalizations current = 916			
09/18	**191,019 / 3,207**	**+8,733 / +184**	**1,248 / 26**
09/19: Trump rally			
NEW! 09/22: test positivity rate = 5.0%			
09/25	**204,331 / 3,409**	**+13,312 / +202**	**1,902 / 29**
09/30: total tests = 3,094,417			
10/01: deaths/million population = 344			
10/02	**214,684 / 3,608**	**+10,353 / +199**	**1,479 / 28**
10/09	**227,431 / 3,747**	**+12,747 / +139**	**1,821 / 20**
10/15: IFR (infection fatality rate) = 1.62%			
10/15: hospitalizations current = 1,140			
10/15: Trump rally			
10/16	**241,623 / 3,910**	**+14,192 / +163**	**2,027 / 23**
10/21: Trump rally			
10/22: test positivity rate = 6.2%			
10/23	**255,708 / 4,114**	**+14,085 / +204**	**2,012 / 29**
10/24: Trump rally			
10/30	**271,830 / 4,332**	**+16,122 / +218**	**2,303 / 31**
10/31: total tests = 4,043,698			
11/01: deaths/million population = 418			
11/03: Election Day			
11/06	**288,569 / 4,582**	**+16,739 / +250**	**2,391 / 36**
11/07: Biden wins election			
11/13	**305,233 / 4,720**	**+16,664 / +138**	**2,381 / 20**
11/15: IFR (infection fatality rate) = 1.54%			
11/15: hospitalizations current = 1,395			
11/20	**328,846 / 4,979**	**+23,613 / +259**	**3,373 / 37**
11/22: test positivity rate = 8.5%			

DATE	CASES / DEATHS	WEEKLY INCREASE	DAILY AVERAGE
11/26: Thanksgiving			
11/27	354,514 / 5,210	+25,668 / +231	3,667 / 33
11/30: total tests = 5,355,690			
12/01: deaths/million population = 512			
12/04	382,534 / 5,467	+28,020 / +257	4,003 / 37
12/11	423,623 / 5,752	+41,089 / +285	5,870 / 41
12/14: first COVID-19 vaccinations given in the U.S.			
12/15: IFR (infection fatality rate) = 1.32%			
12/15: hospitalizations current = 2,735			
12/18	466,104 / 6,125	+42,481 / +373	6,069 / 53
12/22: new U.K. variant identified in the U.S.			
12/22: test positivity rate = 10.3%			
12/25: Christmas			
12/25	508,559 / 6,360	+42,455 / +235	6,065 / 34
12/31: total tests = 6,898,509			
12/31: deaths/million population = 657,747			
01/01: New Year's Day			
01/01: CFR (case fatality rate) = 1.64% (16.4X more deadly than influenza at 0.1%)			
01/01/2021	539,545 / 6,748	+30,986 / +368	4,427 / 53

BONUS: Enjoy additional week from upcoming book: PANDEMIC 2021: The U.S. Edition
    01/06: right-wing mob insurrection at U.S. Capitol as Joe Biden confirmed president
    01/08: Twitter permanently bans Trump's account

01/08	602,774 / 7,328	+63,229 / +580	9,033 / 83

*The daily average column is rounded to the nearest whole person. The infection fatality rate (IFR) is the number of deaths divided by the number of confirmed cases. The case fatality rate (CFR), shown only at the end of the year, is the number of deaths divided by the number of confirmed cases *which have had an outcome* (either recovery or death). The CFR excludes active cases.

CHAPTER 36

~ NORTH DAKOTA *~*

POPULATION AS OF MARCH, 2020: 761,723
Republican Governor Doug Burgum
VOTED RED: Trump 65.1% / Biden 31.8%

DATE	CASES / DEATHS	WEEKLY INCREASE	DAILY AVERAGE
01/30: WHO declares Public Health Emergency of International Concern			
01/31: Trump issues a China "travel ban"			
03/11: WHO declares COVID-19 a pandemic			
03/11: North Dakota's first case			
03/13: North Dakota declares State of Emergency			
03/13: Trump declares a National Emergency			
03/13: Trump issues a Europe "travel ban"			
03/16: schools close			
03/20	**28 / 0**	**+27 / +0**	**4 / 0**
03/27: North Dakota's first death			
03/27	**80 / 1**	**+52 / +1**	**7 / 0**
03/31: total tests = 3,837			
04/03	**186 / 3**	**+106 / +2**	**15 / 0**
04/10	**278 / 6**	**+92 / +3**	**13 / 0**
04/12: Easter			
04/15: IFR (infection fatality rate) = 2.47%			
04/15: hospitalizations current = 13			
04/15: hospitalizations cumulative = 44			
04/17	**439 / 9**	**+161 / +3**	**23 / 0**
04/24	**748 / 15**	**+309 / +6**	**44 / 1**
04/30: total tests = 25,350			
05/01	**1,107 / 23**	**+359 / +8**	**51 / 1**
05/08	**1,425 / 33**	**+318 / +10**	**45 / 1**

DATE	CASES / DEATHS	WEEKLY INCREASE	DAILY AVERAGE
05/10: Mother's Day			
05/15: IFR (infection fatality rate) = 2.39%			
05/15: hospitalizations current = 35			
05/15: hospitalizations cumulative = 130			
05/15	1,761 / 42	+336 / +9	48 / 1
05/22	2,317 / 52	+556 / +10	79 / 1
05/25: Memorial Day			
05/26: George Floyd protests begin			
05/29	2,520 / 59	+203 / +7	29 / 1
05/31: total tests = 70,981			
NEW! 06/01: deaths/million population = 80			
06/05	2,745 / 71	+225 / +12	32 / 2
06/12	3,016 / 74	+271 / +3	39 / 0
06/15: IFR (infection fatality rate) = 2.39%			
06/15: hospitalizations current = 31			
06/15: hospitalizations cumulative = 197			
06/19	3,226 / 76	+210 / +2	30 / 0
06/21: Father's Day			
06/26	3,421 / 78	+195 / +2	28 / 0
06/30: total tests = 106,122			
07/01: deaths/million population = 105			
07/03	3,722 / 80	+301 / +2	43 / 0
07/04: Independence Day			
07/10	4,154 / 85	+432 / +5	62 / 1
07/15: IFR (infection fatality rate) = 1.93%			
07/15: hospitalizations current = 42			
07/15: hospitalizations cumulative = 284			
07/17	4,792 / 90	+638 / +5	91 / 1
07/24	5,614 / 99	+822 / +9	117 / 1
07/31	6,469 / 103	+855 / +4	122 / 1
07/31: total tests = 153,964			
08/01: deaths/million population = 135			
08/07	7,327 / 110	+858 / +7	123 / 1
08/14	8,322 / 121	+995 / +11	142 / 2
08/15: IFR (infection fatality rate) = 1.43%			
08/15: hospitalizations current = 55			
08/15: hospitalizations cumulative = 457			
08/21	9,474 / 132	+1,152 / +11	165 / 2

DATE	CASES / DEATHS	WEEKLY INCREASE	DAILY AVERAGE
08/28	**11,110 / 139**	**+1,636 / +7**	**234 / 1**
08/31: total tests = 209,499			
09/01: deaths/million population = 203			
09/04	**12,973 / 150**	**+1,863 / +11**	**266 / 2**
09/07: Labor Day			
09/11	**14,684 / 164**	**+1,711 / +14**	**244 / 2**
09/15: IFR (infection fatality rate) = 1.07%			
09/15: hospitalizations current = 62			
09/15: hospitalizations cumulative = 657			
09/18	**17,230 / 184**	**+2,546 / +20**	**364 / 3**
NEW! 09/22: test positivity rate = 6.2%			
09/25	**19,885 / 219**	**+2,655 / +35**	**379 / 5**
09/30: total tests = 244,312			
10/01: deaths/million population = 346			
10/02	**22,694 / 264**	**+2,809 / +45**	**401 / 6**
10/09	**26,040 / 321**	**+3,346 / +57**	**478 / 8**
10/15: IFR (infection fatality rate) = 1.25%			
10/15: hospitalizations current = 207			
10/15: hospitalizations cumulative = 1,192			
10/16	**30,517 / 388**	**+4,477 / +67**	**640 / 10**
10/22: test positivity rate = 11%			
10/23	**35,939 / 440**	**+5,422 / +52**	**775 / 7**
10/30	**42,483 / 512**	**+6,544 / +72**	**935 / 10**
10/31: total tests = 294,064			
11/01: deaths/million population = 697			
11/03: Election Day			
11/06	**51,602 / 613**	**+9,119 / +101**	**1,303 / 14**
11/07: Biden wins election			
11/13	**60,602 / 707**	**+9,000 / +94**	**1,286 / 13**
11/14: mask mandate			
11/15: IFR (infection fatality rate) = 1.15%			
11/15: hospitalizations current = 400			
11/15: hospitalizations cumulative = 2,178			
11/20	**70,105 / 818**	**+9,503 / +111**	**1,358 / 16**
11/22: test positivity rate = 14.8%			
11/26: Thanksgiving			
11/27	**77,232 / 902**	**+7,127 / +84**	**1,018 / 12**
11/30: total tests = 351,652			

DATE	CASES / DEATHS	WEEKLY INCREASE	DAILY AVERAGE
12/01: deaths/million population = 1,268			
12/04	**81,949 / 989**	**+4,717 / +87**	**674 / 12**
12/11	**87,214 / 1,130**	**+5,265 / +141**	**752 / 20**
12/14: first COVID-19 vaccinations given in the U.S.			
12/15: IFR (infection fatality rate) = 1.32%			
12/15: hospitalizations current = 277			
12/15: hospitalizations cumulative = 3,073			
12/18	**89,557 / 1,225**	**+2,343 / +95**	**335 / 14**
12/22: new U.K. variant identified in the U.S.			
12/22: test positivity rate = 6.3%			
12/25: Christmas			
12/25	**90,948 / 1,260**	**+1,391 / +35**	**199 / 5**
12/31: total tests = 376,910			
12/31: deaths/million population = 1,695			
01/01: New Year's Day			
01/01: CFR (case fatality rate) = 1.45% (14.3X more deadly than influenza at 0.1%)			
01/01/2021	**92,495 / 1,292**	**+1,547 / +32**	**221 / 5**

BONUS: Enjoy additional week from upcoming book: PANDEMIC 2021: The U.S. Edition
    01/06: right-wing mob insurrection at U.S. Capitol as Joe Biden confirmed president
    01/08: Twitter permanently bans Trump's account

DATE	CASES / DEATHS	WEEKLY INCREASE	DAILY AVERAGE
01/08	**94,438 / 1,352**	**+1,943 / +60**	**278 / 9**

---

*The daily average column is rounded to the nearest whole person. The infection fatality rate (IFR) is the number of deaths divided by the number of confirmed cases. The case fatality rate (CFR), shown only at the end of the year, is the number of deaths divided by the number of confirmed cases *which have had an outcome* (either recovery or death). The CFR excludes active cases.

CHAPTER 37

~ OHIO *~*

POPULATION AS OF MARCH, 2020: 11,747,694
Republican Governor Richard Michael DeWine
VOTED RED: Trump 53.3% / Biden 45.2%

DATE	CASES / DEATHS	WEEKLY INCREASE	DAILY AVERAGE
	01/30: WHO declares Public Health Emergency of International Concern		
	01/31: Trump issues a China "travel ban"		
	03/09: Ohio's first 3 cases		
	03/09: Ohio declares State of Emergency		
	03/11: WHO declares COVID-19 a pandemic		
	03/13: Trump declares a National Emergency		
	03/13: Trump issues a Europe "travel ban"		
03/13	13 / 0	N/A	N/A
	03/16: schools close		
	03/20: Ohio's first death		
03/20	169 / 1	+156 / +1	22 / 0
	03/23: non-essential services close		
	03/23: stay at home order		
03/27	1,137 / 19	+968 / +118	138 / 3
	03/31: total tests = 27,275		
04/03	3,312 / 91	+2,175 / +72	311 / 10
04/10	5,878 / 231	+2,566 / +140	367 / 20
	04/12: Easter		
	04/15: IFR (infection fatality rate) = 4.63%		
	04/15: hospitalizations current = not given		
	04/15: hospitalizations cumulative = 2,156		
04/17	9,107 / 418	+3,229 / +187	461 / 27
04/24	15,169 / 690	+6,062 / +272	866 / 39

PANDEMIC 2020: The U.S. Edition

DATE	CASES / DEATHS	WEEKLY INCREASE	DAILY AVERAGE
	04/30: total tests = 131,379		
05/01	**18,743 / 1,002**	**+3,574 / +312**	**511 / 45**
05/08	**23,016 / 1,306**	**+4,273/ +304**	**610 / 43**
	05/10: Mother's Day		
	05/15: IFR (infection fatality rate) = 5.88%		
	05/15: hospitalizations current = 944		
	05/15: hospitalizations cumulative = 4,791		
05/15	**26,961 / 1,584**	**+3,945 / +278**	**564 / 40**
05/22	**30,865 / 1,879**	**+3,904 / +295**	**558 / 42**
	05/25: Memorial Day		
	05/26: George Floyd protests begin		
05/29	**34,625 / 2,137**	**+3,760 / +258**	**537 / 37**
	05/31: total tests = 381,947		
	NEW! 06/01: deaths/million population = 188		
06/05	**37,792 / 2,363**	**+3,167 / +226**	**452 / 32**
06/12	**40,480 / 2,514**	**+2,688 / +151**	**384 / 22**
	06/15: IFR (infection fatality rate) = 6.20%		
	06/15: hospitalizations current = 513		
	06/15: hospitalizations cumulative = 6,948		
06/19	**43,834 / 2,672**	**+3,354 / +158**	**479 / 23**
	06/21: Father's Day		
06/26	**49,077 / 2,812**	**+5,243 / +140**	**749 / 20**
	06/30: total tests = 787,929		
	07/01: deaths/million population = 248		
07/03	**55,763 / 2,932**	**+6,686 / +120**	**955 / 17**
	07/04: Independence Day		
07/10	**62,884 / 3,037**	**+7,121 / +105**	**1,017 / 15**
	07/15: IFR (infection fatality rate) = 4.44%		
	07/15: hospitalizations current = 1,027		
	07/15: hospitalizations cumulative = 9,209		
07/17	**72,321 / 3,119**	**+9,437 / +82**	**1,348 / 12**
	07/23: mask mandate		
07/24	**81,790 / 3,306**	**+9,469 / +187**	**1,353 / 27**
07/31	**91,179 / 3,495**	**+9,389 / +189**	**1,341 / 27**
	07/31: total tests = 1,463,508		
	08/01: deaths/million population = 301		
08/07	**98,694 / 3,661**	**+7,515 / +166**	**1,074 / 24**
08/14	**106,585 / 3,790**	**+7,891 / +129**	**1,127 / 18**

DATE	CASES / DEATHS	WEEKLY INCREASE	DAILY AVERAGE
	08/15: IFR (infection fatality rate) = 3.55%		
	08/15: hospitalizations current = 899		
	08/15: hospitalizations cumulative = 12,210		
08/21	**113,092 / 3,963**	**+6,507 / +173**	**930 / 25**
08/28	**120,171 / 4,112**	**+7,079 / +149**	**1,011 / 21**
	08/31: total tests = 2,371,204		
	09/01: deaths/million population = 364		
09/04	**128,560 / 4,251**	**+8,389 / +139**	**1,198 / 20**
	09/07: Labor Day		
09/11	**135,477 / 4,406**	**+6,917 / +155**	**988 / 22**
	09/15: IFR (infection fatality rate) = 3.23%		
	09/15: hospitalizations current = 666		
	09/15: hospitalizations cumulative = 14,481		
09/18	**142,831 / 4,618**	**+7,354 / +212**	**1,051 / 30**
	09/21: 2 Trump rallies		
	NEW! 09/22: test positivity rate = 2.8%		
09/25	**149,030 / 4,747**	**+6,199 / +129**	**886 / 18**
	09/30: total tests = 3,262,736		
	10/01: deaths/million population = 420		
10/02	**156,892 / 4,911**	**+7,862 / +164**	**1,123 / 23**
10/09	**166,146 / 5,000**	**+9,254 / +89**	**1,322 / 13**
	10/15: IFR (infection fatality rate) = 2.87%		
	10/15: hospitalizations current = 1,041		
	10/15: hospitalizations cumulative = 16,824		
10/16	**178,050 / 5,061**	**+11,904 / +61**	**1,701 / 9**
	10/22: test positivity rate = 5.0%		
10/23	**193,038 / 5,218**	**+14,988 / +157**	**2,141 / 22**
	10/24: Trump rally		
10/30	**212,823 / 5,341**	**+19,785 / +123**	**2,826 / 18**
	10/31: total tests = 4,459,339		
	11/01: deaths/million population = 459		
	11/03: Election Day		
11/06	**240,178 / 5,536**	**+27,355 / +195**	**3,908 / 28**
	11/07: Biden wins election		
11/13	**282,528 / 5,736**	**+42,350 / +200**	**6,050 / 29**
	11/15: IFR (infection fatality rate) = 1.93%		
	11/15: hospitalizations current = 3,175		
	11/15: hospitalizations cumulative = 22,265		

DATE	CASES / DEATHS	WEEKLY INCREASE	DAILY AVERAGE
11/20	**335,423 / 5,955**	**+52,895 / +219**	**7,556 / 31**
11/22: test positivity rate = 24.7%			
11/26: Thanksgiving			
11/27	**399,808 / 6,346**	**+64,385 / +391**	**9,198 / 56**
11/30: total tests = 6,194,031			
12/01: deaths/million population = 571			
12/04	**456,963 / 6,882**	**+57,155 / +536**	**8,165 / 77**
12/11	**542,209 / 7,428**	**+85,246 / +546**	**12,178 / 78**
12/14: first COVID-19 vaccinations given in the U.S.			
12/15: IFR (infection fatality rate) = 1.32%			
12/15: hospitalizations current = 5,296			
12/15: hospitalizations cumulative = 32,878			
12/18	**605,862 / 7,967**	**+63,653 / +539**	**9,093 / 77**
12/22: new U.K. variant identified in the U.S.			
12/22: test positivity rate = 15.7%			
12/25: Christmas			
12/25	**653,651 / 8,457**	**+47,789 / +490**	**6,827 / 70**
12/31: total tests = 7,680,270			
12/31: deaths/million population = 767			
01/01: New Year's Day			
01/01: CFR (case fatality rate) = 1.59% (15.9X more deadly than influenza at 0.1%)			
01/01/2021	**700,380 / 8,962**	**+46,729 / +505**	**6,676 / 72**

BONUS: Enjoy additional week from upcoming book: PANDEMIC 2021: The U.S. Edition

01/06: right-wing mob insurrection at U.S. Capitol as Joe Biden confirmed president			
01/08: Twitter permanently bans Trump's account			
01/08	**762,603 / 9,545**	**+62,223 / +583**	**8,889 / 83**

*The daily average column is rounded to the nearest whole person. The infection fatality rate (IFR) is the number of deaths divided by the number of confirmed cases. The case fatality rate (CFR), shown only at the end of the year, is the number of deaths divided by the number of confirmed cases *which have had an outcome* (either recovery or death). The CFR excludes active cases.

CHAPTER 38

~ OKLAHOMA *~*

POPULATION AS OF MARCH, 2020: 3,954,821
Republican Governor Kevin Stitt
VOTED RED: Trump 65.4% / Biden 32.3%

DATE	CASES / DEATHS	WEEKLY INCREASE	DAILY AVERAGE
	01/30: WHO declares Public Health Emergency of International Concern		
	01/31: Trump issues a China "travel ban"		
	03/07: Oklahoma's first case		
	03/11: WHO declares COVID-19 a pandemic		
	03/13: Trump declares a National Emergency		
	03/13: Trump issues a Europe "travel ban"		
03/13	3 / 0	N/A	N/A
	03/15: Oklahoma declares State of Emergency		
	03/17: schools close		
	03/19: Oklahoma's first death		
03/20	49 / 1	+46 / +1	7 / 0
03/27	322 / 8	+273 / +7	39 / 1
	03/31: total tests = 1,688		
	04/01: non-essential services close		
04/03	988 / 38	+666 / +30	95 / 4
04/10	1,794 / 88	+806 / +50	115 / 7
	04/12: Easter		
	04/15: IFR (infection fatality rate) = 5.33%		
	04/15: hospitalizations current = 194		
	04/15: hospitalizations cumulative = 510		
04/17	2,465 / 136	+671 / +48	96 / 7
04/24	3,121 / 188	+656 / +52	94 / 7
	04/30: total tests = 58,012		

DATE	CASES / DEATHS	WEEKLY INCREASE	DAILY AVERAGE
05/01	3,748 / 230	+627 / +42	90 / 6
05/08	4,424 / 266	+676 / +36	97 / 5

05/10: Mother's Day
05/15: IFR (infection fatality rate) = 5.60%
05/15: hospitalizations current = 215
05/15: hospitalizations cumulative = 863

05/15	5,086 / 285	+662 / +19	95 / 3
05/22	5,849 / 307	+763 / +22	109 / 3

05/25: Memorial Day
05/26: George Floyd protests begin

05/29	6,338 / 329	+489 / +22	70 / 3

05/31: total tests = 193,118
NEW! 06/01: deaths/million population = 84

06/05	7,003 / 345	+665 / +16	95 / 2
06/12	7,848 / 359	+845 / +14	121 / 2

06/15: IFR (infection fatality rate) = 4.27%
06/15: hospitalizations current = 149
06/15: hospitalizations cumulative = 1,117

06/19	9,706 / 367	+1,858 / +8	265 / 1

06/20: Trump rally
06/21: Father's Day

06/26	12,343 / 377	+2,637 / +10	377 / 1

06/30: total tests = 341,597
07/01: deaths/million population = 98

07/03	15,065 / 398	+2,722 / +21	389 / 3

07/04: Independence Day

07/10	19,092 / 416	+4,027 / +18	575 / 3

07/15: IFR (infection fatality rate) = 1,89%
07/15: hospitalizations current = 561
07/15: hospitalizations cumulative = 2,170

07/17	24,140 / 445	+5,048 / +29	721 / 4
07/24	29,116 / 484	+4,976 / +39	711 / 6
07/31	36,487 / 541	+7,371 / +57	1,053 / 8

07/31: total tests = 644,042
08/01: deaths/million population = 139

08/07	42,255 / 600	+5,768 / +59	824 / 8
08/14	46,897 / 644	+4,642 / +44	663 / 6

08/15: IFR (infection fatality rate) = 1.37%

DATE	CASES / DEATHS	WEEKLY INCREASE	DAILY AVERAGE
	08/15: hospitalizations current = 506		
	08/15: hospitalizations cumulative = 3,998		
08/21	**51,746 / 715**	**+4,849 / +71**	**693 / 10**
08/28	**56,260 / 786**	**+4,514 / +71**	**645 / 10**
	08/31: total tests = 939,500		
	09/01: deaths/million population = 215		
09/04	**62,040 / 846**	**+5,780 / +60**	**826 / 9**
	09/07: Labor Day		
09/11	**67,642 / 888**	**+5,602 / +42**	**800 / 6**
	09/15: IFR (infection fatality rate) = 1.28%		
	09/15: hospitalizations current = 561		
	09/15: hospitalizations cumulative = 5,562		
09/18	**74,567 / 939**	**+6,925 / +51**	**989 / 7**
	NEW! 09/22: test positivity rate = 9.1%		
09/25	**82,520 / 993**	**+7,953 / +54**	**1,136 / 8**
	09/30: total tests = 1,262,313		
	10/01: deaths/million population = 264		
10/02	**89,559 / 1,044**	**+7,039 / +51**	**1,006 / 7**
10/09	**97,088 / 1,091**	**+7,529 / +47**	**1,076 / 7**
	10/15: IFR (infection fatality rate) = 1.10%		
	10/15: hospitalizations current = 781		
	10/15: hospitalizations cumulative = 7,601		
10/16	**105,308 / 1,154**	**+8,220 / +63**	**1,174 / 9**
	10/22: test positivity rate = 9.4%		
10/23	**113,856 / 1,234**	**+8,548 / +80**	**1,221 / 11**
10/30	**121,495 / 1,326**	**+7,639 / +92**	**1,091 / 13**
	10/31: total tests = 1,632,701		
	11/01: deaths/million population = 340		
	11/03: Election Day		
11/06	**131,751 / 1,429**	**+10,256 / +103**	**1,465 / 15**
	11/07: Biden wins election		
11/13	**147,358 / 1,493**	**+15,607 / +64**	**2,230 / 9**
	11/15: IFR (infection fatality rate) = 0.99%		
	11/15: hospitalizations current = 1,247		
	11/15: hospitalizations cumulative = 10,372		
11/20	**167,261 / 1,603**	**+19,903 / +110**	**2,843 / 16**
	11/22: test positivity rate = 39.1%		
	11/26: Thanksgiving		

DATE	CASES / DEATHS	WEEKLY INCREASE	DAILY AVERAGE
11/27	187,567 / 1,704	+20,306 / +101	2,901 / 14

11/30: total tests = 2,151,411
12/01: deaths/million population = 458

12/04	208,875 / 1,860	+21,308 / +156	3,044 / 22
12/11	229,353 / 2,007	+20,478 / +147	2,925 / 21

12/14: first COVID-19 vaccinations given in the U.S.
12/15: IFR (infection fatality rate) = 0.86%
12/15: hospitalizations current = 1,741
12/15: hospitalizations cumulative = 14,408

12/18	251,760 / 2,161	+22,407 / +154	3,201 / 22

12/22: new U.K. variant identified in U.S.
12/22: test positivity rate = 21.1%
12/25: Christmas

12/25	272,553 / 2,328	+20,793 / +167	2,970 / 24

12/31: total tests = 2,669,170
12/31: deaths/million population = 629
01/01: New Year's Day
01/01: CFR (case fatality rate) = 0.96% (9.6X more deadly than influenza at 0.1%)

01/01/2021	290,936 / 2,489	+18,383 / +161	2,626 / 23

BONUS: Enjoy additional week from upcoming book: PANDEMIC 2021: The U.S. Edition
01/06: right-wing mob insurrection at U.S. Capitol as Joe Biden confirmed president
01/08: Twitter permanently bans Trump's account

01/08	320,586 / 2,703	+29,650 / +214	4,236 / 31

*The daily average column is rounded to the nearest whole person. The infection fatality rate (IFR) is the number of deaths divided by the number of confirmed cases. The case fatality rate (CFR), shown only at the end of the year, is the number of deaths divided by the number of confirmed cases *which have had an outcome* (either recovery or death). The CFR excludes active cases.

CHAPTER 39

~ OREGON *~*

POPULATION AS OF MARCH, 2020: 4,301,089
Democratic Governor Kate Brown
VOTED BLUE: Biden 56.5% / Trump 40.4%

DATE	CASES / DEATHS	WEEKLY INCREASE	DAILY AVERAGE
01/30: WHO declares Public Health Emergency of International Concern			
01/31: Trump issues a China "travel ban"			
02/28: Oregon's first case			
03/06	3 / 0	+3 / +0	0 / 0
03/11: Oregon declares State of Emergency			
03/11: WHO declares COVID-19 a pandemic			
03/13: Trump declares a National Emergency			
03/13: Trump issues a Europe "travel ban"			
03/13	30 / 0	+27 / +0	4 / 0
03/14: Oregon's first death			
03/16: schools close			
03/20	114 / 3	+84 / +3	12 / 0
03/27	414 / 12	+300 / +9	43 / 1
03/31: total tests = 12,883			
04/03	899 / 22	+485 / +10	69 / 1
04/10	1,371 / 48	+472 / +26	67 / 4
04/12: Easter			
04/15: IFR (infection fatality rate) = 3.49%			
04/15: hospitalizations current = 305			
04/15: hospitalizations cumulative = 401			
04/17	1,785 / 70	+414 / +22	59 / 3
04/24	2,177 / 86	+392 / +16	56 / 2
04/30: total tests = 53,377			

DATE	CASES / DEATHS	WEEKLY INCREASE	DAILY AVERAGE
05/01	2,579 / 104	+402 / +18	57 / 3
05/08	3,068 / 124	+489 / +20	70 / 3
05/10: Mother's Day			
05/15: IFR (infection fatality rate) = 3.87%			
05/15: hospitalizations current = 161			
05/15: hospitalizations cumulative = 691			
05/15	3,541 / 137	+473 / +13	68 / 2
05/22	3,864 / 147	+323 / +10	46 / 1
05/25: Memorial Day			
05/26: George Floyd protests begin			
05/29	4,131 / 151	+267 / +4	38 / 1
05/31: total tests = 126,795			
NEW! 06/01: deaths/million population = 36			
06/05	4,570 / 161	+439 / +10	63 / 1
06/12	5,377 / 173	+807 / +12	115 / 2
06/15: IFR (infection fatality rate) = 3.09%			
06/15: hospitalizations current = 125			
06/15: hospitalizations cumulative = 899			
06/19	6,572 / 188	+1,195 / +15	171 / 2
06/21: Father's Day			
06/26	7,818 / 202	+1,246 / +14	178 / 2
06/30: total tests = 237,243			
07/01: deaths/million population = 49			
07/01: mask mandate			
07/03	9,636 / 209	+1,818 / +7	260 / 1
07/04: Independence Day			
07/10	11,454 / 232	+1,818 / +23	260 / 3
07/15: IFR (infection fatality rate) = 1.89%			
07/15: hospitalizations current = 207			
07/15: hospitalizations cumulative = 1,290			
07/17	13,802 / 254	+2,348 / +22	335 / 3
07/24	16,104 / 282	+2,302 / +28	329 / 4
07/31	18,492 / 322	+2,388 / +40	341 / 6
07/31: total tests = 403,241			
08/01: deaths/million population = 77			
08/07	20,636 / 348	+2,144 / +26	306 / 4
08/14	22,613 / 385	+1,977 / +37	282 / 5
08/15: IFR (infection fatality rate) = 1.68%			

DATE	CASES / DEATHS	WEEKLY INCREASE	DAILY AVERAGE
	08/15: hospitalizations current = 224		
	08/15: hospitalizations cumulative = 1,863		
08/21	24,421 / 414	+1,808 / +29	258 / 4
08/28	26,054 / 447	+1,633 / +33	233 / 5
	08/31: total tests = 580,107		
	09/01: deaths/million population = 114		
09/04	27,601 / 475	+1,547 / +28	221 / 4
	09/07: Labor Day		
09/11	28,865 / 499	+1,264 / +24	181 / 3
	09/15: IFR (infection fatality rate) = 1.75%		
	09/15: hospitalizations current = 155		
	09/15: hospitalizations cumulative = 2,292		
09/18	30,342 / 521	+1,477 / +22	211 / 3
	NEW! 09/22: test positivity rate = 6.7%		
09/25	32,314 / 542	+1,972 / +21	282 / 3
	09/30: total tests = 695,616		
	10/01: deaths/million population = 133		
10/02	34,163 / 563	+1,849 / +21	264 / 3
10/09	36,526 / 597	+2,363 / +34	338 / 5
	10/15: IFR (infection fatality rate) = 1.59%		
	10/15: hospitalizations current = 199		
	10/15: hospitalizations cumulative = 2,868		
10/16	38,935 / 617	+2,409 / +20	344 / 3
	10/22: test positivity rate = 6.2%		
10/23	41,348 / 649	+2,413 / +32	345 / 5
10/30	44,389 / 675	+3,041 / +26	434 / 4
	10/31: total tests = 861,949		
	11/01: deaths/million population = 164		
	11/03: Election Day		
11/06	48,608 / 716	+4,219 / +41	603 / 6
	11/07: Biden wins election		
11/13	54,937 / 753	+6,329 / +37	904 / 5
	11/15: IFR (infection fatality rate) = 1.34%		
	11/15: hospitalizations current = 356		
	11/15: hospitalizations cumulative = 3,628		
11/20	62,175 / 812	+7,238 / +59	1,034 / 8
	11/22: test positivity rate = 14.3%		
	11/26: Thanksgiving		

DATE	CASES / DEATHS	WEEKLY INCREASE	DAILY AVERAGE
11/27	70,832 / 885	+8,657 / +73	1,237 / 10

11/30: total tests = 2,012,942
12/01: deaths/million population = 226

DATE	CASES / DEATHS	WEEKLY INCREASE	DAILY AVERAGE
12/04	81,437 / 1,003	+10,605 / +118	1,515 / 17
12/11	91,420 / 1,138	+9,983 / +135	1,426 / 19

12/14: first COVID-19 vaccinations given in the U.S.
12/15: IFR (infection fatality rate) = 1.26%
12/15: hospitalizations current = 599
12/15: hospitalizations cumulative = 5,579

DATE	CASES / DEATHS	WEEKLY INCREASE	DAILY AVERAGE
12/18	100,308 / 1,304	+8,888 / +166	1,270 / 24

12/22: new U.K. variant identified in the U.S.
12/22: test positivity rate = 5.2%
12/25: Christmas

DATE	CASES / DEATHS	WEEKLY INCREASE	DAILY AVERAGE
12/25	107,718 / 1,422	+7,410 / +118	1,059 / 17

12/31: total tests = 628,932
12/31: deaths/million population = 350
01/01: New Year's Day
01/01: CFR (case fatality rate) = N/A (active case counts are not available)

DATE	CASES / DEATHS	WEEKLY INCREASE	DAILY AVERAGE
01/01/2021	115,339 / 1,490	+7,621 / +68	1,089 / 10

BONUS: Enjoy additional week from upcoming book: PANDEMIC 2021: The U.S. Edition
01/06: right-wing mob insurrection at U.S. Capitol as Joe Biden confirmed president
01/08: Twitter permanently bans Trump's account

DATE	CASES / DEATHS	WEEKLY INCREASE	DAILY AVERAGE
01/08	122,847 / 1,575	+7,508 / +85	1,073 / 12

*The daily average column is rounded to the nearest whole person. The infection fatality rate (IFR) is the number of deaths divided by the number of confirmed cases. The case fatality rate (CFR), shown only at the end of the year, is the number of deaths divided by the number of confirmed cases *which have had an outcome* (either recovery or death). The CFR excludes active cases.

CHAPTER 40

~ PENNSYLVANIA *~*

POPULATION AS OF MARCH, 2020: 12,820,878
Democratic Governor Tom Wolf
VOTED BLUE: Biden 50.0% / Trump 48.8%

DATE	CASES / DEATHS	WEEKLY INCREASE	DAILY AVERAGE
01/30: WHO declares Public Health Emergency of International Concern			
01/31: Trump issues a China "travel ban"			
03/06: Pennsylvania's first 2 cases			
03/06: Pennsylvania declares Disaster Emergency			
03/11: WHO declares COVID-19 a pandemic			
03/13: Trump declares a National Emergency			
03/13: Trump issues a Europe "travel ban"			
03/13	**41 / 0**	**+39 / 0**	**6 / 0**
03/17: schools close			
03/18: Pennsylvania's first death			
03/20	**268 / 1**	**+227 / +1**	**32 / 0**
03/23: non-essential services close			
03/27	**2,218 / 22**	**+1,950 / +21**	**279 / 3**
03/31: total tests = not given			
04/01: stay at home order			
04/03	**8,420 / 102**	**+6,202 / +80**	**886 / 11**
04/10	**20,340 / 446**	**+11,920 / +344**	**1,703 / 49**
04/12: Easter			
04/15: IFR (infection fatality rate) = 2.91%			
04/15: hospitalizations current = 2,395			
04/15: hospitalizations cumulative = not given for this state			
04/17: mask mandate			
04/17	**29,921 / 957**	**+9,581 / +511**	**1,369 / 73**

DATE	CASES / DEATHS	WEEKLY INCREASE	DAILY AVERAGE
04/24	**40,149 / 1,736**	**+10,228 / +779**	**1,461 / 111**
04/30: total tests = 235,376			
05/01	**49,642 / 2,651**	**+9,493 / +915**	**1,356 / 131**
05/08	**57,471 / 3,717**	**+7,829 / +1,066**	**1,118 / 152**
05/10: Mother's Day			
05/15: IFR (infection fatality rate) = 6.89%			
05/15: hospitalizations current = 1,934			
05/15	**64,261 / 4,429**	**+6,790 / +712**	**970 / 102**
05/22	**70,331 / 5,061**	**+6,070 / +632**	**867 / 90**
05/25: Memorial Day			
05/26: George Floyd protests begin			
05/29	**75,078 / 5,493**	**+4,747 / +432**	**678 / 62**
05/31: total tests = 465,257			
NEW! 06/01: deaths/million population = 437			
06/05	**78,920 / 5,969**	**+3,842 / +476**	**549 / 68**
06/12	**82,582 / 6,248**	**+3,662 / +279**	**523 / 40**
06/15: IFR (infection fatality rate) = 7.55%			
06/15: hospitalizations current = 851			
06/19	**85,293 / 6,456**	**+2,711 / +208**	**387 / 30**
06/21: Father's Day			
06/26	**88,948 / 6,640**	**+3,655 / +184**	**522 / 26**
06/30: total tests = 775,037			
07/01: deaths/million population = 527			
07/03	**93,418 / 6,797**	**+4,470 / +157**	**639 / 22**
07/04: Independence Day			
07/10	**98,574 / 6,936**	**+5,156 / +139**	**737 / 20**
07/15: IFR (infection fatality rate) = 6.86%			
07/15: hospitalizations current = 667			
07/17	**104,172 / 7,068**	**+5,598 / +132**	**800 / 19**
07/24	**110,342 / 7,183**	**+6,170 / +115**	**881 / 16**
07/31	**116,787 / 7,281**	**+6,445 / +98**	**921 / 14**
07/31: total tests = 1,213,731			
08/01: deaths/million population = 569			
08/07	**122,078 / 7,383**	**+5,291 / +102**	**756 / 15**
08/14	**127,774 / 7,535**	**+5,696 / +152**	**814 / 22**
08/15: IFR (infection fatality rate) = 5.87%			
08/15: hospitalizations = 572			
08/20: Trump rally			

DATE	CASES / DEATHS	WEEKLY INCREASE	DAILY AVERAGE
08/21	132,461 / 7,656	+4,687 / +121	670 / 17
08/28	136,824 / 7,741	+4,363 / +85	623 / 12
08/31: total tests = 1,732,180			
09/01: deaths/million population = 614			
09/03: Trump rally			
09/04	142,537 / 7,840	+5,713 / +99	816 / 14
09/07: Labor Day			
09/11	147,744 / 7,932	+5,207 / +92	744 / 13
09/15: IFR (infection fatality rate) = 5.27%			
09/15: hospitalizations = 483			
09/18	153,561 / 8,022	+5,817 / +90	831 / 13
NEW! 09/22: test positivity rate = 6.2%			
09/22: Trump rally			
09/25	159,052 / 8,165	+5,491 / +143	784 / 20
09/26: Trump rally			
09/30: total tests = 2,060,877			
10/01: deaths/million population = 645			
10/02	166,270 / 8,262	+7,218 / +97	1,031 / 14
10/09	174,352 / 8,394	+8,082 / +132	1,155 / 19
10/13: Trump rally			
10/15: IFR (infection fatality rate) = 4.66%			
10/15: hospitalizations = 799			
10/16	184,185 / 8,533	+9,833 / +139	1,405 / 20
10/20: Trump rally			
10/22: test positivity rate = 10%			
10/23	195,659 / 8,703	+11,474 / +170	1,639 / 24
10/26: 3 Trump rallies			
10/30	210,586 / 8,867	+14,927 / +164	2,132 / 23
10/31: total tests = 2,752,937			
11/01: deaths/million population = 695			
11/03: Election Day			
11/06	229,346 / 9,059	+18,760 / +192	2,680 / 27
11/7: Biden wins election			
11/13	260,001 / 9,317	+30,655 / +258	4,379 / 37
11/15: IFR (infection fatality rate) = 3.49%			
11/15: hospitalizations = 2,440			
11/18: mask mandate			
11/20	301,373 / 9,766	+41,372 / +449	5,910 / 64

DATE	CASES / DEATHS	WEEKLY INCREASE	DAILY AVERAGE
11/22: test positivity rate = 25.1%			
11/26: Thanksgiving			
11/27	349,360 / 10,318	+47,987 / +552	6,855 / 79
11/30: total tests = 5,708,285			
12/01: deaths/million population = 846			
12/04	404,699 / 11,220	+55,339 / +902	7,906 / 129
12/11	476,493 / 12,331	+71,794 / +1,111	10,256 / 159
12/14: first COVID-19 vaccinations given in the U.S.			
12/15: IFR (infection fatality rate) = 2.52%			
12/15: hospitalization current = 6,295			
12/18	544,853 / 13,705	+68,360 / +1,374	9,766 / 196
12/22: new U.K. variant identified in the U.S.			
12/22: test positivity rate = 39.1%			
12/25: Christmas			
12/25	602,729 / 14,928	+57,876 / +1,223	8,268 / 175
12/31: total tests = 7,421,572			
12/31: deaths/million population = 1,272			
01/01: New Year's Day			
01/01: CFR (case fatality rate) = 3.66% (36.6X more deadly than influenza at 0.1%)			
01/01/2021	652,959 / 16,286	+50,230 / +1,358	7,176 / 194

BONUS: Enjoy additional week from upcoming book: PANDEMIC 2021: The U.S. Edition
01/06: right-wing mob insurrection at U.S. Capitol as Joe Biden confirmed president
01/08: Twitter permanently bans Trump's account

DATE	CASES / DEATHS	WEEKLY INCREASE	DAILY AVERAGE
01/08	709,244 / 17,475	+56,285 / +1,189	8,041 / 170

---

*The daily average column is rounded to the nearest whole person. The infection fatality rate (IFR) is the number of deaths divided by the number of confirmed cases. The case fatality rate (CFR), shown only at the end of the year, is the number of deaths divided by the number of confirmed cases which have had an outcome *(either recovery or death). The CFR excludes active cases.*

CHAPTER 41

~ RHODE ISLAND *~*

POPULATION AS OF MARCH, 2020: 1,056,161
Democratic Governor Gina Raimondo
VOTED BLUE: Biden 59.4% / Trump 38.6%

DATE	CASES / DEATHS	WEEKLY INCREASE	DAILY AVERAGE
	01/30: WHO declares Public Health Emergency of International Concern		
	01/31: Trump issues a China "travel ban"		
	03/01: Rhode Island's first 2 cases		
03/06	3 / 0	N/A	N/A
	03/09: Rhode Island declares Disaster Emergency		
	03/11: WHO declares COVID-19 a pandemic		
	03/13: Trump declares a National Emergency		
	03/13: Trump issues a Europe "travel ban"		
03/13	19 / 0	+16 / +0	2 / 0
	03/19: Rhode Island's first death		
03/20	74 / 1	+55 / +1	8 / 0
03/27	248 / 3	+174 / +2	25 / 0
	03/31: total tests = 2,463		
04/03	830 / 19	+582 / +16	83 / 2
04/10	2,565 / 70	+1,735 / +51	248 / 7
	04/12: Easter		
	04/15: IFR (infection fatality rate) = 2.47%		
	04/15: hospitalizations current = 229		
	04/15: hospitalization cumulative = 331		
04/17	4,177 / 118	+1,612 / +48	230 / 7
	04/20: mask mandate		
04/24	6,600 / 202	+2,423 / +84	346 / 12
	04/30: total tests = 59,891		

PANDEMIC 2020: The U.S. Edition

DATE	CASES / DEATHS	WEEKLY INCREASE	DAILY AVERAGE
05/01	**8,962 / 279**	**+2,362 / +77**	**337 / 11**
05/08: mask mandate			
05/08	**10,779 / 399**	**+1,817 / +120**	**260 / 17**
05/10: Mother's Day			
05/15: IFR (infection fatality rate) = 3.92%			
05/15: hospitalizations current = 272			
05/15: hospitalization cumulative = 1,372			
05/15	**12,219 / 479**	**+1,440 / +80**	**206 / 11**
05/22	**13,736 / 579**	**+1,517 / +100**	**217 / 14**
05/25: Memorial Day			
05/26: George Floyd protests begin			
05/29	**14,635 / 693**	**+899 / +114**	**128 / 16**
05/31: total tests = 150,317			
NEW! 06/01: deaths/million population = 682			
06/05	**15,441 / 772**	**+806 / +79**	**115 / 11**
06/12	**15,947 / 833**	**+506 / +61**	**72 / 9**
06/15: IFR (infection fatality rate) = 5.29%			
06/15: hospitalizations current = 127			
06/15: hospitalization cumulative = 1,882			
06/19	**16,337 / 894**	**+390 / +61**	**56 / 9**
06/21: Father's Day			
06/26	**16,661 / 927**	**+324 / +33**	**46 / 5**
06/30: total tests = 242,282			
07/01: deaths/million population = 902			
07/03	**16,991 / 960**	**+330 / +33**	**47 / 5**
07/04: Independence Day			
07/10	**17,312 / 976**	**+321 / +16**	**46 / 2**
07/15: IFR (infection fatality rate) = 5.60%			
07/15: hospitalizations current = 59			
07/15: hospitalization cumulative = 2,075			
07/17	**17,793 / 990**	**+481 / +14**	**69 / 2**
07/24	**18,224 / 1,002**	**+431 / +12**	**62 / 2**
07/31	**19,022 / 1,007**	**+798 / +5**	**114 / 1**
07/31: total tests = 365,066			
08/01: deaths/million population = 951			
08/07	**19,611 / 1,014**	**+589 / +7**	**84 / 1**
08/14	**20,335 / 1,021**	**+724 / +7**	**103 / 1**
08/15: IFR (infection fatality rate) = 5.02%			

DATE	CASES / DEATHS	WEEKLY INCREASE	DAILY AVERAGE
	08/15: hospitalizations current = 85		
	08/15: hospitalization cumulative = 2,375		
08/21	**21,022 / 1,030**	**+687 / +9**	**98 / 1**
08/28	**21,683 / 1,046**	**+661 / +16**	**94 / 2**
	08/31: total tests = 557,522		
	09/01: deaths/million population = 996		
09/04	**22,243 / 1,055**	**+560 / +9**	**80 / 1**
	09/07: Labor Day		
09/11	**22,905 / 1,071**	**+662 / +16**	**95 / 2**
	09/15: IFR (infection fatality rate) = 81		
	09/15: hospitalization current = 81		
	09/15: hospitalization cumulative = 2,650		
09/18	**23,620 / 1,088**	**+715 / +17**	**102 / 2**
	NEW! 09/22: test positivity rate = 1.5%		
09/25	**24,181 / 1,107**	**+561 / +19**	**80 / 3**
	09/30: total tests = 797,014		
	10/01: deaths/million population = 1,055		
10/02	**25,046 / 1,118**	**+865 / +11**	**124 / 2**
10/09	**26,294 / 1,130**	**+1,248 / +12**	**178 / 2**
	10/15: IFR (infection fatality rate) = 4.19%		
	10/15: hospitalizations current = 129		
	10/15: hospitalization cumulative = 2,999		
10/16	**27,691 / 1,152**	**+1,397 / +22**	**200 / 3**
	10/22: test positivity rate = 2.4%		
10/23	**30,118 / 1,177**	**+2,427 / +25**	**347 / 4**
10/30	**32,874 / 1,201**	**+2,756 / +24**	**394 / 3**
	10/31: total tests = 1,124,307		
	11/01: deaths/million population = 1,134		
	11/03: Election Day		
11/06	**36,380 / 1,224**	**+3,506 / +23**	**501 / 3**
	11/07: Biden wins election		
11/13	**41,529 / 1,254**	**+5,149 / +30**	**736 / 4**
	11/15: IFR (infection fatality rate) = 3.02%		
	11/15: hospitalizations current = 256		
	11/15: hospitalization cumulative = 3,857		
11/20	**48,001 / 1,294**	**+6,472 / +40**	**925 / 6**
	11/22: test positivity rate = 6.5%		
	11/26: Thanksgiving		

DATE	CASES / DEATHS	WEEKLY INCREASE	DAILY AVERAGE
11/27	**53,954 / 1,346**	**+5,953 / +52**	**850 / 7**
	11/30: total tests = 1,574,531		
	12/01: deaths/million population = 1,313		
12/04	**62,137 / 1,413**	**+8,183 / +67**	**1,169 / 10**
12/11	**70,818 / 1,509**	**+8,681 / +96**	**1,240 / 14**
	12/14: first COVID-19 vaccinations given in the U.S.		
	12/15: IFR (infection fatality rate) = 2.09%		
	12/15: hospitalizations current = 455		
	12/15: hospitalization cumulative = 5,616		
12/18	**77,812 / 1,625**	**+6,994 / +116**	**999 / 17**
	12/22: new U.K. variant identified in the U.S.		
	12/22: test positivity rate = 6.3%		
	12/25: Christmas		
12/25	**82,066 / 1,704**	**+4,254 / +79**	**608 / 11**
	12/31: total tests = 1,974,498		
	12/31: deaths/million population = 1,677		
	01/01: New Year's Day		
	01/01: CFR (case fatality rate) = 2.48% (24.8X more deadly than influenza at 0.1%)		
01/01/2021	**87,949 / 1,777**	**+5,883 / +73**	**840 / 10**

BONUS: Enjoy additional week from upcoming book: PANDEMIC 2021: The U.S. Edition
01/06: right-wing mob insurrection at U.S. Capitol as Joe Biden confirmed president
01/08: Twitter permanently bans Trump's account

01/08	**97,614 / 1,916**	**+9,665 / +139**	**1,381 / 20**

---

*The daily average column is rounded to the nearest whole person. The infection fatality rate (IFR) is the number of deaths divided by the number of confirmed cases. The case fatality rate (CFR), shown only at the end of the year, is the number of deaths divided by the number of confirmed cases *which have had an outcome* (either recovery or death). The CFR excludes active cases.

CHAPTER 42

~ SOUTH CAROLINA *~*

POPULATION AS OF MARCH, 2020: 5,210,095
Republican Governor Henry McMaster
VOTED RED: Trump 55.1% / Biden 43.4%

DATE	CASES / DEATHS	WEEKLY INCREASE	DAILY AVERAGE
01/30: WHO declares Public Health Emergency of International Concern			
01/31: Trump issues a China "travel ban"			
03/07: South Carolina's first 2 cases			
03/11: WHO declares COVID-19 a pandemic			
03/13: South Carolina declares State of Emergency			
03/13: Trump declares a National Emergency			
03/13: Trump issues a Europe "travel ban"			
03/13	13 / 0	N/A	N/A
03/16: South Carolina's first death			
03/16: schools close			
03/20	125 / 3	+112 / +3	16 / 0
03/27	539 / 13	+414 / +10	59 / 1
03/31: total tests = 3,498			
04/03	1,700 / 34	+1,161 / +21	166 / 3
04/10	3,065 / 72	+1,365 / +38	195 / 5
04/12: Easter			
04/15: IFR (infection fatality rate) = 2.93%			
04/15: hospitalizations current = not given			
04/15: hospitalizations cumulative = 675			
04/17	4,086 / 116	+1,021 / +44	146 / 6
04/24	5,070 / 157	+984 / +41	141 / 6
04/30: total tests = 57,014			
05/01	6,258 / 256	+1,188 / +99	170 / 14

DATE	CASES / DEATHS	WEEKLY INCREASE	DAILY AVERAGE
05/08	**7,367 / 320**	**+1,109 / +64**	**158 / 9**
05/10: Mother's Day			
05/15: IFR (infection fatality rate) = 4.52%			
05/15: hospitalizations current = not given			
05/15: hospitalizations cumulative = 1,421			
05/15	**8,407 / 380**	**+1,040 / +60**	**149 / 9**
05/22	**9,638 / 419**	**+1,231 / +39**	**176 / 6**
05/25: Memorial Day			
05/26: George Floyd protests begin			
05/29	**11,131 / 483**	**+1,493 / +64**	**213 / 9**
05/31: total tests = 194,047			
NEW! 06/01: deaths/million population = 96			
06/05	**13,453 / 538**	**+2,322 / +55**	**332 / 8**
06/12	**17,170 / 593**	**+3,717 / +55**	**531 / 8**
06/15: IFR (infection fatality rate) = 3.11%			
06/15: hospitalizations current = 536			
06/15: hospitalizations cumulative = 1,988			
06/19	**22,631 / 639**	**+5,461 / +46**	**780 / 7**
06/21: Father's Day			
06/26	**30,335 / 694**	**+7,704 / +55**	**1,101 / 8**
06/30: total tests = 420.061			
07/01: deaths/million population = 149			
07/03	**41,532 / 793**	**+11,197 / +99**	**1,560 / 14**
07/04: Independence Day			
07/10	**52,419 / 929**	**+10,887 / +136**	**1,555 / 19**
07/15: IFR (infection fatality rate) = 1.60%			
07/15: hospitalizations current = 1,560			
07/15: hospitalizations cumulative = 3,744			
07/17	**66,060 / 1,096**	**+13,641 / +167**	**1,949 / 24**
07/24	**78,607 / 1,385**	**+12,547 / +289**	**1,792 / 41**
07/31	**89,016 / 1,712**	**+10,409 / +327**	**1,487 / 47**
07/31: total tests = 745,198			
08/01: deaths/million population = 340			
08/07	**98,219 / 1,962**	**+9,203 / +250**	**1,315 / 36**
08/14	**104,841 / 2,204**	**+6,622 / +242**	**946 / 35**
08/15: IFR (infection fatality rate) = 2.13%			
08/15: hospitalizations current = 1,246			
08/15: hospitalizations cumulative = 6,852			

DATE	CASES / DEATHS	WEEKLY INCREASE	DAILY AVERAGE
08/21	110,378 / 2,459	+5,537 / +255	791 / 36
08/28	115,951 / 2,655	+5,573 / +196	796 / 28
	08/31: total tests = 1,058,938		
	09/01: deaths/million population = 559		
09/04	123,325 / 2,846	+7,374 / +191	1,053 / 27
	09/07: Labor Day		
09/11	129,046 / 3,028	+5,721 / +182	817 / 26
	09/15: IFR (infection fatality rate) = 2.32%		
	09/15: hospitalizations current = 745		
	09/15: hospitalizations cumulative = 8,502		
09/18	136,318 / 3,177	+7,272 / +149	1,039 / 21
	NEW! 09/22: test positivity rate = 7.5%		
09/25	143,902 / 3,297	+7,584 / +120	1,083 / 17
	09/30: total tests = 1,456,923		
	10/01: deaths/million population = 662		
10/02	149,185 / 3,409	+5,283 / +112	755 / 16
10/09	155,676 / 3,530	+6,491 / +121	927 / 17
	10/15: IFR (infection fatality rate) = 2.24%		
	10/15: hospitalizations current = 769		
	10/15: hospitalizations cumulative = 9,798		
10/16	162,253 / 3,615	+6,577 / +85	940 / 12
	10/22: test positivity rate = 6.2%		
10/23	168,549 / 3,777	+6,296 / +162	899 / 23
10/30	175,594 / 3,896	+7,045 / +119	1,006 / 17
	10/31: total tests = 1,993,561		
	11/01: deaths/million population = 764		
	11/03: Election Day		
11/06	182,872 / 4,005	+7,278 / +109	1,040 / 16
	11/07: Biden wins election		
11/13	192,101 / 4,101	+9,229 / +96	1,318 / 14
	11/15: IFR (infection fatality rate) = 2.10%		
	11/15: hospitalizations current = 752		
	11/15: hospitalizations cumulative = 11,211		
11/20	203,151 / 4,231	+11,050 / +130	1,579 / 19
	11/22: test positivity rate = 7.3%		
	11/26: Thanksgiving		
11/27	213,120 / 4,346	+9,969 / +115	1,424 / 16
	11/30: total tests = 2,749,657		

DATE	CASES / DEATHS	WEEKLY INCREASE	DAILY AVERAGE
12/01: deaths/million population = 863			
12/04	**226,013 / 4,496**	**+12,893 / +150**	**1,842 / 21**
12/11	**245,226 / 4,673**	**+19,213 / +177**	**2,745 / 25**
12/14: first COVID-19 vaccinations given in the U.S.			
12/15: IFR (infection fatality rate) = 1.85%			
12/15: hospitalizations current = 1,046			
12/15: hospitalizations cumulative = 12,960			
12/18	**267,076 / 4,872**	**+21,850 / +199**	**3,121 / 28**
12/22: new U.K. variant identified in the U.S.			
12/22: test positivity rate = 12.2%			
12/25: Christmas			
12/25	**285,028 / 5,043**	**+17,952 / +171**	**2,565 / 24**
12/31: total tests = 3,663,351			
12/31: deaths/million population = 1,029			
01/01: New Year's Day			
01/01: CFR (case fatality rate) = 3.39% (33.9X more deadly than influenza at 0.1%)			
01/01/2021	**307,507 / 5,296**	**+22,479 / +253**	**3,211 / 36**

BONUS: Enjoy additional week from upcoming book: PANDEMIC 2021: The U.S. Edition
   01/06: right-wing mob insurrection at U.S. Capitol as Joe Biden confirmed president
   01/08: Twitter permanently bans Trump's account

01/08	**344,176 / 5,695**	**+26,669 / +399**	**3,810 / 57**

*The daily average column is rounded to the nearest whole person. The infection fatality rate (IFR) is the number of deaths divided by the number of confirmed cases. The case fatality rate (CFR), shown only at the end of the year, is the number of deaths divided by the number of confirmed cases *which have had an outcome* (either recovery or death). The CFR excludes active cases.

CHAPTER 43

~ SOUTH DAKOTA *~*

POPULATION AS OF MARCH, 2020: 903,027
Republican Governor Kristi L. Noem
VOTED RED: Trump 61.8% / Biden 35.6%

DATE	CASES / DEATHS	WEEKLY INCREASE	DAILY AVERAGE
01/30: WHO declares Public Health Emergency of International Concern			
01/31: Trump issues a China "travel ban"			
03/10: South Dakota's first 5 cases			
03/11: WHO declares COVID-19 a pandemic			
03/13: South Dakota declares State of Emergency			
03/13: Trump declares a National Emergency			
03/13: Trump issues a Europe "travel ban"			
03/13	9 / 0	N/A	N/A
03/16: schools close			
03/18: South Dakota's first death			
03/20	14 / 1	+5 / +1	1 / 0
03/27	58 / 1	+44 / +0	6 / 0
03/31: total tests = 3,579			
04/03	187 / 2	129 / +1	18 / 0
04/10	536 / 6	+349 / +4	50 / 1
04/12: Easter			
04/15: IFR (infection fatality rate) = 4.96%			
04/15: hospitalizations current = not given			
04/15: hospitalizations cumulative = 51			
04/17	1,411 / 7	+875 / +1	125 / 0
04/24	2,040 / 10	+629 / +3	90 / 0
04/30: total tests = 17,791			
05/01	2,525 / 21	+485 / +11	69 / 2

DATE	CASES / DEATHS	WEEKLY INCREASE	DAILY AVERAGE
05/08	**3,144 / 31**	**+619 / +10**	**88 / 1**

05/10: Mother's Day
05/15: IFR (infection fatality rate) = 1.13%
05/15: hospitalizations current = 80
05/15: hospitalizations cumulative = 296

05/15	**3,887 / 44**	**+743 / +13**	**106 / 2**
05/22	**4,356 / 50**	**+469 / +6**	**67 / 1**

05/25: Memorial Day
05/26: George Floyd protests begin

05/29	**4,866 / 59**	**+510 / +9**	**73 / 1**

05/31: total tests = 42,938
NEW! 06/01: deaths/million population = 69

06/05	**5,277 / 65**	**+411 / +6**	**59 / 1**
06/12	**5,742 / 74**	**+465 / +9**	**66 / 1**

06/15: IFR (infection fatality rate) = 1.27%
06/15: hospitalizations current = 93
06/15: hospitalizations cumulative = 544

06/19	**6,158 / 81**	**+416 / +7**	**59 / 1**

06/21: Father's Day

06/26	**6,535 / 88**	**+377 / +7**	**54 / 1**

06/30: total tests = 80,088
07/01: deaths/million population = 105
07/03: Trump rally

07/03	**6,764 / 91**	**+229 / +3**	**33 / 0**

07/04: Independence Day

07/10	**7,401 / 107**	**+637 / +16**	**91 / 2**

07/15: IFR (infection fatality rate) = 1.45%
07/15: hospitalizations current = 59
07/15: hospitalizations cumulative = 752

07/17	**7,789 / 116**	**+388 / +9**	**55 / 1**
07/24	**8,200 / 122**	**+411 / +6**	**59 / 1**
07/31	**8,764 / 130**	**+564 / +8**	**81 / 1**

07/31: total tests = 111,635
08/01: deaths/million population = 151

08/07	**9,371 / 144**	**+607 / +14**	**87 / 2**
08/14	**10,024 / 150**	**+653 / +6**	**93 / 1**

08/15: IFR (infection fatality rate) = 1.50%
08/15: hospitalizations current = 63

DATE	CASES / DEATHS	WEEKLY INCREASE	DAILY AVERAGE
	08/15: hospitalizations cumulative = 913		
08/21	**10,884 / 159**	**+860 / +9**	**123 / 1**
08/28	**12,517 / 165**	**+1,633 / +6**	**233 / 1**
	08/31: total tests = 153,907		
	09/01: deaths/million population = 196		
09/04	**14,596 / 170**	**+2,079 / +5**	**297 / 1**
	09/07: Labor Day		
09/11	**16,117 / 177**	**+1,521 / +7**	**217 / 1**
	09/15: IFR (infection fatality rate) = 1.08%		
	09/15: hospitalizations current = 133		
	09/15: hospitalizations cumulative = 1,195		
09/18	**18,075 / 198**	**+1,958 / +21**	**280 / 3**
	NEW! 09/22: test positivity rate = 17.9%		
09/25	**20,554 / 216**	**+2,479 / +18**	**354 / 3**
	09/30: total tests = 196,261		
	10/01: deaths/million population = 268		
10/02	**23,522 / 237**	**+2,968 / +21**	**424 / 3**
10/09	**27,215 / 277**	**+3,693 / +40**	**528 / 6**
	10/15: IFR (infection fatality rate) = 0.98%		
	10/15: hospitalizations current = 304		
	10/15: hospitalizations cumulative = 2,000		
10/16	**31,805 / 307**	**+4,590 / +30**	**656 / 4**
	10/22: test positivity rate = 35.2%		
10/23	**37,202 / 356**	**+5,397 / +49**	**771 / 7**
10/30	**44,559 / 415**	**+7,357 / +59**	**1,051 / 8**
	10/31: total tests = 259,532		
	11/01: deaths/million population = 434		
	11/03: Election Day		
11/06	**52,639 / 510**	**+8,080 / +95**	**1,154 / 14**
	11/07: Biden wins election		
11/13	**62,327 / 568**	**+9,688 / +58**	**1,384 / 8**
	11/15: IFR (infection fatality rate) = 0.98%		
	11/15: hospitalizations current = 553		
	11/15: hospitalizations cumulative = 3,644		
11/20	**71,070 / 741**	**+8,743 / +173**	**1,249 / 25**
	11/22: test positivity rate = 48.2%		
	11/26: Thanksgiving		
11/27	**78,280 / 888**	**+7,210 / +147**	**1,030 / 21**

DATE	CASES / DEATHS	WEEKLY INCREASE	DAILY AVERAGE
11/30: total tests = 332,540			
12/01: deaths/million population = 1,125			
12/04	**84,398 / 1,064**	**+6,118 / +176**	**874 / 25**
12/11	**89,672 / 1,210**	**+5,274 / +146**	**753 / 21**
12/14: first COVID-19 vaccinations given in the U.S.			
12/15: IFR (infection fatality rate) = 1.38%			
12/15: hospitalizations current = 435			
12/15: hospitalizations cumulative = 5,242			
12/18	**93,772 / 1,329**	**+4,100 / +119**	**586 / 17**
12/22: new U.K. variant identified in the U.S.			
12/22: test positivity rate = 38.1%			
12/25: Christmas			
12/25	**96,546 / 1,430**	**+2,774 / +101**	**396 / 14**
12/31: total tests = 372,640			
12/31: deaths/million population = 1,682			
01/01: New Year's Day			
01/01: CFR (case fatality rate) = 1.59% (15.9X more deadly than influenza at 0.1%)			
01/01/2021	**99,164 / 1,488**	**+2,618 / +58**	**374 / 8**

BONUS: Enjoy additional week from upcoming book: PANDEMIC 2021: The U.S. Edition

01/06: right-wing mob insurrection at U.S. Capitol as Joe Biden confirmed president
01/08: Twitter permanently bans Trump's account

DATE	CASES / DEATHS	WEEKLY INCREASE	DAILY AVERAGE
01/08	**102,580 / 1,556**	**+3,416 / +68**	**488 / 10**

*The daily average column is rounded to the nearest whole person. The infection fatality rate (IFR) is the number of deaths divided by the number of confirmed cases. The case fatality rate (CFR), shown only at the end of the year, is the number of deaths divided by the number of confirmed cases *which have had an outcome* (either recovery or death). The CFR excludes active cases.

CHAPTER 44

~ TENNESSEE *~*

POPULATION AS OF MARCH, 2020: 6,897,576
Republican Governor Bill Lee
VOTED RED: Trump 60.7% / Biden 37.4%

DATE	CASES / DEATHS	WEEKLY INCREASE	DAILY AVERAGE
01/30: WHO declares Public Health Emergency of International Concern			
01/31: Trump issues a China "travel ban"			
03/08: Tennessee's first 3 cases			
03/11: WHO declares COVID-19 a pandemic			
03/12: Tennessee declares State of Emergency			
03/13: Trump declares a National Emergency			
03/13: Trump issues a Europe "travel ban"			
03/13	26 / 0	N/A	N/A
03/20: schools close			
03/20	228 / 0	+202 / +0	29 / 0
03/24: Tennessee's first 2 deaths			
03/27	1,203 / 6	+975 / +6	139 / 1
03/30: non-essential services close			
03/31: total tests = 17,184			
04/02: stay at home order			
04/03	3,067 / 37	+1,864 / +31	266 / 4
04/10	4,862 / 98	+1,825 / +61	261 / 9
04/12: Easter			
04/15: IFR (infection fatality rate) = 2.29%			
04/15: hospitalizations current = 412			
04/15: hospitalizations cumulative = 663			
04/17	6,589 / 142	+1,727 / +44	247 / 6
04/24	8,726 / 168	+2,137 / +26	305 / 4

DATE	CASES / DEATHS	WEEKLY INCREASE	DAILY AVERAGE
04/30: total tests = 168,406			
05/01	**11,891 / 204**	**+3,165 / +36**	**452 / 5**
05/08	**14,441 / 241**	**+2,550 / +37**	**364 / 5**
05/10: Mother's Day			
05/15: IFR (infection fatality rate) = 1.71%			
05/15: hospitalizations current = 535			
05/15: hospitalizations cumulative = 1,454			
05/15	**16,970 / 290**	**+2,529 / +49**	**361 / 7**
05/22	**19,394 / 315**	**+2,424 / +25**	**346 / 4**
05/25: Memorial Day			
05/26: George Floyd protests begin			
05/29	**22,085 / 360**	**+2,691 / +45**	**384 / 6**
05/31: total tests = 427,046			
NEW! 06/01: deaths/million population = 53			
06/05	**25,520 / 408**	**+3,435 / +48**	**491 / 7**
06/12	**29,126 / 468**	**+3,606 / +60**	**515 / 9**
06/15: IFR (infection fatality rate) = 1.55%			
06/15: hospitalizations current = 642			
06/15: hospitalizations cumulative = 2,106			
06/19	**34,017 / 515**	**+4,891 / +47**	**699 / 7**
06/21: Father's Day			
06/26	**39,444 / 577**	**+5,427 / +62**	**775 / 9**
06/30: total tests = 793,127			
07/01: deaths/million population = 89			
07/03	**48,712 / 633**	**+9,268 / +56**	**1,324 / 8**
07/04: Independence Day			
07/10	**59,546 / 723**	**+10,834 / +90**	**1,548 / 13**
07/15: IFR (infection fatality rate) = 1.13%			
07/15: hospitalizations current = 1,282			
07/15: hospitalizations cumulative = 3,434			
07/17	**73,819 / 815**	**+14,273 / +92**	**2,039 / 13**
07/24	**89,078 / 938**	**+15,259 / +123**	**2,180 / 18**
07/31	**105,959 / 1,060**	**+16,881 / +122**	**2,412 / 17**
07/31: total tests = 1,512,224			
08/01: deaths/million population = 156			
08/07	**118,782 / 1,206**	**+12,823 / +146**	**1,832 / 21**
08/14	**130,458 / 1,326**	**+11,676 / +120**	**1,668 / 17**
08/15: IFR (infection fatality rate) = 1.02%			

DATE	CASES / DEATHS	WEEKLY INCREASE	DAILY AVERAGE
	08/15: hospitalizations current = 1,307		
	08/15: hospitalizations cumulative = 5,813		
08/21	140,844 / 1,549	+10,386 / +223	1,484 / 32
08/28	150,815 / 1,701	+9,971 / +152	1,424 / 22
	08/31: total tests = 2,306,032		
	09/01: deaths/million population = 273		
09/04	160,597 / 1,837	+9,782 / +136	1,397 / 19
	09/07: Labor Day		
09/11	169,859 / 2,025	+9,262 / +188	1,323 / 27
	09/15: IFR (infection fatality rate) = 1.21%		
	09/15: hospitalizations current = 888		
	09/15: hospitalizations cumulative = 7,858		
09/18	180,497 / 2,196	+10,638 / +171	1,520 / 24
	NEW! 09/22: test positivity rate = 5.6%		
09/25	189,454 / 2,352	+8,957 / +156	1,280 / 22
	09/30: total tests = 2,910,999		
	10/01: deaths/million population = 368		
10/02	198,403 / 2,515	+8,951 / +163	1,279 / 23
10/09	211,033 / 2,732	+12,630 / +217	1,804 / 31
	10/15: IFR (infection fatality rate) = 1.29%		
	10/15: hospitalizations current = 1,331		
	10/15: hospitalizations cumulative = 9,416		
10/16	223,493 / 2,871	+12,460 / +139	1,780 / 20
	10/22: test positivity rate = 9.0%		
10/23	241,513 / 3,076	+18,020 / +205	2,574 / 29
10/30	259,488 / 3,341	+17,975 / +265	2,568 / 38
	10/31: total tests = 3,657,005		
	11/01: deaths/million population = 491		
	11/03: Election Day		
11/06	273,144 / 3,541	+13,656 / +200	1,951 / 29
	11/07: Biden wins election		
11/13	300,458 / 3,852	+27,314 / +311	3,902 / 44
	11/15: IFR (infection fatality rate) = 1.25%		
	11/15: hospitalizations current = 1,972		
	11/15: hospitalizations cumulative = 11,141		
11/20	331,532 / 4,202	+31,074 / +350	4,439 / 50
	11/22: test positivity rate = 14.6%		
	11/26: Thanksgiving		

DATE	CASES / DEATHS	WEEKLY INCREASE	DAILY AVERAGE
11/27	356,716 / 4,526	+25,184 / +324	3,598 / 46

11/30: total tests = 4,574,275
12/01: deaths/million population = 686

12/04	392,608 / 4,876	+35,892 / +350	5,127 / 50
12/11	436,262 / 5,327	+43,654 / +451	6,236 / 64

12/14: first COVID-19 vaccinations given in the U.S.
12/15: IFR (infection fatality rate) = 1.19%
12/15: hospitalizations current = 3,062
12/15: hospitalizations cumulative = 13,332

12/18	503,651 / 5,960	+67,389 / +633	9,627 / 90

12/22: new U.K. variant identified in the U.S.
12/22: test positivity rate = 19.2%
12/25: Christmas

12/25	555,727 / 6,436	+52,076 / +476	7,439 / 68

12/31: total tests = 5,571,715
12/31: deaths/million population = 1,011
01/01: New Year's Day
01/01: CFR (case fatality rate) = 1.34% (13.4X more deadly than influenza at 0.1%)

01/01/2021	586,802 / 6,907	+31,075 / +471	4,439 / 67

BONUS: Enjoy additional week from upcoming book: PANDEMIC 2021: The U.S. Edition
01/06: right-wing mob insurrection at U.S. Capitol as Joe Biden confirmed president
01/08: Twitter permanently bans Trump's account

01/08	640,606 / 7,618	+53,804 / +711	7,686 / 102

*The daily average column is rounded to the nearest whole person. The infection fatality rate (IFR) is the number of deaths divided by the number of confirmed cases. The case fatality rate (CFR), shown only at the end of the year, is the number of deaths divided by the number of confirmed cases *which have had an outcome* (either recovery or death). The CFR excludes active cases.

CHAPTER 45

~ TEXAS *~*

POPULATION AS OF MARCH, 2020: 29,472,295
Republican Governor Greg Abbott
VOTED RED: Trump 52.0% / Biden 46.5%

DATE	CASES / DEATHS	WEEKLY INCREASE	DAILY AVERAGE
01/30: WHO declares Public Health Emergency of International Concern			
01/31: Trump issues a China "travel ban"			
03/06: first 5 cases			
03/06	5 / 0	N/A	N/A
03/11: WHO declares COVID-19 a pandemic			
03/13: State of Disaster declared			
03/13: Trump declares a National Emergency			
03/13: Trump issues a Europe "travel ban"			
03/13	22 / 0	+17 / +0	2 / 0
03/17: first death			
03/20	175 / 5	+153 / +5	22 / 1
03/27	1,731 / 23	+1,556 / +18	222 / 3
03/31: total tests = 35,880			
04/03	5,330 / 90	+3,599 / +67	514 / 10
04/10	11,426 / 222	+6,096 / +132	871 / 19
04/12: Easter			
04/15: IFR (infection fatality rate) = 2.34%			
04/15: hospitalizations current = 1,538			
04/15: hospitalizations cumulative = not given for this state			
04/17	17,760 / 439	+6,334 / +217	905 / 31
04/24	23,170 / 601	+5,410 / +162	773 / 23
04/30: total tests = 379,648			
05/01	29,893 / 849	+6,723 / +248	960 / 35

DATE	CASES / DEATHS	WEEKLY INCREASE	DAILY AVERAGE
05/08	**37,727 / 1,079**	**+7,834 / +230**	**1,119 / 33**

05/10: Mother's Day
05/15: IFR (infection fatality rate) = 2.80%
05/15: hospitalizations current = 1,716

05/15	**46,787 / 1,308**	**+9,060 / +229**	**1,294 / 33**
05/22	**54,616 / 1,512**	**+7,829 / +204**	**1,118 / 29**

05/25: Memorial Day
05/26: George Floyd protests begin

05/29	**62,126 / 1,654**	**+7,510 / +142**	**1,073 / 20**

05/31: total tests = 1,054,793
NEW! 06/01: deaths/million population = 58

06/05	**73,286 / 1,828**	**+11,160 / +174**	**1,594 / 25**
06/12	**85,641 / 1,966**	**+12,355 / +138**	**1,765 / 20**

06/15: IFR (infection fatality rate) = 2.21%
06/15: hospitalizations current = 2,326

06/19	**107,158 / 2,173**	**+21,517 / +207**	**3,074 / 30**

06/21: Father's Day

06/26	**142,766 / 2,367**	**+35,608 / +194**	**5,087 / 28**

06/30: total tests = 2,119,036
07/01: deaths/million population = 88
07/03: mask mandate

07/03	**190,387 / 2,621**	**+47,621 / +254**	**6,803 / 36**

07/04: Independence Day

07/10	**251,076 / 3,150**	**+60,689 / +529**	**8,670 / 76**

07/15: IFR (infection fatality rate) = 1.22%
07/15: hospitalizations current = 10,471

07/17	**322,556 / 3,932**	**+71,480 / +782**	**10,211 / 112**
07/24	**385,948 / 4,932**	**+63,392 / +1,000**	**9,056 / 143**
07/31	**443,026 / 6,998**	**+57,078 / +2,066**	**8,154 / 295**

07/31: total tests = 3,990,030
08/01: deaths/million population = 251

08/07	**497,406 / 8,344**	**+54,380 / +1,346**	**7,769 / 192**
08/14	**548,911 / 9,736**	**+51,505 / +1,392**	**7,358 / 199**

08/15: IFR (infection fatality rate) = 1.78%
08/15: hospitalizations current = 6,481

08/21	**597,253 / 11,553**	**+48,342 / +1,817**	**6,906 / 260**
08/28	**631,118 / 12,667**	**+33,865 / +1,114**	**4,838 / 159**

08/31: total tests = 5,687,163

DATE	CASES / DEATHS	WEEKLY INCREASE	DAILY AVERAGE
09/01: deaths/million population = 472			
09/04	**661,505 / 13,561**	**+30,387 / +894**	**4,341 / 128**
09/07: Labor Day			
09/11	**686,471 / 14,345**	**+24,966 / +784**	**3,567 / 112**
09/15: IFR (infection fatality rate) = 2.09%			
09/15: hospitalizations current = 3,311			
09/18	**718,174 / 15,078**	**+31,703 / +733**	**4,529 / 105**
NEW! 09/22: test positivity rate = 11.3%			
09/25	**766,471 / 15,726**	**+48,297 / +648**	**6,900 / 93**
09/30: total tests = 6,900,580			
10/01: deaths/million population = 564			
10/02	**797,144 / 16,345**	**+30,673 / +619**	**4,382 / 88**
10/09	**829,453 / 16,991**	**+32,309 / +646**	**4,616 / 92**
10/15: IFR (infection fatality rate) = 2.03%			
10/15: hospitalizations current = 4,263			
10/16	**863,169 / 17,491**	**+33,716 / +500**	**4,817 / 71**
10/22: test positivity rate = 8.4%			
10/23	**903,286 / 17,954**	**+40,117 / +463**	**5,731 / 66**
10/30	**949,971 / 18,607**	**+46,685 / +653**	**6,669 / 93**
10/31: total tests = 8,965,178			
11/01: deaths/million population = 642			
11/03: Election Day			
11/06	**1,007,155 / 19,154**	**+57,184 / +547**	**8,169 / 78**
11/07: Biden wins election			
11/13	**1,078,194 / 19,946**	**+71,039 / +792**	**10,148 / 113**
11/15: IFR (infection fatality rate) = 1.84%			
11/15: hospitalizations current = 7,274			
11/15: hospitalizations cumulative =			
11/20	**1,161,219 / 20,956**	**+83,025 / +1,010**	**11,861 / 144**
11/22: test positivity rate = 23.4%			
11/26: Thanksgiving			
11/27	**1,235,838 / 21,834**	**+74,619 / +878**	**10,660 / 125**
11/30: total tests = 12,190,111			
12/01: deaths/million population = 776			
12/04	**1,331,516 / 22,977**	**+95,678 / +1,143**	**13,668 / 163**
12/11	**1,425,119 / 24,298**	**+93,603 / +1,321**	**13,372 / 189**
12/14: first COVID-19 vaccinations given in the U.S.			
12/15: IFR (infection fatality rate) = 1.64%			

DATE	CASES / DEATHS	WEEKLY INCREASE	DAILY AVERAGE
12/15: hospitalizations current = 9,472			
12/18	**1,572,594 / 25,663**	**+147,475 / +1,365**	**21,068 / 195**
12/22: new U.K. variant identified in the U.S.			
12/22: test positivity rate = 16.7%			
12/25: Christmas			
12/25	**1,666,099 / 27,109**	**+93,505 / +1,446**	**13,358 / 207**
12/31: total tests = 15,699,242			
12/31: deaths/million population = 973			
01/01: New Year's Day			
01/01: CFR (case fatality rate) = 1.91% (19.1X more deadly than influenza at 0.1%)			
01/01/2021	**1,784,569 / 28,506**	**+118,470 / +1,397**	**16,924 / 200**

BONUS: Enjoy additional week from upcoming book: PANDEMIC 2021: The U.S. Edition
01/06: right-wing mob insurrection at U.S. Capitol as Joe Biden confirmed president
01/08: Twitter permanently bans Trump's account

DATE	CASES / DEATHS	WEEKLY INCREASE	DAILY AVERAGE
01/08	**1,941,212 / 30,190**	**+156,643 / +1,684**	**22,378 / 241**

*The daily average column is rounded to the nearest whole person. The infection fatality rate (IFR) is the number of deaths divided by the number of confirmed cases. The case fatality rate (CFR), shown only at the end of the year, is the number of deaths divided by the number of confirmed cases *which have had an outcome* (either recovery or death). The CFR excludes active cases.

CHAPTER 46

~ UTAH *~*

POPULATION AS OF MARCH, 2020: 3,282,115
Republican Governor Gary Herbert
VOTED RED: Trump 58.1% / Biden 37.6%

DATE	CASES / DEATHS	WEEKLY INCREASE	DAILY AVERAGE
01/30: WHO declares Public Health Emergency of International Concern			
01/31: Trump issues a China "travel ban"			
03/06: first case			
03/06: State of Emergency declared			
03/06	1 / 0	N/A	N/A
03/11: WHO declares COVID-19 a pandemic			
03/13: Trump declares a National Emergency			
03/13: Trump issues a Europe "travel ban"			
03/13	9 / 0	+8 / +0	1 / 0
03/16: schools close			
03/20	121 / 0	+112 / +0	16 / 0
03/22: first death			
03/27	574 / 4	+453 / +4	65 / 1
03/31: total tests = 1,111			
04/03	1,424 / 10	+850 / +6	121 / 1
04/10	2,102 / 17	+678 / +7	97 / 1
04/12: Easter			
04/15: IFR (infection fatality rate) = 0.79%			
04/15: hospitalizations current = not given			
04/15: hospitalizations cumulative = 221			
04/17	2,805 / 23	+703 / +6	100 / 1
04/24	3,782 / 39	+977 / +16	140 / 2
04/30: total tests = 112,804			

DATE	CASES / DEATHS	WEEKLY INCREASE	DAILY AVERAGE
05/01	4,828 / 46	+1,046 / +7	149 / 1
05/08	5,919 / 61	+1,091 / +15	156 / 2

05/10: Mother's Day
05/15: IFR (infection fatality rate) = 1.11%
05/15: hospitalizations current = 161
05/15: hospitalizations cumulative = 566

05/15	6,913 / 77	+994 / +16	142 / 2
05/22	8,057 / 93	+1,144 / +16	163 / 2

05/25: Memorial Day
05/26: George Floyd protests begin

05/29	9,264 / 107	+1,207 / +14	172 / 2

05/31: total tests = 210,105
NEW! 06/01: deaths/million population = 34

06/05	11,252 / 120	+1,988 / +13	284 / 2
06/12	13,577 / 139	+2,325 / +19	332 / 3

06/15: IFR (infection fatality rate) = 0.98%
06/15: hospitalizations current = 184
06/15: hospitalizations cumulative = 1,041

06/19	16,425 / 155	+2,848 / +16	407 / 2

06/21: Father's Day

06/26	20,050 / 166	+3,625 / +11	518 / 2

06/30: total tests = 340,753
07/01: deaths/million population = 54

07/03	23,866 / 181	+3,816 / +15	545 / 2

07/04: Independence Day

07/10	28,223 / 207	+4,357 / +26	622 / 4

07/15: IFR (infection fatality rate) = 0.75%
07/15: hospitalizations current = 250
07/15: hospitalizations cumulative = 1,913

07/17	32,572 / 235	+4,349 / +28	621 / 4
07/24	36,962 / 273	+4,390 / +38	627 / 5
07/31	40,196 / 304	+3,234 / +31	462 / 4

07/31: total tests = 631,309
08/01: deaths/million population = 97

08/07	43,375 / 335	+3,179 / +31	454 / 4
08/14	45,976 / 360	+2,601 / +25	372 / 4

08/15: IFR (infection fatality rate) = 0.57%
08/15: hospitalizations current = 186

DATE	CASES / DEATHS	WEEKLY INCREASE	DAILY AVERAGE
08/15: hospitalizations cumulative = 2,760			
08/21	48,445 / 383	+2,469 / +23	353 / 3
08/28	50,948 / 407	+2,503 / +24	358 / 3
08/31: total tests = 851,482			
09/01: deaths/million population = 131			
09/04	53,839 / 419	+2,891 / +12	413 / 2
09/07: Labor Day			
09/11	56,675 / 431	+2,836 / +12	405 / 2
09/15: IFR (infection fatality rate) = 0.74%			
09/15: hospitalizations current = 178			
09/15: hospitalizations cumulative = 3,361			
09/18	61,775 / 437	+5,100 / +6	729 / 1
NEW! 09/22: test positivity rate = 13.9%			
09/25	68,530 / 448	+6,755 / +11	965 / 2
09/30: total tests = 1,099,333			
10/01: deaths/million population = 148			
10/02	75,157 / 474	+6,627 / +26	947 / 4
10/09	83,290 / 505	+8,133 / +31	1,162 / 4
10/15: IFR (infection fatality rate) = 0.58%			
10/15: hospitalizations current = 277			
10/15: hospitalizations cumulative = 4,511			
10/16	91,957 / 537	+8,667 / +32	1,238 / 5
10/22: test positivity rate = 16.1%			
10/23	101,509 / 567	+9,552 / +30	1,365 / 4
10/30	112,932 / 601	+11,423 / +34	1,632 / 5
10/31: total tests = 1,477,706			
11/01: deaths/million population = 192			
11/03: Election Day			
11/06	127,279 / 649	+14,347 / +48	2,050 / 7
11/07: Biden wins election			
11/09: mask mandate			
11/13	145,789 / 701	+18,510 / +52	2,644 / 7
11/15: IFR (infection fatality rate) = 0.47%			
11/15: hospitalizations current = 502			
11/15: hospitalizations cumulative = 6,769			
11/20	170,584 / 773	+24,795 / +72	3,542 / 10
11/22: test positivity rate = 20.2%			
11/26: Thanksgiving			

DATE	CASES / DEATHS	WEEKLY INCREASE	DAILY AVERAGE
11/27	190,044 / 849	+19,460 / +76	2,780 / 11

11/30: total tests = 2,087,151
12/01: deaths/million population = 283

| 12/04 | 209,170 / 925 | +19,126 / +76 | 2,732 / 11 |
| 12/11 | 228,129 / 1,025 | +18,959 / +100 | 2,708 / 14 |

12/14: first COVID-19 vaccinations given in the U.S.
12/15: IFR (infection fatality rate) = 0.45%
12/15: hospitalizations current = 568
12/15: hospitalizations cumulative = 9,585

| 12/18 | 246,562 / 1,140 | +18,433 / +115 | 2,633 / 16 |

12/22: new U.K. variant identified in the U.S.
12/22: test positivity rate = 17.6%
12/25: Christmas

| 12/25 | 263,087 / 1,204 | +16,525 / +64 | 2,361 / 9 |

12/31: total tests = 2,673,611
12/31: deaths/million population = 396
01/01: New Year's Day
01/01: CFR (case fatality rate) = 0.56% (5.6X more deadly than influenza at 0.1%)

| 01/01/2021 | 276,612 / 1,269 | +13,525 / +65 | 1,932 / 9 |

BONUS: Enjoy additional week from upcoming book: PANDEMIC 2021: The U.S. Edition
01/06: right-wing mob insurrection at U.S. Capitol as Joe Biden confirmed president
01/08: Twitter permanently bans Trump's account

| 01/08 | 301,110 / 1,381 | +24,498 / +112 | 3,500 / 16 |

---

*The daily average column is rounded to the nearest whole person. The infection fatality rate (IFR) is the number of deaths divided by the number of confirmed cases. The case fatality rate (CFR), shown only at the end of the year, is the number of deaths divided by the number of confirmed cases *which have had an outcome* (either recovery or death). The CFR excludes active cases.

CHAPTER 47

~ VERMONT *~*

POPULATION AS OF MARCH, 2020: 628,061
Republican Governor Phil Scott
VOTED BLUE: Biden 66.1% / Trump 30.7%

DATE	CASES / DEATHS	WEEKLY INCREASE	DAILY AVERAGE
01/30: WHO declares Public Health Emergency of International Concern			
01/31: Trump issues a China "travel ban"			
03/07: first case			
03/11: WHO declares COVID-19 a pandemic			
03/13: Vermont declares State of Emergency			
03/13: Trump declares a National Emergency			
03/13: Trump issues a Europe "travel ban"			
03/13	**1 / 0**	**N/A**	**N/A**
03/18: schools close			
03/19: first 2 deaths			
03/20	**29 / 2**	**+28 / +2**	**4 / 0**
03/24: stay at home order			
03/25: non-essential services close			
03/27	**184 / 10**	**+155 / +8**	**11 / 1**
03/31: total tests = 1,732			
04/3	**389 / 17**	**+205 / +7**	**29 / 1**
04/10	**679 / 24**	**+290 / +7**	**41 / 1**
04/12: Easter			
04/15: IFR (infection fatality rate) = 3.95%			
04/15: hospitalizations current = 63			
04/15: hospitalizations cumulative = not given for this state			
04/17	**779 / 35**	**+100 / +11**	**14 / 2**
04/24	**827 / 44**	**+48 / +9**	**7 / 1**

DATE	CASES / DEATHS	WEEKLY INCREASE	DAILY AVERAGE
04/30: total tests = 16,491			
05/01	**879 / 50**	**+52 / +6**	**7 / 1**
05/08	**919 / 53**	**+40 / +3**	**6 / 0**
05/10: Mother's Day			
05/15: IFR (infection fatality rate) = 5.68%			
05/15: hospitalizations current = 17			
05/15	**933 / 53**	**+14 / +0**	**2 / 0**
05/22	**952 / 54**	**+19 / +1**	**3 / 0**
05/25: Memorial Day			
05/26: George Floyd protests begin			
05/29	**975 / 55**	**+23 / +1**	**3 / 0**
05/31: total tests = 32,667			
NEW! 06/01: deaths/million population = 88			
06/05	**1,027 / 55**	**+52 / +0**	**7 / 0**
06/12	**1,119 / 55**	**+92 / +0**	**13 / 0**
06/15: IFR (infection fatality rate) = 4.88%			
06/15: hospitalizations current = 16			
06/19	**1,144 / 56**	**+25 / +1**	**4 / 0**
06/21: Father's Day			
06/26	**1,198 / 56**	**+54 / +0**	**8 / 0**
06/30: total tests = 67,341			
07/01: deaths/million population = 90			
07/03	**1,236 / 56**	**+38 / +0**	**5 / 0**
07/04: Independence Day			
07/10	**1,277 / 56**	**+41 / +0**	**6 / 0**
07/15: IFR (infection fatality rate) = 4.25%			
07/15: hospitalizations current = 19			
07/17	**1,334 / 56**	**+57 / +0**	**8 / 0**
07/24	**1,385 / 56**	**+51 / +0**	**7 / 0**
07/31	**1,414 / 57**	**+29 / +1**	**4 / 0**
07/31: total tests = 94,368			
08/01: deaths/million population = 91			
08/01: mask mandate			
08/07	**1,448 / 58**	**+34 / +1**	**5 / 0**
08/14	**1,501 / 58**	**+53 / +0**	**8 / 0**
08/15: IFR (infection fatality rate) = 3.84%			
08/15: hospitalizations current = 14			
08/21	**1,541 / 58**	**+40 / +0**	**6 / 0**

DATE	CASES / DEATHS	WEEKLY INCREASE	DAILY AVERAGE
08/31: total tests = 143,088			
09/01: deaths/million population = 93			
09/011/64	**1,642 / 58**	**+53 / +0**	**8 / 0**
09/07: Labor Day			
09/11	**1,668 / 58**	**+26 / +0**	**4 / 0**
09/15: IFR (infection fatality rate) = 3.41%			
09/15: hospitalizations current = 7			
09/18	**1,706 / 58**	**+38 / +0**	**5 / 0**
NEW! 09/22: test positivity rate = 0.3%			
09/25	**1,731 / 58**	**+25 / +0**	**4 / 0**
09/30: total tests = 164,859			
10/01: deaths/million population = 93			
10/02	**1,768 / 58**	**+37 / +0**	**5 / 0**
10/09	**1,846 / 58**	**+78 / +0**	**11 / 0**
10/15: IFR (infection fatality rate) = 3.05%			
10/15: hospitalizations current = 6			
10/16	**1,915 / 58**	**+69 / +0**	**10 / 0**
10/22: test positivity rate = 1.4%			
10/23	**2,016 / 58**	**+101 / +0**	**14 / 0**
10/30	**2,155 / 58**	**+139 / +0**	**20 / 0**
10/31: total tests = 189,680			
11/01: deaths/million population = 93			
11/03: Election Day			
11/06	**2,326 / 58**	**+171 / +0**	**24 / 0**
11/07: Biden wins election			
11/13	**2,743 / 59**	**+417 / +1**	**60 / 0**
11/15: IFR (infection fatality rate) = 2.04%			
11/15: hospitalizations current = 20			
11/20	**3,459 / 62**	**+716 / +3**	**102 / 0**
11/22: test positivity rate = 2.5%			
11/26: Thanksgiving			
11/27	**4,005 / 67**	**+546 / +5**	**78 / 1**
11/30: total tests = 225,958			
12/01: deaths/million population = 119			
12/04	**4,763 / 77**	**+758 / +10**	**108 / 1**
12/11	**5,541 / 93**	**+778 / +16**	**111 / 2**
12/14: first COVID-19 vaccinations given in the U.S.			

DATE	CASES / DEATHS	WEEKLY INCREASE	DAILY AVERAGE
12/15: IFR (infection fatality rate) = 1.69%			
12/15: hospitalizations current = 20			
12/18	**6,243 / 107**	**+702 / +14**	**100 / 2**
12/22: new U.K. variant identified in the U.S.			
12/22: test positivity rate = 2.0%			
12/25: Christmas			
12/25	**6,887 / 120**	**+644 / +13**	**92 / 2**
12/31: total tests = 697,705			
12/31: deaths/million population = 218			
01/01: New Year's Day			
01/01: CFR (case fatality rate) = 2.67% (26.7X more deadly than influenza at 0.1%)			
01/01/2021	**7,412 / 136**	**+525 / +16**	**75 / 2**

BONUS: Enjoy additional week from upcoming book: PANDEMIC 2021: The U.S. Edition
01/06: right-wing mob insurrection at U.S. Capitol as Joe Biden confirmed president
01/08: Twitter permanently bans Trump's account

01/08	**8,619 / 156**	**+1,207 / +20**	**172 / 3**

*The daily average column is rounded to the nearest whole person. The infection fatality rate (IFR) is the number of deaths divided by the number of confirmed cases. The case fatality rate (CFR), shown only at the end of the year, is the number of deaths divided by the number of confirmed cases *which have had an outcome* (either recovery or death). The CFR excludes active cases.

CHAPTER 48

~ VIRGINIA *~*

POPULATION AS OF MARCH, 2020: 8,626,207
Democratic Governor Ralph Northam
VOTED BLUE: Biden 54.1% / Trump 44.0%

DATE	CASES / DEATHS	WEEKLY INCREASE	DAILY AVERAGE
	01/30: WHO declares Public Health Emergency of International Concern		
	01/31: Trump issues a China "travel ban"		
	03/07: Virginia's first case		
	03/11: WHO declares COVID-19 a pandemic		
	03/12: Virginia declares State of Emergency		
	03/13: Trump declares a National Emergency		
	03/13: Trump issues a Europe "travel ban"		
03/13	30 / 0	N/A	N/A
	03/14: Virginia's first death		
	03/16: schools close		
03/20	114 / 2	+84 / +2	12 / 0
03/27	615 / 15	+501 / +13	72 / 2
	03/30: stay at home order		
	03/31: total tests = 12,038		
04/03	2,012 / 46	+1,397 / +31	200 / 4
04/10	4,509 / 121	+2,497 / +75	357 / 11
	04/12: Easter		
	04/15: IFR (infection fatality rate) = 3.00%		
	04/15: hospitalizations current = 1,298		
	04/15: hospitalizations cumulative = not given		
	04/17: Trump tweets LIBERATE VIRGINIA		
04/17	7,491 / 231	+2,982 / +110	426 / 16
04/24	11,594 / 410	+4,103 / +179	586 / 26

DATE	CASES / DEATHS	WEEKLY INCREASE	DAILY AVERAGE
04/30: total tests = 92,178			
05/01	16,901 / 581	+5,307 / +171	758 / 24
05/08	22,342 / 812	+5,441 / +231	777 / 33
05/10: Mother's Day			
05/15: IFR (infection fatality rate) = 3.41%			
05/15: hospitalizations current = 1,511			
05/15: hospitalizations cumulative = 3,657			
05/15	28,672 / 977	+6,330 / +165	904 / 24
05/22	34,950 / 1,136	+6,278 / +159	897 / 23
05/25: Memorial Day			
05/26: George Floyd protests begin			
05/29: mask mandate			
05/29	42,533 / 1,358	+7,583 / +222	1,083 / 32
05/31: total tests = 340,856			
NEW! 06/01: deaths/million population = 161			
06/05	48,532 / 1,453	+5,999 / +95	857 / 14
06/12	53,211 / 1,534	+4,679 / +81	668 / 12
06/15: IFR (infection fatality rate) = 2.83%			
06/15: hospitalizations current = 902			
06/15: hospitalizations cumulative = 5,588			
06/19	56,793 / 1,602	+3,582 / +68	512 / 10
06/21: Father's Day			
06/26	60,570 / 1,700	+3,777 / +98	540 / 14
06/30: total tests = 711,093			
07/01: deaths/million population = 209			
07/03	64,393 / 1,845	+3,823 / +145	546 / 21
07/04: Independence Day			
07/10	68,931 / 1,958	+4,538 / +113	648 / 16
07/15: IFR (infection fatality rate) = 2.71%			
07/15: hospitalizations current = 1,081			
07/15: hospitalizations cumulative = 6,905			
07/17	75,433 / 2,013	+6,502 / +55	929 / 8
07/24	82,364 / 2,067	+6,931 / +54	990 / 8
07/31	89,888 / 2,174	+7,524 / +107	1,075 / 15
07/31: total tests = 1,211,622			
08/01: deaths/million population = 260			
08/07	97,882 / 2,317	+7,994 / +143	1,142 / 20
08/14	104,838 / 2,370	+6,956 / +53	994 / 8

DATE	CASES / DEATHS	WEEKLY INCREASE	DAILY AVERAGE
	08/15: IFR (infection fatality rate) = 2.25%		
	08/15: hospitalizations current = 1,271		
	08/15: hospitalizations cumulative = 8,701		
08/21	**110,860 / 2,436**	**+6,022 / +66**	**860 / 9**
08/28	**117,592 / 2,550**	**+6,732 / +114**	**962 / 16**
	08/31: total tests = 1,783,802		
	09/01: deaths/million population = 314		
09/04	**124,779 / 2,662**	**+7,187 / +112**	**1,027 / 16**
	09/07: Labor Day		
09/11	**131,640 / 2,711**	**+6,861 / +49**	**980 / 7**
	09/15: IFR (infection fatality rate) = 2.09%		
	09/15: hospitalizations current = 1,015		
	09/15: hospitalizations cumulative = 10,337		
09/18	**138,702 / 2,949**	**+7,062 / +238**	**1,009 / 34**
	NEW! 09/22: test positivity rate = 5.2%		
09/25	**144,433 / 3,136**	**+5,731 / +187**	**819 / 27**
	09/25: Trump rally		
	09/30: total tests = 2,246,923		
	10/01: deaths/million population = 381		
10/02	**149,687 / 3,250**	**+5,254 / +114**	**751 / 16**
10/09	**156,649 / 3,344**	**+6,962 / +94**	**995 / 13**
	10/15: IFR (infection fatality rate) = 2.08%		
	10/15: hospitalizations current = 1,009		
	10/15: hospitalizations cumulative = 11,704		
10/16	**164,124 / 3,408**	**+7,475 / +64**	**1,068 / 9**
	10/22: test positivity rate = 5.7%		
10/23	**171,284 / 3,539**	**+7,160 / +131**	**1,023 / 19**
10/30	**179,639 / 3,643**	**+8,355 / +104**	**1,194 / 15**
	10/31: total tests = 2,833,250		
	11/01: deaths/million population = 428		
	11/03: Election Day		
11/06	**188,770 / 3,682**	**+9,131 / +39**	**1,304 / 6**
	11/07: Biden wins election		
11/13	**199,262 / 3,785**	**+10,492 / +103**	**1,499 / 15**
	11/15: IFR (infection fatality rate) = 1.88%		
	11/15: hospitalizations current = 1,284		
	11/15: hospitalizations cumulative = 13,504		
11/20	**213,331 / 3,912**	**+14,069 / +127**	**2,010 / 18**

DATE	CASES / DEATHS	WEEKLY INCREASE	DAILY AVERAGE
11/22: test positivity rate = 8.8%			
11/26: Thanksgiving			
11/27	**230,444 / 4,044**	**+17,113 / +132**	**2,445 / 19**
11/30: total tests = 3,852,413			
12/01: deaths/million population = 482			
12/04	**247,380 / 4,160**	**+16,936 / +116**	**2,419 / 17**
12/11	**274,438 / 4,370**	**+27,058 / +210**	**3,865 / 30**
12/14: first COVID-19 vaccinations given in the U.S.			
12/15: IFR (infection fatality rate) = 1.55%			
12/15: hospitalizations current = 2,361			
12/15: hospitalizations cumulative = 16,187			
12/18	**299,388 / 4,598**	**+24,950 / +228**	**3,564 / 33**
12/22: new U.K. variant identified in the U.S.			
12/22: test positivity rate = 10.5%			
12/25: Christmas			
12/25	**327,993 / 4,820**	**+28,605 / +222**	**4,086 / 32**
12/31: total tests = 5,148,590			
12/31: deaths/million population = 595			
01/01: New Year's Day			
01/01: CFR (case fatality rate) = 2.67% (26.7X more deadly than influenza at 0.1%)			
01/01/2021	**354,766 / 5,081**	**+26,773 / +261**	**3,825 / 37**

BONUS: Enjoy additional week from upcoming book: PANDEMIC 2021: The U.S. Edition
01/06: right-wing mob insurrection at U.S. Capitol as Joe Biden confirmed president
01/08: Twitter permanently bans Trump's account

DATE	CASES / DEATHS	WEEKLY INCREASE	DAILY AVERAGE
01/08	**387,917 / 5,312**	**+33,151 / +231**	**4,736 / 33**

*The daily average column is rounded to the nearest whole person. The infection fatality rate (IFR) is the number of deaths divided by the number of confirmed cases. The case fatality rate (CFR), shown only at the end of the year, is the number of deaths divided by the number of confirmed cases *which have had an outcome* (either recovery or death). The CFR excludes active cases.

CHAPTER 49

~ WASHINGTON *~*

POPULATION AS OF MARCH, 2020: 7,797,095
Democratic Governor Jay Inslee
VOTED BLUE: Biden 58.0% / Trump 38.8%

DATE	CASES / DEATHS	WEEKLY INCREASE	DAILY AVERAGE
01/30: WHO declares Public Health Emergency of International Concern			
01/31: Trump issues a China "travel ban"			
02/29: Washington declares State of Emergency			
03/02: Washington's first 22 cases / first 11 deaths			
03/06	99 / 26	N/A	N/A
03/11: WHO declares COVID-19 a pandemic			
03/11: schools close			
03/13: Trump declares a National Emergency			
03/13: Trump issues a Europe "travel ban"			
03/13	601 / 49	+502 / +23	72 / 3
03/20	1,658 / 111	+1,057 / +62	151 / 9
03/24: stay at home order			
03/25: non-essential services close			
03/27	4,057 / 220	+2,399 / +109	343 / 16
03/31: total tests = 65,462			
04/03	7,068 / 368	+3,011 / +148	430 / 21
04/10	9,635 / 523	+2,567 / +155	367 / 22
04/12: Easter			
04/15: IFR (infection fatality rate) = 5.30%			
04/15: hospitalizations current = 645			
04/15: hospitalizations cumulative = not given			
04/17	11,159 / 599	+1,524 / +76	218 / 11
04/24	13,176 / 723	+2,017 / +124	288 / 18

DATE	CASES / DEATHS	WEEKLY INCREASE	DAILY AVERAGE
04/30: total tests = 188,981			
05/01	**15,161 / 832**	**+1,985 / +109**	**284 / 16**
05/08	**17,196 / 914**	**+2,035 / +82**	**291 / 12**
05/10: Mother's Day			
05/15: IFR (infection fatality rate) = 5.35%			
05/15: hospitalizations current = 626			
05/15: hospitalizations cumulative = not given			
05/15	**18,779 / 1,005**	**+1,583 / +91**	**226 / 13**
05/22	**20,176 / 1,071**	**+1,397 / +66**	**200 / 9**
05/25: Memorial Day			
05/26: George Floyd protests begin			
05/29	**22,097 / 1,116**	**+1,921 / +45**	**274 / 6**
05/31: total tests = 354,354			
NEW! 06/01: deaths/million population = 145			
06/05	**24,258 / 1,160**	**+2,161 / +44**	**309 / 6**
06/12	**26,087 / 1,202**	**+1,829 / +42**	**261 / 6**
06/15: IFR (infection fatality rate) = 4.55%			
06/15: hospitalizations current = 357			
06/15: hospitalizations cumulative = 3,856			
06/19	**28,526 / 1,248**	**+2,439 / +46**	**348 / 7**
06/21: Father's Day			
06/26: mask mandate			
06/26	**31,863 / 1,305**	**+3,337 / +57**	**477 / 8**
06/30: total tests = 557,275			
07/01: deaths/million population = 176			
07/03	**35,641 / 1,352**	**+3,778 / +47**	**540 / 7**
07/04: Independence Day			
07/10	**40,435 / 1,424**	**+4,794 / +72**	**685 / 10**
07/15: IFR (infection fatality rate) = 3.21%			
07/15: hospitalizations current = 497			
07/15: hospitalizations cumulative = 4,788			
07/17	**46,506 / 1,442**	**+6,071 / +18**	**867 / 3**
07/24	**52,508 / 1,505**	**+6,002 / +63**	**857 / 9**
07/31	**58,240 / 1,573**	**+5,732 / +68**	**819 / 10**
07/31: total tests = 973,654			
08/01: deaths/million population = 209			
08/07	**63,187 / 1,659**	**+4,947 / +86**	**707 / 12**
08/14	**68,018 / 1,757**	**+4,831 / +98**	**690 / 14**

DATE	CASES / DEATHS	WEEKLY INCREASE	DAILY AVERAGE
08/15: IFR (infection fatality rate) = 2.58%			
08/15: hospitalizations current = 529			
08/15: hospitalizations cumulative = 6,206			
08/21: Trump rally			
08/21	**71,875 / 1,850**	**+3,857 / +93**	**551 / 13**
08/28	**75,443 / 1,905**	**+3,568 / +55**	**510 / 8**
08/31: total tests = 1,550,477			
09/01: deaths/million population = 256			
09/04	**78,684 / 1,953**	**+3,241 / +48**	**463 / 7**
09/07: Labor Day			
09/11	**81,490 / 1,991**	**+2,806 / +38**	**401 / 5**
09/15: IFR (infection fatality rate) = 2.42%			
09/15: hospitalizations current = 348			
09/15: hospitalizations cumulative = 7,127			
09/18	**84,457 / 2,037**	**+2,967 / +46**	**424 / 7**
NEW! 09/22: test positivity rate = 2.9%			
09/25	**88,004 / 2,100**	**+3,547 / +63**	**507 / 9**
09/30: total tests = 1,905,759			
10/01: deaths/million population = 282			
10/02	**91,723 / 2,145**	**+3,719 / +45**	**531 / 6**
10/09	**95,639 / 2,193**	**+3,916 / +48**	**559 / 7**
10/15: IFR (infection fatality rate) = 2.25%			
10/15: hospitalizations current = 373			
10/15: hospitalizations cumulative = 7,883			
10/16	**100,223 / 2,244**	**+4,584 / +51**	**655 / 7**
10/22: test positivity rate = 3.4%			
10/23	**104,867 / 2,299**	**+4,644 / +55**	**663 / 8**
10/30	**110,396 / 2,366**	**+5,529 / +67**	**790 / 10**
10/31: total tests = 2,450,122			
11/01: deaths/million population = 311			
11/03: Election Day			
11/06	**118,487 / 2,452**	**+8,091 / +86**	**1,156 / 12**
11/07: Biden wins election			
11/13	**130,782 / 2,530**	**+12,295 / +78**	**1,756 / 11**
11/15: IFR (infection fatality rate) = 1.89%			
11/15: hospitalizations current = 658			
11/15: hospitalizations cumulative = 9,281			
11/20	**145,951 / 2,636**	**+15,169 / +106**	**2,167 / 15**

DATE	CASES / DEATHS	WEEKLY INCREASE	DAILY AVERAGE
	11/22: test positivity rate = 8.9%		
	11/26: Thanksgiving		
11/27	**164,331 / 2,723**	**+18,380 / +87**	**2,626 / 12**
	11/30: total tests = 2,894,367		
	12/01: deaths/million population = 377		
12/04	**181,220 / 2,958**	**+16,889 / +235**	**2,413 / 34**
12/11	**202,802 / 2,996**	**+21,582 / +38**	**3,083 / 5**
	12/14: first COVID-19 vaccinations given in the U.S.		
	12/15: IFR (infection fatality rate) = 1.45%		
	12/15: hospitalizations current = 1,144		
	12/15: hospitalizations cumulative = 12,649		
12/18	**223,470 / 3,200**	**+20,668 / +204**	**2,953 / 29**
	12/22: new U.K. variant identified in the U.S.		
	12/22: test positivity rate = 6.2%		
	12/25: Christmas		
12/25	**236,201 / 3,351**	**+12,731 / +151**	**1,819 / 22**
	12/31: total tests = 3,836,820		
	12/31: deaths/million population = 468		
	01/01: New Year's Day		
	01/01: CFR (case fatality rate) = 3.39% (33.9X more deadly than influenza at 0.1%)		
01/01/2021	**250,821 / 3,573**	**+14,620 / +222**	**2,089 / 32**

BONUS: Enjoy additional week from upcoming book: PANDEMIC 2021: The U.S. Edition
> *01/06: right-wing mob insurrection at U.S. Capitol as Joe Biden confirmed president*
> *01/08: Twitter permanently bans Trump's account*

| **01/08** | **271,989 / 3,812** | **+21,168 / +239** | **3,024 / 34** |

---

*The daily average column is rounded to the nearest whole person. The infection fatality rate (IFR) is the number of deaths divided by the number of confirmed cases. The case fatality rate (CFR), shown only at the end of the year, is the number of deaths divided by the number of confirmed cases *which have had an outcome* (either recovery or death). The CFR excludes active cases.

CHAPTER 50

~ WEST VIRGINIA *~*

POPULATION AS OF MARCH, 2020: 1,778,070
Republican Governor Jim Justice
VOTED RED: Trump 68.6% / Biden 29.7%

DATE	CASES / DEATHS	WEEKLY INCREASE	DAILY AVERAGE
01/30: WHO declares Public Health Emergency of International Concern			
01/31: Trump issues a China "travel ban"			
03/11: WHO declares COVID-19 a pandemic			
03/13: Trump declares a National Emergency			
03/13: Trump issues a Europe "travel ban"			
03/14: West Virginia schools close			
03/16: West Virginia declares State of Preparedness			
03/17: West Virginia's first case			
03/20	**7 / 0**	**N/A**	**N/A**
03/24: non-essential services close			
03/25: stay at home order			
03/27	**101 / 0**	**+94 / +0**	**13 / 0**
03/30: West Virginia's first death			
03/31: total tests = 3,110			
04/03	**281 / 2**	**+180 / +2**	**26 / 0**
04/10	**574 / 5**	**+293 / +3**	**42 / 0**
04/12: Easter			
04/15: IFR (infection fatality rate) = 1.67%			
04/15: hospitalizations current = 82			
04/15: hospitalizations cumulative = not given for this state			
04/17	**775 / 16**	**+201 / +11**	**29 / 2**
04/24	**1,010 / 32**	**+235 / +16**	**34 / 2**
04/30: total tests = 45,210			

DATE	CASES / DEATHS	WEEKLY INCREASE	DAILY AVERAGE
05/01	1,151 / 47	+141 / +15	20 / 2
05/08	1,323 / 52	+172 / +5	25 / 1
05/10: Mother's Day			
05/15: IFR (infection fatality rate) = 4.42%			
05/15: hospitalizations current = 57			
05/15	1,447 / 64	+124 / +12	18 / 2
05/22	1,705 / 72	+258 / +8	37 / 1
05/25: Memorial Day			
05/26: George Floyd protests begin			
05/29	1,972 / 74	+267 / +2	38 / 0
05/31: total tests = 96,369			
NEW! 06/01: deaths/million population = 43			
06/05	2,119 / 84	+147 / +10	21 / 1
06/12	2,249 / 88	+130 / +4	19 / 1
06/15: IFR (infection fatality rate) = 3.79%			
06/15: hospitalizations current = 25			
06/19	2,468 / 88	+219 / +0	31 / 0
06/21: Father's Day			
06/26	2,730 / 92	+262 / +4	37 / 1
06/30: total tests = 171,663			
07/01: deaths/million population = 52			
07/03	3,126 / 93	+396 / +1	57 / 0
07/04: Independence Day			
07/07: mask mandate			
07/10	3,983 / 95	+857 / +2	122 / 0
07/15: IFR (infection fatality rate) = 2.15%			
07/15: hospitalizations current = 63			
07/17	4,783 / 100	+800 / +5	114 / 1
07/24	5,695 / 103	+912 / +3	130 / 0
07/31	6,642 / 116	+947 / +13	135 / 2
07/31: total tests = 283,848			
08/01: deaths/million population = 65			
08/07	7,433 / 127	+791 / +11	113 / 2
08/14	8,274 / 157	+841 / +30	120 / 4
08/15: IFR (infection fatality rate) = 1.89%			
08/15: hospitalizations current = 132			
08/21	9,066 / 170	+793 / +13	113 / 2
08/28	9,824 / 202	+758 / +32	108 / 5

DATE	CASES / DEATHS	WEEKLY INCREASE	DAILY AVERAGE
08/31: total tests = 453,285			
09/01: deaths/million population = 136			
09/04	**11,037 / 243**	**+1,213 / +41**	**173 / 6**
09/07: Labor Day			
09/11	**12,174 / 263**	**+1,137 / +20**	**162 / 3**
09/15: IFR (infection fatality rate) = 2.16%			
09/15: hospitalizations current = 155			
09/18	**13,683 / 297**	**+1,509 / +34**	**216 / 5**
NEW! 09/22: test positivity rate = 4.4%			
09/25	**14,953 / 330**	**+1,270 / +33**	**181 / 5**
09/30: total tests = 576,026			
10/01: deaths/million population = 198			
10/02	**16,307 / 355**	**+1,354 / +25**	**193 / 4**
10/09	**17,707 / 376**	**+1,400 / +21**	**200 / 3**
10/15: IFR (infection fatality rate) = 2.06%			
10/15: hospitalizations current = 180			
10/16	**19,580 / 396**	**+1,873 / +20**	**268 / 3**
10/22: test positivity rate = 4.1%			
10/23	**21,392 / 422**	**+1,812 / +26**	**258 / 4**
10/30	**23,990 / 451**	**+2,598 / +29**	**371 / 4**
10/31: total tests = 776,609			
11/01: deaths/million population = 255			
11/03: Election Day			
11/06	**27,087 / 487**	**+3,097 / +36**	**442 / 5**
11/07: Biden wins election			
11/13	**31,639 / 565**	**+4,552 / +78**	**650 / 11**
11/14: mask mandate			
11/15: IFR (infection fatality rate) = 1.73%			
11/15: hospitalizations current = 365			
11/20	**38,480 / 639**	**+6,841 / +74**	**977 / 11**
11/22: test positivity rate = 7.6%			
11/26: Thanksgiving			
11/27	**45,046 / 712**	**+6,566 / +73**	**938 / 10**
11/30: total tests = 1,152,045			
12/01: deaths/million population = 434			
12/04	**52,172 / 799**	**+7,126 / +87**	**1,018 / 12**
12/11	**60,637 / 938**	**+8,465 / +139**	**1,209 / 20**
12/14: first COVID-19 vaccinations given in the U.S.			

DATE	CASES / DEATHS	WEEKLY INCREASE	DAILY AVERAGE
12/15: IFR (infection fatality rate) = 1.54%			
12/15: hospitalizations current = 774			
12/18	**69,751 / 1,091**	**+9,114 / +153**	**1,302 / 22**
12/22: new U.K. variant identified in the U.S.			
12/22: test positivity rate = 11.6%			
12/25: Christmas			
12/25	**78,836 / 1,247**	**+9,085 / +156**	**1,298 / 22**
12/31: total tests = 1,518,917			
12/31: deaths/million population = 759			
01/01: New Year's Day			
01/01: CFR (case fatality rate) = 2.21% (22.1X more deadly than influenza at 0.1%)			
01/01/2021	**87,820 / 1,361**	**+8,984 / +114**	**1,283 / 16**

BONUS: Enjoy additional week from upcoming book: PANDEMIC 2021: The U.S. Edition
01/06: right-wing mob insurrection at U.S. Capitol as Joe Biden confirmed president
01/08: Twitter permanently bans Trump's account

DATE	CASES / DEATHS	WEEKLY INCREASE	DAILY AVERAGE
01/08	**97,898 / 1,554**	**+10,078 / +192**	**1,440 / 27**

*The daily average column is rounded to the nearest whole person. The infection fatality rate (IFR) is the number of deaths divided by the number of confirmed cases. The case fatality rate (CFR), shown only at the end of the year, is the number of deaths divided by the number of confirmed cases *which have had an outcome* (either recovery or death). The CFR excludes active cases.

CHAPTER 51

~ WISCONSIN *~*

POPULATION AS OF MARCH, 2020: 5,851,754
Democratic Governor Tony Evers
VOTED BLUE: Biden 49.4% / Trump 48.8%

DATE	CASES / DEATHS	WEEKLY INCREASE	DAILY AVERAGE
01/30: WHO declares Public Health Emergency of International Concern			
01/31: Trump issues a China "travel ban"			
02/05: Wisconsin's first case			
03/06	1 / 0	N/A	N/A
03/11: WHO declares COVID-19 a pandemic			
03/12: Wisconsin declares Public Health Emergency			
03/13: Trump declares a National Emergency			
03/13: Trump issues a Europe "travel ban"			
03/13	19 / 0	+18 / +0	3 / 0
03/18: Wisconsin schools close			
03/19: Wisconsin's first 2 deaths			
03/20	206 / 3	+ 187 / +3	27 / 0
03/25: non-essential services close			
03/25: stay at home order			
03/27	842 / 13	+636 / +10	91 / 1
03/31: total tests = 17,077			
04/03	1,916 / 37	+1,074 / +24	153 / 3
04/10	3,068 / 128	+1,152 / +91	165 / 13
04/12: Easter			
04/15: IFR (infection fatality rate) = 4.89%			
04/15: hospitalizations current = 406			
04/15: hospitalizations cumulative = 1,091			
04/17	4,045 / 205	+977 / +77	140 / 11

DATE	CASES / DEATHS	WEEKLY INCREASE	DAILY AVERAGE
04/24	**5,356 / 262**	**+1,311 / +57**	**187 / 8**
04/30: total tests = 78,230			
05/01	**7,314 / 327**	**+1,958 / +65**	**280 / 9**
05/08	**9,590 / 384**	**+2,276 / +57**	**325 / 8**
05/10: Mother's Day			
05/15: IFR (infection fatality rate) = 3.81%			
05/15: hospitalizations current = 356			
05/15: hospitalizations cumulative = 1,977			
05/15	**11,685 / 445**	**+2,095 / +61**	**299 / 9**
05/22	**14,396 / 496**	**+2,711 / +51**	**387 / 7**
05/25: Memorial Day			
05/26: George Floyd protests begin			
05/29	**17,707 / 568**	**+3,311 / +72**	**473 / 10**
05/31: total tests = 261,876			
NEW! 06/01: deaths/million population = 102			
06/05	**20,249 / 633**	**+2,542 / +65**	**363 / 9**
06/12	**22,518 / 691**	**+2,269 / +58**	**324 / 8**
06/15: IFR (infection fatality rate) = 3.03%			
06/15: hospitalizations current = 284			
06/15: hospitalizations cumulative = 3,061			
06/19	**24,154 / 730**	**+1,636 / +39**	**234 / 6**
06/21: Father's Day			
06/26	**26,747 / 766**	**+2,593 / +36**	**370 / 5**
06/30: total tests = 571,201			
07/01: deaths/million population = 135			
07/03	**30,317 / 796**	**+3,570 / +30**	**510 / 4**
07/04: Independence Day			
07/10	**34,753 / 814**	**+4,436 / +18**	**634 / 3**
07/15: IFR (infection fatality rate) = 2.14%			
07/15: hospitalizations current = 295			
07/15: hospitalizations cumulative = 3,923			
07/17	**40,507 / 833**	**+5,754 / +19**	**822 / 3**
07/24	**46,917 / 878**	**+6,410 / +45**	**916 / 6**
07/31	**52,940 / 934**	**+6,023 / +56**	**860 / 8**
07/31: total tests = 935,089			
08/01: deaths/million population = 163			
08/01: mask mandate			
08/07	**58,768 / 990**	**+5,828 / +56**	**833 / 8**

DATE	CASES / DEATHS	WEEKLY INCREASE	DAILY AVERAGE
08/14	64,227 / 1,025	+5,459 / +35	780 / 5

08/15: IFR (infection fatality rate) = 1.60%
08/15: hospitalizations current = 337
08/15: hospitalizations cumulative = 5,275
08/17: Trump rally

| 08/21 | 69,059 / 1,068 | +4,832 / +43 | 690 / 6 |
| 08/28 | 73,981 / 1,113 | +4,922 / +45 | 703 / 6 |

08/31: total tests = 1,297,578
09/01: deaths/million population = 201
09/01: Trump rally

| 09/04 | 79,354 / 1,153 | +5,373 / +40 | 768 / 6 |

09/07: Labor Day

| 09/11 | 86,250 / 1,197 | +6,896 / +44 | 985 / 6 |

09/15: IFR (infection fatality rate) = 1.34%
09/15: hospitalizations current = 343
09/15: hospitalizations cumulative = 6,406
09/17: Trump rally

| 09/18 | 97,279 / 1,238 | +11,029 / +41 | 1,576 / 6 |

NEW! 09/22: test positivity rate = 17.3%

| 09/25 | 110,828 / 1,274 | +13,549 / +36 | 1,936 / 5 |

09/30: total tests = 1,573,477
10/01: deaths/million population = 232

| 10/02 | 127,906 / 1,353 | +17,078 / +79 | 2,440 / 11 |
| 10/09 | 144,818 / 1,440 | +16,912 / +87 | 2,416 / 12 |

10/15: IFR (infection fatality rate) = 0.96%
10/15: hospitalizations current = 1,043
10/15: hospitalizations cumulative = 8,892

| 10/16 | 166,186 / 1,574 | +21,368 / +134 | 3,053 / 19 |

10/17: Trump rally
10/22: test positivity rate = 14.1%

| 10/23 | 190,478 / 1,745 | +24,292 / +171 | 3,470 / 24 |

10/24 & 10/27: Trump rallies

| 10/30 | 220,092 / 1,972 | +29,614 / +227 | 4,231 / 32 |

10/31: total tests = 2,052,006
11/01: deaths/million population = 352
11/03: Election Day

| 11/06 | 256,065 / 2,256 | +35,973 / +284 | 5,139 / 41 |

11/07: Biden wins election

DATE	CASES / DEATHS	WEEKLY INCREASE	DAILY AVERAGE
11/13	**301,165 / 2,573**	**+45,100 / +317**	**6,443 / 45**
11/15: IFR (infection fatality rate) = 0.84%			
11/15: hospitalizations current = 2,097			
12/15: hospitalizations cumulative = 14,381			
11/20	**344,945 / 2,954**	**+43,780 / +381**	**6,254 / 54**
11/22: test positivity rate = 15.3%			
11/26: Thanksgiving			
11/27	**375,837 / 3,257**	**+30,892 / +303**	**4,413 / 43**
11/30: total tests = 2,557,706			
12/01: deaths/million population = 601			
12/04	**404,555 / 3,625**	**+28,718 / +368**	**4,103 / 53**
12/11	**429,957 / 3,991**	**+25,402 / +366**	**3,629 / 52**
12/14: first COVID-19 vaccinations given in the U.S.			
12/15: IFR (infection fatality rate) = 0.93%			
12/15: hospitalizations current = 1,461			
12/15: hospitalizations cumulative = 19,510			
12/18	**451,676 / 4,315**	**+21,719 / +324**	**3,103 / 46**
12/22: new U.K. variant identified in the U.S.			
12/22: test positivity rate = 11.0%			
12/25: Christmas			
12/25	**467,899 / 4,679**	**+16,223 / +364**	**2,318 / 52**
12/31: total tests = 2,840,064			
12/31: deaths/million population = 836			
01/01: New Year's Day			
01/01: CFR (case fatality rate) = 1.07% (10.7X more deadly than influenza at 0.1%)			
01/01/2021	**483,007 / 4,869**	**+15,108 / +190**	**2,158 / 27**

BONUS: *Enjoy additional week from upcoming book: PANDEMIC 2021: The U.S. Edition*
01/06: right-wing mob insurrection at U.S. Capitol as Joe Biden confirmed president
01/08: Twitter permanently bans Trump's account

DATE	CASES / DEATHS	WEEKLY INCREASE	DAILY AVERAGE
01/08	**502,012 / 5,119**	**+19,005 / +250**	**2,715 / 36**

*The daily average column is rounded to the nearest whole person. The infection fatality rate (IFR) is the number of deaths divided by the number of confirmed cases. The case fatality rate (CFR), shown only at the end of the year, is the number of deaths divided by the number of confirmed cases *which have had an outcome* (either recovery or death). The CFR excludes active cases.

CHAPTER 52

~ WYOMING *~*

POPULATION AS OF MARCH, 2020: 567,025
Republican Governor Mark Gordon
VOTED RED: Trump 69.9% / Biden 26.6%

DATE	CASES / DEATHS	WEEKLY INCREASE	DAILY AVERAGE
01/30: WHO declares Public Health Emergency of International Concern			
01/31: Trump issues a China "travel ban"			
03/11: WHO declares COVID-19 a pandemic			
03/12: Wyoming's first case			
03/13: Wyoming declares State of Emergency			
03/13: Trump declares a National Emergency			
03/13: Trump issues a Europe "travel ban"			
03/13	2 / 0	N/A	N/A
03/19: Wyoming schools close			
03/20	20 / 0	+18 / +0	3 / 0
03/27	73 / 0	+53 / +0	8 / 0
03/31: total tests = 1,934			
04/03	165 / 0	+92 / +0	13 / 0
04/10	253 / 0	+88 / +0	13 / 0
04/12: Easter			
04/13: Wyoming's first death			
04/15: IFR (infection fatality rate) = 0.69%			
04/15: hospitalizations current = 19			
04/15: hospitalizations cumulative = 43			
04/17	412 / 2	+159 / +2	23 / 0
04/24	473 / 7	+61 / +5	9 / 1
04/30: total tests = 8,833			
05/01	566 / 7	+93 / +0	13 / 0

DATE	CASES / DEATHS	WEEKLY INCREASE	DAILY AVERAGE
05/08	644 / 7	+78 / +0	11 / 0
05/10: Mother's Day			
05/15: IFR (infection fatality rate) = 0.98%			
05/15: hospitalizations current = 8			
05/15: hospitalizations cumulative = 68			
05/15	716 / 7	+72 / +0	10 / 0
05/22	803 / 12	+87 / +5	12 / 1
05/25: Memorial Day			
05/26: George Floyd protests begin			
05/29	891 / 15	+88 / +3	13 / 0
05/31: total tests = 24,083			
NEW! 06/01: deaths/million population = 30			
06/05	933 / 17	+42 / +2	6 / 0
06/12	1,027 / 18	+94 / +1	13 / 0
06/15: IFR (infection fatality rate) = 1.67%			
06/15: hospitalizations current = 4			
06/15: hospitalizations cumulative = 93			
06/19	1,173 / 20	+146 / +2	21 / 0
06/21: Father's Day			
06/26	1,368 / 20	+195 / +0	28 / 0
06/30: total tests = 45,969			
07/01: deaths/million population = 35			
07/30	1,582 / 20	+214 / +0	31 / 0
07/04: Independence Day			
07/10	1,790 / 21	+208 / +1	30 / 0
07/15: IFR (infection fatality rate) = 1.11%			
07/15: hospitalizations current = 17			
07/15: hospitalizations cumulative = 131			
07/17	2,069 / 24	+279 / +3	40 / 0
07/24	2,405 / 25	+336 / +1	48 / 0
07/31	2,726 / 26	+321 / +1	46 / 0
07/31: total tests = 77,429			
08/01: deaths/million population = 45			
08/07	3,000 / 28	+274 / +2	39 / 0
08/14	3,183 / 30	+183 / +2	26 / 0
08/15: IFR (infection fatality rate) = 0.93%			
08/15: hospitalizations current = 13			
08/15: hospitalizations cumulative = 191			

DATE	CASES / DEATHS	WEEKLY INCREASE	DAILY AVERAGE
08/21	3,524 / 37	+341 / +7	49 / 1
08/28	3,763 / 37	+239 / +0	34 / 0
	08/31: total tests = 121,596		
	09/01: deaths/million population = 73		
09/04	3,989 / 42	+226 / +5	32 / 1
	09/07: Labor Day		
09/11	4,264 / 42	+275 / +0	39 / 0
	09/15: IFR (infection fatality rate) = 1.04%		
	09/15: hospitalizations current = 16		
	09/15: hospitalizations cumulative = 230		
09/18	4,747 / 49	+483 / +7	69 / 1
	NEW! 09/22: test positivity rate = 11.3%		
09/25	5,420 / 50	+673 / +1	
	09/30: total tests = 165,242		
	10/01: deaths/million population = 92		
10/02	6,214 / 53	+794 / +3	113 / 0
10/09	7,335 / 54	+1,121 / +1	160 / 0
	10/15: IFR (infection fatality rate) = 0.68%		
	10/15: hospitalizations current = 51		
	10/15: hospitalizations cumulative = 354		
10/16	8,665 / 57	+1,330 / +3	190 / 0
	10/22: test positivity rate = 31.4%		
10/23	10,545 / 68	+1,880 / +11	269 / 2
10/30	13,028 / 87	+2,483 / +19	355 / 3
	10/31: total tests = 250,713		
	11/01: deaths/million population = 150		
	11/03: Election Day		
11/06	16,405 / 105	+3,377 / +18	482 / 3
	11/07: Biden wins election		
11/13	21,341 / 127	+4,936 / +22	705 / 3
	11/15: IFR (infection fatality rate) = 0.64%		
	11/15: hospitalizations current = 189		
	11/15: hospitalizations cumulative = 580		
11/20	27,129 / 176	+5,788 / +49	827 / 7
	11/22: test positivity rate = 77.2%		
	11/26: Thanksgiving		
11/27	31,773 / 215	+4,644 / +39	663 / 6
	11/30: total tests = 419,587		

DATE	CASES / DEATHS	WEEKLY INCREASE	DAILY AVERAGE
12/01: deaths/million population = 397			
12/04	35,737 / 257	+3,964 / +42	566 / 6
12/11	38,785 / 321	+3,048 / +64	435 / 9
12/14: first COVID-19 vaccinations given in the U.S.			
12/15: IFR (infection fatality rate) = 0.82%			
12/15: hospitalizations current = 178			
12/15: hospitalizations cumulative = 971			
12/18	41,359 / 351	+2,574 / +30	368 / 4
12/22: new U.K. variant found in the U.S.			
12/22: test positivity rate = 5.9%			
12/25: Christmas			
12/25	42,663 / 373	+1,304 / +22	186 / 3
12/31: total tests = 501,784			
12/31: deaths/million population = 757			
01/01: New Year's Day			
01/01: CFR (case fatality rate) = 1.02% (10.2X more deadly than influenza at 0.1%)			
01/01/2021	44,409 / 438	+1,746 / +65	249 / 9

BONUS: Enjoy additional week from upcoming book: PANDEMIC 2021: The U.S. Edition

 01/06: right-wing mob insurrection at U.S. Capitol as Joe Biden confirmed president
 01/08: Twitter permanently bans Trump's account

01/08	46,647 / 489	+2,238 / +51	320 / 7

*The daily average column is rounded to the nearest whole person. The infection fatality rate (IFR) is the number of deaths divided by the number of confirmed cases. The case fatality rate (CFR), shown only at the end of the year, is the number of deaths divided by the number of confirmed cases *which have had an outcome* (either recovery or death). The CFR excludes active cases.

CHAPTER 53

~ DISTRICT OF *~*
COLOMBIA (D.C.)

POPULATION AS OF MARCH, 2020: 720,687

DATE	CASES / DEATHS	WEEKLY INCREASE	DAILY AVERAGE
01/30: WHO declares Public Health Emergency of International Concern			
01/31: Trump issues a China "travel ban"			
03/07: DC's first 2 cases			
03/11: WHO declares COVID-19 a pandemic			
03/11: DC declares Public Health Emergency			
03/13: Trump declares a National Emergency			
03/13: Trump issues a Europe "travel ban"			
03/13	10 / 0	+8 / +0	1 / 0
03/16: schools close			
03/20: first death			
03/20	77 / 1	+67 / +1	10 / 0
03/25: non-essential services close			
03/27	304 / 4	+227 / +3	32 / 0
03/30: stay-at-home order			
03/31: total tests = 4,070			
04/03: mask mandate			
04/03	902 / 21	+598 / +17	85 / 2
04/10	1,778 / 47	+876 / +26	125 / 4
04/12: Easter			
04/15: IFR (infection fatality rate) = 3.28%			
04/15: hospitalizations current = 313			
04/15: hospitalizations cumulative = not available for D.C.			
04/17	2,476 / 86	+698 / +39	100 / 6

DATE	CASES / DEATHS	WEEKLY INCREASE	DAILY AVERAGE
04/24	**3,528 / 153**	**+1,052 / +67**	**150 / 10**
04/30: total tests = 22,004			
05/01	**4,658 / 231**	**+1,130 / +78**	**161 / 11**
05/08	**5,899 / 304**	**+1,241 / +73**	**177 / 10**
05/10: Mother's Day			
05/15: IFR (infection fatality rate) = 5.31%			
05/15: hospitalizations current = 393			
05/15	**6,871 / 368**	**+972 / +64**	**139 / 9**
05/22	**7,893 / 418**	**+1,022 / +50**	**146 / 7**
05/25: Memorial Day			
05/26: George Floyd protests begin			
05/29	**8,538 / 460**	**+645 / +42**	**92 / 6**
05/31: total tests = 45,629			
NEW! 06/01: deaths/million population = 649			
06/05	**9,199 / 479**	**+661 / +19**	**94 / 3**
06/12	**9,654 / 506**	**+455 / +27**	**65 / 4**
06/15: IFR (infection fatality rate) = 5.26%			
06/15: hospitalizations current = 191			
06/19	**9,952 / 530**	**+298 / +24**	**43 / 3**
06/21: Father's Day			
06/26	**10,185 / 546**	**+233 / +16**	**33 / 2**
06/30: total tests = 97,295			
07/01: deaths/million population = 784			
07/03	**10,435 / 555**	**+250 / +9**	**36 / 1**
07/04: Independence Day			
07/10	**10,743 / 568**	**+308 / +13**	**44 / 2**
07/15: IFR (infection fatality rate) = 5.18%			
07/15: hospitalizations current = 95			
07/17	**11,115 / 577**	**+372 / +9**	**53 / 1**
07/22: mask mandate			
07/24	**11,649 / 581**	**+534 / +4**	**76 / 1**
07/31	**12,126 / 585**	**+477 / +4**	**68 / 1**
07/31: total tests = 188,741			
08/01: deaths/million population = 829			
08/07	**12,589 / 589**	**+463 / +4**	**66 / 1**
08/14	**13,118 / 594**	**+529 / +5**	**76 / 1**
08/15: IFR (infection fatality rate) = 4.54%			
08/15: hospitalizations current = 81			

DATE	CASES / DEATHS	WEEKLY INCREASE	DAILY AVERAGE
08/21	13,469 / 602	+351 / +8	50 / 1
08/28	13,851 / 605	+382 / +3	55 / 0
08/31: total tests = 307,864			
09/01: deaths/million population = 866			
09/04	14,186 / 611	+335 / +6	48 / 1
09/07: Labor Day			
09/11	14,493 / 616	+307 / +5	44 / 1
09/15: IFR (infection fatality rate) = 4.21%			
09/15: hospitalizations current = 89			
09/18	14,852 / 619	+359 / +3	51 / 0
NEW! 09/22: test positivity rate = 1.3%			
09/25	15,163 / 623	+311 / +4	44 / 1
09/30: total tests = 394,118			
10/01: deaths/million population = 189			
10/02	15,423 / 629	+260 / +6	37 / 1
10/09	15,843 / 634	+420 / +5	60 / 1
10/15: IFR (infection fatality rate) = 3.95%			
10/15: hospitalizations current = 88			
10/16	16,255 / 641	+412 / +7	59 / 1
10/22: test positivity rate = 1.3%			
10/23	16,609 / 642	+354 / +1	51 / 0
10/30	17,144 / 646	+535 / +4	76 / 1
10/31: total tests = 520,436			
11/01: deaths/million population = 915			
11/03: Election Day			
11/06	17,792 / 652	+648 / +6	93 / 1
11/07: Biden wins election			
11/13	18,666 / 657	+874 / +5	125 / 1
11/15: IFR (infection fatality rate) = 3.48%			
11/15: hospitalizations current = 104			
11/20	19,808 / 669	+1,142 / +12	163 / 2
11/22: test positivity rate = 3.5%			
11/26: Thanksgiving			
11/27	20,937 / 677	+1,129 / +8	161 / 1
11/30: total tests = 701,485			
12/01: deaths/million population = 978			
12/04	22,480 / 693	+1,543 / +16	220 / 2
12/11	24,357 / 709	+1,877 / +16	268 / 2

DATE	CASES / DEATHS	WEEKLY INCREASE	DAILY AVERAGE
	12/14: first COVID-19 vaccinations given in the U.S.		
	12/15: IFR (infection fatality rate) = 2.84%		
	12/15: hospitalizations current = 224		
12/18	26,104 / 728	+1,747 / +19	250 / 3
	12/22: new U.K. variant identified in the U.S.		
	12/22: test positivity rate = 3.3%		
	12/25: Christmas		
12/25	27,436 / 756	+1,332 / +28	190 / 4
	12/31: total tests = 896,524		
	12/31: deaths/million population = 1,049		
	01/01: New Year's Day		
01/01/2021	29,252 / 788	+1,816 / +32	259 / 5

BONUS: Enjoy additional week from upcoming book: PANDEMIC 2021: The U.S. Edition
01/06: right-wing mob insurrection at U.S. Capitol as Joe Biden confirmed president
01/08: Twitter permanently bans Trump's account

DATE	CASES / DEATHS	WEEKLY INCREASE	DAILY AVERAGE
01/08	31,107 / 809	+1,855 / +21	265 / 3

*The daily average column is rounded to the nearest whole person. The infection fatality rate (IFR) is the number of deaths divided by the number of confirmed cases. The case fatality rate (CFR), shown only at the end of the year, is the number of deaths divided by the number of confirmed cases *which have had an outcome* (either recovery or death). The CFR excludes active cases.

SECTION III

U.S.
TERRIOTORIES

CHAPTER 54

~ PUERTO RICO *~*

POPULATION AS OF MARCH, 2020: 2,877,655

DATE	CASES / DEATHS	WEEKLY INCREASE	DAILY AVERAGE
	03/13: Puerto Rico's first 3 cases		
03/13	3 / 0	N/A	N/A
03/20	14 / 0	+11 / +0	2 / 0
	03/21: Puerto Rico's first death		
03/27	79 / 3	+65 / +3	9 / 0
	03/31: total tests = 2,709		
04/03	378 / 15	+299 / +12	43 / 2
04/10	725 / 39	+347 / +24	50 / 3
	04/15: IFR (infection fatality rate) = 5.24%		
04/17	1,068 / 58	+343 / +19	49 / 3
04/24	1,276 / 77	+208 / +19	30 / 3
	04/30: total tests = 12,633		
05/01	1,575 / 94	+299 / +17	43 / 2
05/08	2,156 / 107	+581 / +13	83 / 2
	05/15: IFR (infection fatality rate) = 4.80%		
05/15	2,542 / 122	+386 / +15	55 / 2
05/22	3,030 / 126	+488 / +4	70 / 1
05/29	3,647 / 132	+617 / +6	88 / 1
	05/31: total tests = 13,022		
	NEW! 06/01: deaths/million population = 47		
06/05	4,620 / 141	+973 / +9	139 / 1
06/12	5,536 / 146	+916 / +5	131 / 1
	06/15: IFR (infection fatality rate) = 2.50%		
06/19	6,195 / 147	+659 / +1	94 / 0
06/26	6,922 / 151	+727 / +4	104 / 1

DATE	CASES / DEATHS	WEEKLY INCREASE	DAILY AVERAGE
	06/30: total tests = 359,473		
	07/01: deaths/million population = 53		
07/03	7,683 / 154	+761 / +3	109 / 0
07/10	9,137 / 159	+1,454 / +5	208 / 1
	07/15: IFR (infection fatality rate) = 1.65%		
07/17	11,120 / 177	+1,983 / +18	283 / 3
07/24	13,967 / 191	+2,847 / +14	407 / 2
07/31	16,781 / 219	+2,814 / +28	402 / 4
	07/31: total tests = 464,073		
	08/01: deaths/million population = 78		
08/07	20,686 / 265	+3,905 / +46	558 / 7
08/14	25,128 / 317	+4,442 / +52	635 / 7
	08/15: IFR (infection fatality rate) = 1.28%		
08/21	28,846 / 375	+3,718 / +58	531 / 8
08/28	31,988 / 424	+3,142 / +49	449 / 7
	08/31: total tests = no longer given		
	09/01: deaths/million population = 137		
09/04	34,241 / 455	+2,253 / +31	322 / 4
09/11	36,581 / 523	+2,340 / +68	334 / 10
	09/15: IFR (infection fatality rate) = 1.96%		
09/18	39,684 / 599	+3,103 / +76	443 / 11
09/25	44,905 / 635	+5,221 / +36	
	10/01: deaths/million population = 199		
10/02	49,747 / 673	+4,842 / +38	692 / 5
10/09	52,892 / 720	+3,145 / +47	449 / 7
	10/15: IFR (infection fatality rate) = 1.35%		
10/16	56,412 / 758	+3,520 / +38	503 / 5
10/23	60,984 / 791	+4,572 / +33	653 / 5
10/30	65,743 / 820	+4,759 / +29	680 / 4
	11/01: deaths/million population = 246		
11/06	70,519 / 862	+4,776 / +42	682 / 6
11/13	76,535 / 914	+6,016 / +52	859 / 7
	11/15: IFR (infection fatality rate) = 1.19%		
11/20	82,904 / 991	+6,369 / +77	910 / 11
11/27	90,705 / 1,076	+7,801 / +85	1,114 / 12
	12/01: deaths/million population = 350		
12/04	96,382 / 1,173	+5,677 / +97	811 / 14
12/11	106,866 / 1,249	+10,484 / +76	1,498 / 11

DATE	CASES / DEATHS	WEEKLY INCREASE	DAILY AVERAGE
12/15: IFR (infection fatality rate) = 1.17%			
12/18	115,192 / 1,333	+8,326 / +84	1,189 / 12
12/25	122,881 / 1,432	+7,689 / +99	1,098 / 14
12/31: CFR (case fatality rate) = 2.26% (22.6X more deadly than influenza at 0.1%)			
01/01: deaths/million population = 498			
01/01/2021	133,270 / 1,521	+10,389 / +89	1,484 / 13

BONUS: Enjoy additional week from upcoming book: PANDEMIC 2021: The U.S. Edition

| 01/08 | 139,835 / 1,592 | +6,565 / +71 | 938 / 10 |

*The daily average column is rounded to the nearest whole person. The infection fatality rate (IFR) is the number of deaths divided by the number of confirmed cases. The case fatality rate (CFR), shown only at the end of the year, is the number of deaths divided by the number of confirmed cases *which have had an outcome* (either recovery or death). The CFR excludes active cases.

CHAPTER 55

~ GUAM *~*

POPULATION AS OF MARCH, 2020: 162,742

DATE	CASES / DEATHS	WEEKLY INCREASE	DAILY AVERAGE
03/15: Guam's first case			
03/22: Guam's first death			
Prior to 04/10, daily data could not be obtained other than date of 1st case and death.			
04/10	133 / 5	N/A	N/A
04/15: IFR (infection fatality rate) = 3.70%			
04/17	135 / 5	+2 / +0	0 / 0
04/24	141 / 5	+6 / +0	1 / 0
04/30: total tests = 605			
05/01	146 / 5	+5 / +0	1 / 0
05/08	151 / 5	+5 / +0	1 / 0
05/15: IFR (infection fatality rate) = 3.25%			
05/15	154 / 5	+3 / +0	0 / 0
05/22	165 / 5	+11 / +0	2 / 0
05/29	172 / 5	+7 / +0	1 / 0
05/31: total tests = 5,803			
NEW! 06/01: deaths/million population = 31			
06/05	179 / 5	+7 / +0	1 / 0
06/12	183 / 5	+4 / +0	1 / 0
06/15: IFR (infection fatality rate) = 2.70%			
06/19	200 / 5	+17 / +0	3 / 0
06/26	247 / 5	+47 / +0	7 / 0
06/30: total tests = 12,969			
07/01: deaths/million population = 31			
07/03	280 / 5	+33 / +0	5 / 0
07/10	310 / 5	+30 / +0	4 / 0

DATE	CASES / DEATHS	WEEKLY INCREASE	DAILY AVERAGE
07/15: IFR (infection fatality rate) = 1.60%			
07/17	314 / 5	+4 / +0	1 / 0
07/24	337 / 5	+23 / +0	3 / 0
07/31	356 / 5	+19 / +0	3 / 0
07/31: total tests = 22,018			
08/01: deaths/million population = 31			
08/07	411 / 5	+55 / +0	8 / 0
08/14	502 / 5	+91 / +0	13 / 0
08/15: IFR (infection fatality rate) = 1.00%			
08/21	767 / 6	+265 / +1	38 / 0
08/28	1,287 / 10	+520 / +4	74 / 1
08/31: total tests = 40,268			
09/01: deaths/million population = 61			
09/04	1,619 / 14	+332 / +4	47 / 1
09/11	1,863 / 23	+244 / +9	35 / 1
09/15: IFR (infection fatality rate) = 1.42%			
09/18	2,074 / 31	+211 / +8	30 / 1
09/25	2,286 / 39	+212 / +8	30 / 1
09/30: total tests = 51,300			
10/01: deaths/million population = 301			
10/02	2,617 / 49	+331 / +10	47 / 1
10/09	2,989 / 58	+372 / +9	53 / 1
10/15: IFR (infection fatality rate) = 1.78%			
10/16	3,538 / 63	+549 / +5	78 / 1
10/23	4,141 / 69	+603 / +6	86 / 1
10/30	4,628 / 79	+487 / +10	70 / 1
10/31: total tests = 67,452			
11/01: deaths/million population = 485			
11/06	5,077 / 88	+449 / +9	64 / 1
11/13	5,924 / 93	+847 / +5	121 / 1
11/15: IFR (infection fatality rate) = 1.54%			
11/20	6,452 / 103	+528 / +10	75 / 1
11/27	6,768 / 112	+316 / +9	45 / 1
11/30: total tests = 87,320			
12/01: deaths/million population = 694			
12/04	6,959 / 113	+191 / +1	27 / 0
12/11	7,079 / 115	+120 / +2	17 / 0
12/15: IFR (infection fatality rate) = 1.66%			

DATE	CASES / DEATHS	WEEKLY INCREASE	DAILY AVERAGE
12/18	7,193 / 119	+114 / +4	16 / 1
12/25	7,268 / 121	+75 / +2	11 / 0

12/31: total tests = 101,046
01/01: deaths/million population = 744
12/31: CFR (case fatality rate) = 1.76% (17.6X more deadly than influenza at 0.1%)

01/01/2021	7,326 / 122	+58 / +1	8 / 0

BONUS: Enjoy additional week from upcoming book: PANDEMIC 2021: The U.S. Edition

01/08	7,399 / 124	+73 / +2	10 / 0

*The daily average column is rounded to the nearest whole person. The infection fatality rate (IFR) is the number of deaths divided by the number of confirmed cases. The case fatality rate (CFR), shown only at the end of the year, is the number of deaths divided by the number of confirmed cases *which have had an outcome* (either recovery or death). The CFR excludes active cases.

CHAPTER 56

~ U.S. VIRGIN ISLANDS *~*

POPULATION AS OF MARCH, 2020: 107,268

DATE	CASES / DEATHS	WEEKLY INCREASE	DAILY AVERAGE
03/13: U.S. Virgin Islands' first case			
03/13	1 / 0	N/A	N/A
03/20	6 / 0	+5 / +0	1 / 0
03/27	19 / 0	+13 / +0	2 / 0
03/31: total tests = not given			
04/03	40 / 0	+21 / +0	3 / 0
04/05: U.S. Virgin Islands' first death			
04/10	51 / 1	+11 / +1	2 / 0
04/15: IFR (infection fatality rate) = 5.66%			
04/17	51 / 2	+0 / +1	0 / 0
04/24	54 / 3	+3 / +1	0 / 0
04/30: total tests = 872			
05/01	66 / 4	+12 / +1	2 / 0
05/08	68 / 4	+2 / +0	0 / 0
05/15: IFR (infection fatality rate) = 8.70%			
05/15	69 / 6	+1 / +2	0 / 0
05/22	69 / 6	+0 / +0	0 / 0
05/29	69 / 6	+0 / +0	0 / 0
05/31: total tests = 1,708			
NEW! 06/01: deaths/million population = 56			
06/05	71 / 6	+2 / +0	0 / 0
06/12	72 / 6	+1 / +0	0 / 0
06/15: IFR (infection fatality rate) = 8.22%			
06/19	73 / 6	+1 / +0	0 / 0
06/26	81 / 6	+8 / +0	1 / 0

DATE	CASES / DEATHS	WEEKLY INCREASE	DAILY AVERAGE
	06/30: total tests = 2,907		
	07/01: deaths/million population = 56		
07/03	**98 / 6**	**+17 / +0**	**2 / 0**
07/10	**153 / 6**	**+55 / +0**	**8 / 0**
	07/15: IFR (infection fatality rate) = 2.47%		
07/17	**263 / 6**	**+110 / +0**	**16 / 0**
07/24	**336 / 7**	**+73 / +1**	**10 / 0**
07/31	**406 / 8**	**+70 / +1**	**10 / 0**
	07/31: total tests = 9,193		
	08/01: deaths/million population = 75		
08/07	**522 / 9**	**+116 / +1**	**17 / 0**
08/14	**704 / 9**	**+182 / +0**	**26 / 0**
	08/15: IFR (infection fatality rate) = 1.23%		
08/21	**932 / 10**	**+228 / +1**	**33 / 0**
08/28	**1,075 / 14**	**+143 / +4**	**20 / 1**
	08/31: total tests = 17,231		
	09/01: deaths/million population = 140		
09/04	**1,150 / 16**	**+75 / +2**	**11 / 0**
09/11	**1,201 / 18**	**+51 / +2**	**7 / 0**
	09/15: IFR (infection fatality rate) = 1.55%		
09/18	**1,242 / 19**	**+41 / +1**	**6 / 0**
09/25	**1,269 / 19**	**+27 / +0**	**4 / 0**
	09/30: total tests = 21,023		
	10/01: deaths/million population = 186		
10/02	**1,324 / 20**	**+55 / +1**	**8 / 0**
10/09	**1,326 / 20**	**+2 / +0**	**0 / 0**
	10/15: IFR (infection fatality rate) = 1.51%		
10/16	**1,329 / 21**	**+3 / +1**	**0 / 0**
10/23	**1,346 / 21**	**+17 / +0**	**2 / 0**
10/30	**1,362 / 21**	**+16 / +0**	**2 / 0**
	10/31: total tests = 24,460		
	11/01: deaths/million population = 196		
11/06	**1,390 / 23**	**+28 / +2**	**4 / 0**
11/13	**1,434 / 23**	**+44 / +0**	**6 / 0**
	11/15: IFR (infection fatality rate) = 1.60%		
11/20	**1,482 / 23**	**+48 / +0**	**7 / 0**
11/27	**1,536 / 23**	**+54 / +0**	**8 / 0**
	11/30: total tests = 29,090		

DATE	CASES / DEATHS	WEEKLY INCREASE	DAILY AVERAGE
12/01: deaths/million population = 214			
12/04	1,613 / 23	+77 / +0	11 / 0
12/11	1,791 / 23	+178 / +0	25 / 0
12/15: IFR (infection fatality rate) = 1.24%			
12/18	1,910 / 23	+119 / +0	17 / 0
12/25	1,979 / 23	+69 / +0	10 / 0
12/31: total tests = 35,411			
01/01: deaths/million population = 214			
12/31: CFR (case fatality rate) = 1.25% (12.5X more deadly than influenza at 0.1%)			
01/01/2021	2,036 / 23	+57 / +0	8 / 0

BONUS: Enjoy additional week from upcoming book: PANDEMIC 2021: The U.S. Edition

01/08	2,130 / 24	+94 / +1	13 / 0

---

*The daily average column is rounded to the nearest whole person. The infection fatality rate (IFR) is the number of deaths divided by the number of confirmed cases. The case fatality rate (CFR), shown only at the end of the year, is the number of deaths divided by the number of confirmed cases *which have had an outcome* (either recovery or death). The CFR excludes active cases.

CHAPTER 57

~ NORTHERN *~*
MARIANA ISLANDS

POPULATION AS OF MARCH, 2020: 55,144

DATE	CASES / DEATHS	WEEKLY INCREASE	DAILY AVERAGE
03/28: Northern Mariana Islands' first 2 cases			
03/30: Northern Mariana Islands' first death			
Prior to 04/10, daily data could not be obtained other than date of 1st case and date of 1st death.			
04/10	11 / 2	+9 / +1	1 / 0
04/15: IFR (infection fatality rate) = 18.18%			
04/17	13 / 2	+2 / +0	0 / 0
04/24	14 / 2	+1 / +0	0 / 0
04/30: total tests = 948			
05/01	14 / 2	+0 / +0	0 / 0
05/08	15 / 2	+1 / +0	0 / 0
05/15: IFR (infection fatality rate) = 10.53%			
05/15	19 / 2	+4 / +0	1 / 0
05/22	22 / 2	+3 / +0	0 / 0
05/29	22 / 2	+0 / +0	0 / 0
05/31: total tests = 6,008			
06/05	26 / 2	+4 / +0	1 / 0
06/12	30 / 2	+4 / +0	1 / 0
06/15: IFR (infection fatality rate) = 6.67%			
06/19	30 / 2	+0 / +0	0 / 0
06/26	31 / 2	+1 / +0	0 / 0
06/30: total tests = 8,217			
07/03	31 / 2	+0 / +0	0 / 0

DATE	CASES / DEATHS	WEEKLY INCREASE	DAILY AVERAGE
07/10	31 / 2	+0 / +0	0 / 0
07/15: IFR (infection fatality rate) = 5.56%			
07/17	37 / 2	+6 / +0	1 / 0
07/24	38 / 2	+1 / +0	0 / 0
07/31	42 / 2	+4 / +0	1 / 0
07/31: total tests = 12,745			
08/07	47 / 2	+5 / +0	1 / 0
08/14	50 / 2	+3 / +0	0 / 0
08/15: IFR (infection fatality rate) = 4.00%			
08/21	54 / 2	+4 / +0	1 / 0
08/28	54 / 2	+0 / +0	0 / 0
08/31: total tests = 17,626			
09/04	57 / 2	+3 / +0	0 / 0
09/11	59 / 2	+2 / +0	0 / 0
09/15: IFR (infection fatality rate) = 3.28%			
09/18	62 / 2	+3 / +0	0 / 0
09/25	69 / 2	+7 / +0	1 / 0
09/30: total tests = 19,835			
10/02	73 / 2	+4 / +0	1 / 0
10/09	75 / 2	+2 / +0	0 / 0
10/15: IFR (infection fatality rate) = 2.50%			
10/16	80 / 2	+5 / +0	1 / 0
10/23	88 / 2	+8 / +0	1 / 0
10/30	92 / 2	+4 / +0	1 / 0
10/31: total tests = 22,633			
11/06	98 / 2	+6 / +0	1 / 0
11/13	100 / 2	+2 / +0	0 / 0
11/15: IFR (infection fatality rate) = 1.96%			
11/20	103 / 2	+3 / +0	0 / 0
11/27	104 / 2	+1 / +0	0 / 0
11/30: total tests = 23,944			
12/04	106 / 2	+2 / +0	0 / 0
12/11	113 / 2	+7 / +0	1 / 0
12/15: IFR (infection fatality rate) = 1.77%			
12/18	115 / 2	+2 / +0	0 / 0
12/25	118 / 2	+3 / +0	0 / 0
12/31: total tests =24,927			

DATE	CASES / DEATHS	WEEKLY INCREASE	DAILY AVERAGE

12/31: CFR (case fatality rate) = not calculable for this island (missing active cases)
01/01: deaths/million population = 36

DATE	CASES / DEATHS	WEEKLY INCREASE	DAILY AVERAGE
01/01/2021	122 / 2	+4 / +0	1 / 0

BONUS: Enjoy additional week from upcoming book: PANDEMIC 2021: The U.S. Edition

| 01/08 | 125/ 2 | +3 / +0 | 0 / 0 |

*The daily average column is rounded to the nearest whole person. The infection fatality rate (IFR) is the number of deaths divided by the number of confirmed cases. The case fatality rate (CFR), shown only at the end of the year, is the number of deaths divided by the number of confirmed cases *which have had an outcome* (either recovery or death). The CFR excludes active cases.

CHAPTER 58

~ AMERICAN *~*
SAMOA

POPULATION AS OF MARCH, 2020: 720,687

AMERICAN SAMOA

There has, as of the publication of this book, been only three diagnosed cases of COVID-19 in American Samoa. All three were identified on November 9, 2020. There have been no deaths.

SECTION IV

U.S.
COMMUNITIES

CHAPTER 59

~ U.S. MILITARY *~*

DATE	CASES / DEATHS	WEEKLY INCREASE	DAILY AVERAGE
04/09/20 US Military added as new category on worldometers.info			
04/10	3,366 / 13	N/A	N/A
04/15: IFR (infection fatality rate) = 0.36%			
04/17	4,849 / 19	+1,483 / +6	212 / 1
04/24	6,213 / 26	+1,364 / +7	195 / 1
04/30: total tests = not given			
05/01	7,145 / 27	+932 / +1	133 / 0
05/08	7,826 / 27	+681 / +0	97 / 0
05/15: IFR (infection fatality rate) = 0.32%			
05/15	8,374 / 27	+548 / +0	78 / 0
05/22	8,950 / 32	+576 / +5	82 / 1
05/29	9,449 / 36	+499 / +4	71 / 1
06/05	10,462 / 36	+1,013 / +0	145 / 0
06/12	11,439 / 36	+977 / +0	140 / 0
06/15: IFR (infection fatality rate) = 0.30%			
06/19	13,232 / 36	+1,793 / +0	256 / 0
06/26	15,577 / 37	+2,345 / +1	335 / 0
07/03	18,071 / 38	+2,494 / +1	356 / 0
07/10	23,842 / 41	+5,771 / +3	824 / 0
07/15: IFR (infection fatality rate) = 0.16%			
07/17	29,047 / 46	+5,205 / +5	744 / 1
07/24	34,491 / 54	+5,444 / +8	778 / 1
07/31	39,591 / 66	+5,100 / +12	729 / 2
08/07	43,634 / 72	+4,043 / +6	578 / 1
08/14	47,513 / 74	+3,879 / +2	554 / 0
08/15: IFR (infection fatality rate) = 0.16%			
08/21	51,238 / 77	+3,725 / +3	532 / 0
08/28	54,124 / 80	+2,886 / +3	412 / 0
09/04	56,719 / 88	+2,595 / +8	371 / 1
09/11	59,091 / 90	+2,372 / +2	339 / 0
09/15: IFR (infection fatality rate) = 0.15%			

DATE	CASES / DEATHS	WEEKLY INCREASE	DAILY AVERAGE
09/18	61,827 / 92	+2,736 / +2	391 / 0
09/25	64,602 / 95	+2,775 / +3	396 / 0
10/02	67,329 / 97	+2,727 / +2	390 / 0
10/09	70,527 / 99	+3,198 / +2	457 / 0
10/15: IFR (infection fatality rate) = 0.14%			
10/16	73,111 / 100	+2,584 / +1	369 / 0
10/23	78,227 / 103	+5,116 / +3	731 / 0
10/30	83,146 / 108	+4,919 / +5	703 / 1
11/06	89,133 / 111	+5,987 / +3	855 / 0
11/13	6,646 / 112	+7,513 / +1	1,073 / 0
11/15: IFR (infection fatality rate) = 0.12%			
11/20	108,562 / 119	+11,916 / +7	1,702 / 1
11/27	110,982 / 124	+2,420 / +5	346 / 1
12/04	125,947 / 136	+14,965 / +12	2,138 / 2
12/11	136,672 / 151	+10,725 / +15	1,532 / 2
12/15: IFR (infection fatality rate) = 0.11%			
12/18	147,760 / 160	+11,088 / +9	1,584 / 1
12/25	154,620 / 165	+6,860 / +5	980 / 1
01/01/2021	162,764 / 180	+8,144 / +15	1,163 / 2

BONUS: Enjoy additional week from upcoming book: PANDEMIC 2021: The U.S. Edition

01/08	179,408 / 203	+16,644 / +23	2,378 / 3

*The daily average column is rounded to the nearest whole person. The infection fatality rate (IFR) is the number of deaths divided by the number of confirmed cases. The case fatality rate (CFR), shown only at the end of the year, is the number of deaths divided by the number of confirmed cases *which have had an outcome* (either recovery or death). The CFR excludes active cases.

CHAPTER 60

~ VETERAN AFFAIRS *~*

DATE	CASES / DEATHS	WEEKLY INCREASE	DAILY AVERAGE
04/25/20 Veteran Affairs added as new category on worldometers.info			
04/30: total tests = 107,178			
05/01	9,015 / 513	N/A	N/A
05/08	10,666 / 841	+1,651 / +328	236 / 47
05/15: IFR (infection fatality rate) = 8.28%			
05/15	11,897 / 985	+1,231 / +144	176 / 21
05/22	13,070 / 1,112	+1,173 / +127	168 / 18
05/29	13,657 / 1,200	+587 / +88	84 / 13
05/31: total tests = 179,287			
06/05	15,555 / 1,337	+1,898 / +137	271 / 20
06/12	16,865 / 1,422	+1,310 / +85	187 / 12
06/15: IFR (infection fatality rate) = 8.38%			
06/19	18,330 / 1,504	+1,465 / +82	209 / 12
06/26	20,828 / 1,574	+2,498 / +70	357 / 10
06/30: total tests = 314,216			
07/03	24,111 / 1,668	+3,283 / +94	469 / 13
07/10	27,716 / 1,758	+3,605 / +90	515 / 13
07/15: IFR (infection fatality rate) = 6.02%			
07/17	31,858 / 1,860	+4,142 / +102	592 / 15
07/24	35,311 / 1,967	+3,453 / +107	493 / 15
07/31	39,067 / 2,112	+3,756 / +145	537 / 21
07/31: total tests = 473,633			
08/07	42,488 / 2,248	+3,421 / +136	489 / 19
08/14	45,998 / 2,419	+3,510 / +171	501 / 24
08/15: IFR (infection fatality rate) = 5.27%			
08/21	48,896 / 2,552	+2,898 / +133	414 / 19
08/28	51,416 / 2,807	+2,520 / +255	360 / 36
08/31: total tests = 620,853			
09/04	53,405 / 3,044	+1,989 / +237	284 / 34
09/11	55,361 / 3,145	+1,956 / +101	279 / 14
09/15: IFR (infection fatality rate) = 5.69%			

DATE	CASES / DEATHS	WEEKLY INCREASE	DAILY AVERAGE
09/18	57,483 / 3,249	+2,122 / +104	303 / 15
09/25	59,842 / 3,343	+2,359 / +94	337 / 13
09/30: total tests = 737,201			
10/02	62,200 / 3,455	+2,358 / +112	337 / 16
10/09	64,864 / 3,585	+2,664 / +130	381 / 19
10/15: IFR (infection fatality rate) = 5.50%			
10/16	67,594 / 3,692	+2,730 / +107	390 / 15
10/23	71,227 / 3,797	+3,633 / +105	519 / 15
10/30	75,584 / 3,961	+4,357 / +164	622 / 23
10/31: total tests = 846,889			
11/06	80,529 / 4,128	+4,945 / +167	706 / 24
11/13	87,488 / 4,290	+6,959 / +162	994 / 23
11/15: IFR (infection fatality rate) = 4.86%			
11/20	96,146 / 4,529	+8,658 / +239	1,237 / 34
11/27	108,343 / 4,857	+12,197 / +328	1,742 / 47
11/30: total tests = 1.021,895			
12/04	118,448 / 5,129	+10,105 / +272	1,444 / 39
12/11	129,979 / 5,542	+11,531 / +413	1,647 / 59
12/15: IFR (infection fatality rate) = 4.26%			
12/18	143,353 / 6,208	+13,374 / +666	1,911 / 95
12/25: Christmas			
12/25	146,557 / 6,303	+3,204 / +95	458 / 14
12/31: total tests =1,154,839			
01/01/2021	155,679 / 6,670	+9,122 / +367	1,303 / 52

BONUS: *Enjoy additional week from upcoming book: PANDEMIC 2021: The U.S. Edition*

01/08	176,567 / 7,153	+20,888 / +483	2,984 / 69

*The daily average column is rounded to the nearest whole person. The infection fatality rate (IFR) is the number of deaths divided by the number of confirmed cases. The case fatality rate (CFR), shown only at the end of the year, is the number of deaths divided by the number of confirmed cases *which have had an outcome* (either recovery or death). The CFR excludes active cases.

CHAPTER 61

~ NAVAJO NATION *~*

DATE	CASES / DEATHS	WEEKLY INCREASE	DAILY AVERAGE
04/10/20 Navajo Nation added as new category on worldometers.info			
04/10	558 / 22	N/A	N/A
04/15: IFR (infection fatality rate) = 3.94%			
04/17	1,042 / 41	+484 / +19	69 / 3
04/24	1,360 / 52	+318 / +11	45 / 1
04/30: total tests = 10,216			
05/01	2,141 / 71	+781 / +19	112 / 3
05/08	2,757 / 88	+616 / +17	88 / 2
05/15: IFR (infection fatality rate) = 3.50%			
05/15	3,632 / 127	+875 / +39	125 / 6
05/22	4,434 / 147	+802 / +20	115 / 3
05/29	5,044 / 167	+610 / +20	87 / 3
05/31: total tests = 29,903			
06/05	5,730 / 264	+686 / +97	98 / 14
06/12	6,470 / 303	+740 / +39	106 / 6
06/15: IFR (infection fatality rate) = 4.70%			
06/19	6,832 / 324	+362 / +21	52 / 3
06/26	7,278 / 348	+446 / +24	64 / 3
06/30: total tests = 51,699			
07/03	7,613 / 369	+335 / +21	48 / 3
07/10	8,042 / 386	+429 / +17	61 / 2
07/15: IFR (infection fatality rate) = 4.84%			
07/17	8,486 / 407	+444 / +21	63 / 3
07/24	8,768 / 434	+282 / +27	40 / 4
07/31	9,019 / 454	+251 / +20	36 / 3
07/31: total tests = 75,792			
08/07	9,257 / 468	+238 / +14	34 / 2
08/14	9,394 / 478	+137 / +10	20 / 1
08/15: IFR (infection fatality rate) = 5.09%			
08/21	9,531 / 489	+137 / +11	20 / 2
08/28	9,780 / 500	+249 / +11	36 / 2

DATE	CASES / DEATHS	WEEKLY INCREASE	DAILY AVERAGE
08/31: total tests = 92,206			
09/04	9,871 / 504	+91 / +4	13 / 1
09/11	9,933 / 530	+62 / +26	9 / 4
09/15: IFR (infection fatality rate) = 5.37%			
09/18	10,090 / 544	+157 / +14	22 / 2
09/25	10,167 / 551	+77 / +7	11 / 1
09/30: total tests = 102,753			
10/02	10,404 / 558	+237 / +7	34 / 1
10/09	10,632 / 564	+228 / +6	33 / 1
10/15: IFR (infection fatality rate) = 5.30%			
10/16	10,819 / 571	+187 / +7	27 / 1
10/23	11,101 / 574	+282 / +3	40 / 0
10/30	11,694 / 578	+593 / +4	85 / 1
10/31: total tests = 124,712			
11/06	12,288 / 591	+594 / +13	85 / 2
11/13	12,971 / 596	+683 / +5	98 / 1
11/15: IFR (infection fatality rate) = 4.50%			
11/20	14,085 / 618	+1,114 / +22	159 / 3
11/27	15,616 / 640	+1,531 / +22	219 / 3
11/30: total tests = 166,820			
12/04	17,310 / 663	+1,694 / +23	242 / 3
12/11	18,943 / 699	+1,633 / +36	233 / 5
12/15: IFR (infection fatality rate) = 3.65%			
12/18	20,575 / 742	+1,632 / +43	233 / 6
12/22: test positivity rate			
12/25	21,833 / 762	+1,258 / +20	180 / 3
12/31: total tests = 197,696			
01/01/2021	23,429 / 813	+1,596 / +51	228 / 7

BONUS: Enjoy additional week from upcoming book: PANDEMIC 2021: The U.S. Edition

01/08	24,521 / 844	+1,092 / +31	156 / 4

*The daily average column is rounded to the nearest whole person. The infection fatality rate (IFR) is the number of deaths divided by the number of confirmed cases. The case fatality rate (CFR), shown only at the end of the year, is the number of deaths divided by the number of confirmed cases *which have had an outcome* (either recovery or death). The CFR excludes active cases.

CHAPTER 62

~ FEDERAL PRISONS *~*

DATE	CASES / DEATHS	WEEKLY INCREASE	DAILY AVERAGE
04/19/20 Federal Prisons added as new category on worldometers.info			
04/24	977 / 24	N/A	N/A
04/30: total tests = not given			
05/01	2,185 / 36	+1,208 / +12	173 / 2
05/08	3,330 / 45	+1,145 / +9	164 / 1
05/15: IFR (infection fatality rate) = 1.52%			
05/15	3,629 / 55	+299 / +10	43 / 1
05/22	3,629 / 59	+0 / +4	0 / 1
05/29	5,679 / 64	+2,050 / +5	293 / 1
05/31: total tests = not given			
06/05	6,477 / 78	+798 / +14	114 / 2
06/12	6,833 / 81	+356 / +3	51 / 0
06/15: IFR (infection fatality rate) = 1.25%			
06/19	7,039 / 86	+206 / +5	29 / 1
06/26	7,301 / 90	+262 / +4	37 / 1
06/30: total tests = 22,110			
07/03	7,798 / 93	+497 / +3	71 / 0
07/10	8,749 / 95	+951 / +2	136 / 0
07/15: IFR (infection fatality rate) = 0.99%			
07/17	10,069 / 98	+1,320 / +3	189 / 0
07/24	11,318 / 100	+1,249 / +2	178 / 0
07/31	11,751 / 104	+433 / +4	62 / 1
07/31: total tests = 36,894			
08/07	12,249 / 112	+498 / +8	71 / 1
08/14	12,665 / 114	+416 / +2	59 / 0
08/15: IFR (infection fatality rate) = 0.90%			
08/21	13,280 / 117	+615 / +3	88 / 0
08/28	13,732 / 118	+452 / +1	65 / 0
08/31: total tests = 51,208			
09/04	14,328 / 120	+596 / +2	85 / 0
09/11	14,952 / 120	+624 / +0	89 / 0

DATE	CASES / DEATHS	WEEKLY INCREASE	DAILY AVERAGE
09/15: IFR (infection fatality rate) = 0.80%			
09/18	15,705 / 123	+753 / +3	108 / 0
09/25	16,447 / 126	+742 / +3	106 / 0
09/30: total tests = 59,865			
10/02	17,033 / 126	+586 / +0	15 / 0
10/09	17,329 / 127	+296 / +1	42 / 0
10/15: IFR (infection fatality rate) = 0.70%			
10/16	18,365 / 128	+1,036 / +1	148 / 0
10/23	19,148 / 130	+783 / +2	112 / 0
10/30	20,119 / 131	+971 / +1	139 / 0
10/31: total tests = 69,571			
11/06	21,233 / 136	+1,114 / +5	159 / 1
11/13	23,082 / 139	+1,849 / +3	264 / 1
11/15: IFR (infection fatality rate) = 0.60%			
11/20	25,195 / 143	+2,113 / +4	302 / 1
11/27	27,669 / 147	+2,474 / +4	353 / 1
11/30: total tests = 81,528			
12/04	30,933 / 151	+3,264 / +4	466 / 1
12/11	35,075 / 157	+4,142 / +6	592 / 1
12/15: IFR (infection fatality rate) = 0.45%			
12/18	37,934 / 170	+2,859 / +13	408 / 2
12/25	40,639 / 174	+2,705 / +4	386 / 1
12/31: total tests = 90,766			
01/01/2021	44,187 / 181	+3,549 / +7	507 / 1

BONUS: Enjoy additional week from upcoming book: PANDEMIC 2021: The U.S. Edition

DATE	CASES / DEATHS	WEEKLY INCREASE	DAILY AVERAGE
01/08	47,175 / 186	+2,988 / +5	427 / 1

*The daily average column is rounded to the nearest whole person. The infection fatality rate (IFR) is the number of deaths divided by the number of confirmed cases. The case fatality rate (CFR), shown only at the end of the year, is the number of deaths divided by the number of confirmed cases *which have had an outcome* (either recovery or death). The CFR excludes active cases.

SECTION V

YEAR-END SUMMARIES

CALIFORNIA: YEAR-END STATS
CASE COUNT RANK = #1
TOTAL CASES = 2,289,539
CASES/MILLION = 58,173
TOTAL DEATHS = 25,967
DEATHS/MILLION = 657
TOTAL TESTS = 33,058,311
TESTS/MILLION = 836,660
HOSPITALIZATIONS CURRENT = 21,449
HOSPITALIZATIONS CUMULATIVE = N/A
IFR (INFECTION FATALITY RATE) = 1.13%
CFR (CASE FATALITY RATE) = 2.61%
POPULATION ON 03/01/20 = 39,937,489
POPULATION ON 12/31/20 = 39,512,223

FLORIDA: YEAR-END STATS
CASE COUNT RANK = #3
TOTAL CASES = 1,323,315
CASES/MILLION = 61,613
TOTAL DEATHS = 21,673
DEATHS/MILLION = 1,009
TOTAL TESTS = 15,703,599
TESTS/MILLION = 731,157
HOSPITALIZATIONS CURRENT = 6,363
HOSPITALIZATIONS CUMULATIVE = 63,741
IFR (INFECTION FATALITY RATE) = 1.64%
CFR (CASE FATALITY RATE) = 2.86%
POPULATION ON 03/01/20 = 21,992,985
POPULATION ON 12/31/20 = 21,477,737

ILLINOIS: YEAR-END STATS
CASE COUNT RANK = #5
TOTAL CASES = 963,389
CASES/MILLION = 76,594
TOTAL DEATHS = 17,978
DEATHS/MILLION = 1,434
TOTAL TESTS = 13,374,665
TESTS/MILLION = 1,055,465
HOSPITALIZATIONS CURRENT = 4,093
HOSPITALIZATIONS CUMULATIVE = N/A
IFR (INFECTION FATALITY RATE) = 1.87%
CFR (CASE FATALITY RATE) = 2.54%
POPULATION ON O3/01/20 = 12,659,682
POPULATION ON 12/31/20 = 12,671,821

TEXAS: YEAR-END STATS
CASE COUNT RANK = #2
TOTAL CASES = 1,776,304
CASES/MILLION = 61,261
TOTAL DEATHS = 28,227
DEATHS/MILLION = 973
TOTAL TESTS = 15,699,242
TESTS/MILLION = 541,430
HOSPITALIZATIONS CURRENT = 12,268
HOSPITALIZATIONS CUMULATIVE = N/A
IFR (INFECTION FATALITY RATE) = 1.59%
CFR (CASE FATALITY RATE) = 1.91%
POPULATION ON 03/01/20 = 29,472,295
POPULATION ON 12/31/20 = 28,995,881

NEW YORK: YEAR-END STATS
CASE COUNT RANK = #4
TOTAL CASES = 1,015,573
CASES/MILLION = 52,885
TOTAL DEATHS = 38,007
DEATHS/MILLION = 1,961
TOTAL TESTS = 25,504,313
TESTS/MILLION = 1,311,036
HOSPITALIZATIONS CURRENT = 7,935
HOSPITALIZATIONS CUMULATIVE = 89,995
IFR (INFECTION FATALITY RATE) = 3.74%
CFR (CASE FATALITY RATE) = 7.38%
POPULATION ON 03/01/20 = 19,440,469
POPULATION ON 12/31/20 = 19,453,561

OHIO: YEAR-END STATS
CASE COUNT RANK = #6
TOTAL CASES = 700,380
CASES/MILLION = 59,917
TOTAL DEATHS = 8,962
DEATHS/MILLION = 767
TOTAL TESTS = 7,680,270
TESTS/MILLION = 657,045
HOSPITALIZATIONS CURRENT = 4,367
HOSPITALIZATIONS CUMULATIVE = 38,334
IFR (INFECTION FATALITY RATE) = 1.28%
CFR (CASE FATALITY RATE) = 1.59%
POPULATION ON 03/01/20
POPULATION ON 12/31/2020 = 11,689,100

GEORGIA: YEAR-END STATS

CASE COUNT RANK = #7
TOTAL CASES = 666,452
CASES/MILLION = 63,819
TOTAL DEATHS = 10,934
DEATHS/MILLION = 1,032
TOTAL TESTS = 5,806,022
TESTS/MILLION = 546,839
HOSPITALIZATIONS CURRENT = 4,937
HOSPITALIZATIONS CUMULATIVE = 42,084
IFR (INFECTION FATALITY RATE) = 1.64%
CFR (CASE FATALITY RATE) = 3.07%
POPULATION ON 03/01/20 = 10,736,059
POPULATION ON 12/31/20 = 10,617,423

TENNESSEE: YEAR-END STATS

CASE COUNT RANK = #9
TOTAL CASES = 586,802
CASES/MILLION = 85,926
TOTAL DEATHS = 6,907
DEATHS/MILLION = 1,011
TOTAL TESTS = 5,571,715
TESTS/MILLION = 815,870
HOSPITALIZATIONS CURRENT = 3,429
HOSPITALIZATIONS CUMULATIVE = 14,531
IFR (INFECTION FATALITY RATE) = 1.18%
CFR (CASE FATALITY RATE) = 1.34%
POPULATION ON 03/01/20 = 6,897,576
POPULATION ON 12/31/20 = 6,829,174

ARIZONA: YEAR-END STATS

CASE COUNT RANK = #11
TOTAL CASES = 520,207
CASES/MILLION = 72,852
TOTAL DEATHS = 8,864
DEATHS/MILLION = 1,239
TOTAL TESTS = 3,269,908
TESTS/MILLION = 449,242
HOSPITALIZATIONS CURRENT = 4,564
HOSPITALIZATIONS CUMULATIVE = 37,257
IFR (INFECTION FATALITY RATE) = 1.70%
CFR (CASE FATALITY RATE) = 10.61%
POPULATION ON 03/01/20 = 7,378,494
POPULATION ON 12/31/20 = 7,278,717

PENNSYLVANIA: YEAR-END STATS

CASE COUNT RANK = #8
TOTAL CASES = 646,060
CASES/MILLION = 51,004
TOTAL DEATHS = 16,073
DEATHS/MILLION = 1,272
TOTAL TESTS = 7,421,572
TESTS/MILLION = 579,720
HOSPITALIZATIONS CURRENT = 5,677
HOSPITALIZATIONS CUMULATIVE = N/A
IFR (INFECTION FATALITY RATE) = 2.49%
CFR (CASE FATALITY RATE) = 3.66%
POPULATION ON 03/01/20 = 12,820,878
POPULATION ON 12/31/20 = 12,801,989

NORTH CAROLINA: YEAR-END STATS

CASE COUNT RANK = #10
TOTAL CASES = 539,545
CASES/MILLION = 51,444
TOTAL DEATHS = 6,748
DEATHS/MILLION = 643
TOTAL TESTS = 6,898,509
TESTS/MILLION = 657,747
HOSPITALIZATIONS CURRENT = 3,472
HOSPITALIZATIONS CUMULATIVE = N/A
IFR (INFECTION FATALITY RATE) = 1.25%
CFR (CASE FATALITY RATE) = 1.64%
POPULATION ON 03/01/20 = 10,611,862
POPULATION ON 12/31/20 = 10,488,084

MICHIGAN: YEAR-END STATS

CASE COUNT RANK = #12
TOTAL CASES = 528,621
CASES/MILLION = 52,932
TOTAL DEATHS = 13,018
DEATHS/MILLION = 1,304
TOTAL TESTS = 8,630,181
TESTS/MILLION = 864,154
HOSPITALIZATIONS CURRENT = 2,758
HOSPITALIZATIONS CUMULATIVE = N/A
IFR (INFECTION FATALITY RATE) = 2.46%
CFR (CASE FATALITY RATE) = 3.93%
POPULATION ON 03/01/20 = 10,045,029
POPULATION ON 12/31/20 = 9,986,857

INDIANA: YEAR-END STATS
CASE COUNT RANK = #13
TOTAL CASES = 511,485
CASES/MILLION = 76,910
TOTAL DEATHS = 8,263
DEATHS/MILLION = 1,243
TOTAL TESTS = 5,730,043
TESTS/MILLION = 851,137
HOSPITALIZATIONS CURRENT = 2,842
HOSPITALIZATIONS CUMULATIVE = 34,999
IFR (INFECTION FATALITY RATE) = 1.62%
CFR (CASE FATALITY RATE) = 2.33%
POPULATION ON 03/01/20 = 6,745,354
POPULATION ON 12/31/20 = 6,732,219

WISCONSIN : YEAR-END STATS
CASE COUNT RANK = #15
TOTAL CASES = 481,102
CASES/MILLION = 82,956
TOTAL DEATHS = 4,859
DEATHS/MILLION = 836
TOTAL TESTS = 2,840,064
TESTS/MILLION = 487,780
HOSPITALIZATIONS CURRENT = 1,074
HOSPITALIZATIONS CUMULATIVE = 21,350
IFR (INFECTION FATALITY RATE) = 1.01%
CFR (CASE FATALITY RATE) = 1.07%
POPULATION ON 03/01/20 = 5,851,754
POPULATION ON 12/31/20 = 5,822,434

MINNESOTA: YEAR-END STATS
CASE COUNT RANK = #17
TOTAL CASES = 415,302
CASES/MILLION = 73,640
TOTAL DEATHS = 5,382
DEATHS/MILLION = 954
TOTAL TESTS = 5,574,962
TESTS/MILLION = 988,533
HOSPITALIZATIONS CURRENT = 895
HOSPITALIZATIONS CUMULATIVE = 21,864
IFR (INFECTION FATALITY RATE) = 1.30%
CFR (CASE FATALITY RATE) = 1.34%
POPULATION ON 03/01/20 = 5,700,671
POPULATION ON 12/31/20 = 5,639,632

NEW JERSEY: YEAR-END STATS
CASE COUNT RANK = #14
TOTAL CASES = 487,350
CASES/MILLION = 55,386
TOTAL DEATHS = 19,109
DEATHS/MILLION = 2,173
TOTAL TESTS = 7,792,714
TESTS/MILLION = 877,342
HOSPITALIZATIONS CURRENT = 3,716
HOSPITALIZATIONS CUMULATIVE = 47,326
IFR (INFECTION FATALITY RATE) = 3.92%
CFR (CASE FATALITY RATE) = 6.65%
POPULATION ON 03/01/20 = 8,936,574
POPULATION ON 12/31/20 = 8,882,190

MISSOURI: YEAR-END STATS
CASE COUNT RANK = #16
TOTAL CASES = 417,272
CASES/MILLION = 68,884
TOTAL DEATHS = 6,010
DEATHS/MILLION = 988
TOTAL TESTS = 4,080,302
TESTS/MILLION = 664,823
HOSPITALIZATIONS CURRENT = 2,777
HOSPITALIZATIONS CUMULATIVE = N/A
IFR (INFECTION FATALITY RATE) = 1.44%
CFR (CASE FATALITY RATE) = 4.50%
POPULATION ON 03/01/20 = 6,169,270
POPULATION ON 12/31/20 = 6,137,428

MASSACHUSETTS: YEAR-END STATS
CASE COUNT RANK = #18
TOTAL CASES = 375,178
CASES/MILLION = 54,433
TOTAL DEATHS = 12,423
DEATHS/MILLION = 1,802
TOTAL TESTS = 10,944,699
TESTS/MILLION = 1,587,914
HOSPITALIZATIONS CURRENT = 2,271
HOSPITALIZATIONS CUMULATIVE = 16,098
IFR (INFECTION FATALITY RATE) = 3.31%
CFR (CASE FATALITY RATE) = 4.21%
POPULATION ON 03/01/20 = 6,976,597
POPULATION ON 12/31/20 = 6,892,503

ALABAMA: YEAR-END STATS
CASE COUNT RANK = #19
TOTAL CASES = 361,226
CASES/MILLION = 74,594
TOTAL DEATHS = 4,827
DEATHS/MILLION = 994
TOTAL TESTS = 1,973,198
TESTS/MILLION = 402,432
HOSPITALIZATIONS CURRENT = 2,815
HOSPITALIZATIONS CUMULATIVE = 34,184
IFR (INFECTION FATALITY RATE) = 1.34%
CFR (CASE FATALITY RATE) = 2.35%
POPULATION ON 03/01/20 = 4,908,621
POPULATION ON 12/31/20 = 4,903,185

COLORADO: YEAR-END STATS
CASE COUNT RANK = #21
TOTAL CASES = 334,097
CASES/MILLION = 58,016
TOTAL DEATHS = 4,814
DEATHS/MILLION = 836
TOTAL TESTS = 2,135,590
TESTS/MILLION = 370,844
HOSPITALIZATIONS CURRENT = 1,086
HOSPITALIZATIONS CUMULATIVE = 18,598
IFR (INFECTION FATALITY RATE) = 1.44%
CFR (CASE FATALITY RATE) = 6.46%
POPULATION ON 03/01/20 = 5,845,526
POPULATION ON 12/31/20 = 5,758,736

SOUTH CAROLINA: YEAR-END STATS
CASE COUNT RANK = #23
TOTAL CASES = 307,507
CASES/MILLION = 59,725
TOTAL DEATHS = 5,296
DEATHS/MILLION = 1,029
TOTAL TESTS = 3,663,351
TESTS/MILLION = 711,508
HOSPITALIZATIONS CURRENT = 2,025
HOSPITALIZATIONS CUMULATIVE = 14,390
IFR (INFECTION FATALITY RATE) = 1.72%
CFR (CASE FATALITY RATE) = 3.39%
POPULATION 03/01/20 = 5,210,095
POPULATION ON 12/31/20 = 5,148,714

VIRGINIA: YEAR-END STATS
CASE COUNT RANK = #20
TOTAL CASES = 349,584
CASES/MILLION = 41,563
TOTAL DEATHS = 5,032
DEATHS/MILLION = 595
TOTAL TESTS = 5,148,590
TESTS/MILLION = 603,096
HOSPITALIZATIONS CURRENT = 2,744
HOSPITALIZATIONS CUMULATIVE = 18,041
IFR (INFECTION FATALITY RATE) = 1.44%
CFR (CASE FATALITY RATE) = 14.20%
POPULATION ON 03/01/20 = 8,626,207
POPULATION ON 12/31/20 = 8,535,519

LOUISIANA: YEAR-END STATS
CASE COUNT RANK = #22
TOTAL CASES = 315,275
CASES/MILLION = 67,819
TOTAL DEATHS = 7,448
DEATHS/MILLION = 1,611
TOTAL TESTS = 4,400,149
TESTS/MILLION = 946,514
HOSPITALIZATIONS CURRENT = 1,731
HOSPITALIZATIONS CUMULATIVE = N/A
IFR (INFECTION FATALITY RATE) = 2.36%
CFR (CASE FATALITY RATE) = 2.76%
POPULATION ON 03/01/20 = 4,645,184
POPULATION ON 12/31/20 = 4,648,794

OKLAHOMA: YEAR-END STATS
CASE COUNT RANK = #24
TOTAL CASES = 290,936
CASES/MILLION = 73,525
TOTAL DEATHS = 2,489
DEATHS/MILLION = 629
TOTAL TESTS = 2,669,170
TESTS/MILLION = 647,549
HOSPITALIZATIONS CURRENT = 1,924
HOSPITALIZATIONS CUMULATIVE = 17,059
IFR (INFECTION FATALITY RATE) = 0.86%
CFR (CASE FATALITY RATE) = 0.96%
POPULATION ON 03/01/20 = 3,958,821
POPULATION ON 12/31/20 = 3,956,971

IOWA: YEAR-END STATS
CASE COUNT RANK = #25
TOTAL CASES = 280,673
CASES/MILLION = 89,590
TOTAL DEATHS = 3,891
DEATHS/MILLION = 1,235
TOTAL TESTS = 1,360,191
TESTS/MILLION = 431,113
HOSPITALIZATIONS CURRENT = 600
HOSPITALIZATIONS CUMULATIVE = N/A
IFR (INFECTION FATALITY RATE) =   1.39%
CFR (CASE FATALITY RATE) = 1.59%
POPULATION ON 03/01/20 = 3,179,849
POPULATION ON 12/31/20 = 3,155,070

UTAH: YEAR END STATS
CASE COUNT RANK = #27
TOTAL CASES = 276,612
CASES/MILLION = 86,281
TOTAL DEATHS = 1,269
DEATHS/MILLION = 396
TOTAL TESTS = 2,673,611
TESTS/MILLION = 833,951
HOSPITALIZATIONS CURRENT = 565
HOSPITALIZATIONS CUMULATIVE = 10,956
IFR (INFECTION FATALITY RATE) = 0.46%
CFR (CASE FATALITY RATE) = 0.56%
POPULATION ON 03/01/20 = 3,282,115
POPULATION ON 12/31/20 = 3,205,958

WASHINGTON: YEAR-END STATS
CASE COUNT RANK = #29
TOTAL CASES = 249,800
CASES/MILLION = 32,804
TOTAL DEATHS = 3,564
DEATHS/MILLION = 468
TOTAL TESTS = 3,836,820
TESTS/MILLION = 503,857
HOSPITALIZATIONS CURRENT = 1,088
HOSPITALIZATIONS CUMULATIVE = 14,571
IFR (INFECTION FATALITY RATE) = 1.43%
CFR (CASE FATALITY RATE) = 3.39%
POPULATION ON 03/01/20 = 7,797,095
POPULATION ON 12/31/20 = 7,614,893

MARYLAND: YEAR-END STATS
CASE COUNT RANK = #26
TOTAL CASES = 276,662
CASES/MILLION = 46,350
TOTAL DEATHS = 5,895
DEATHS/MILLION = 983
TOTAL TESTS = 5,761,534
TESTS/MILLION = 953,000
HOSPITALIZATIONS CURRENT = 1,773
HOSPITALIZATIONS CUMULATIVE = 26,636
IFR (INFECTION FATALITY RATE) =   2.13%
CFR (CASE FATALITY RATE) = 38.84%
POPULATION ON 03/01/20 = 6,083,116
POPULATION ON 12/31/20 = 6,045,680

KANSAS: YEAR-END STATS
CASE COUNT RANK = #28
TOTAL CASES = 265,262
CASES/MILLION = 59,374
TOTAL DEATHS = 2,623
DEATHS/MILLION = 587
TOTAL TESTS = 3,414,879
TESTS/MILLION = 764,353
HOSPITALIZATIONS CURRENT = 1,673
HOSPITALIZATIONS CUMULATIVE = 13,488
IFR (INFECTION FATALITY RATE) = 0.99%
CFR (CASE FATALITY RATE) = 6.66%
POPULATION ON 03/01/20 = 4,499,692
POPULATION ON 12/31/20 = 4,467,673

KANSAS: YEAR-END STATS
CASE COUNT RANK = #30
TOTAL CASES = 224,795
CASES/MILLION = 78,174
TOTAL DEATHS = 2,741
DEATHS/MILLION = 988
TOTAL TESTS = 1,012,506
TESTS/MILLION = 347,544
HOSPITALIZATIONS CURRENT = 767
HOSPITALIZATIONS CUMULATIVE = 6,760
IFR (INFECTION FATALITY RATE) = 1.22%
CFR (CASE FATALITY RATE) = 1.91%
POPULATION ON 03/01/20 = 2,910,357
POPULATION ON 12/31/20 = 2,913,314

NEVADA: YEAR-END STATS
CASE COUNT RANK = #31
TOTAL CASES = 224,731
CASES/MILLION = 73,713
TOTAL DEATHS = 3,125
DEATHS/MILLION = 1,021
TOTAL TESTS = 2,095,778
TESTS/MILLION = 680,413
HOSPITALIZATIONS CURRENT = 1,927
HOSPITALIZATIONS CUMULATIVE = N/A
IFR (INFECTION FATALITY RATE) = 1.39%
CFR (CASE FATALITY RATE) = 2.71%
POPULATION ON 03/01/20 = 3,139,658
POPULATION ON 12/31/20 = 3,080,156

MISSISSIPPI: YEAR-END STATS
CASE COUNT RANK = #33
TOTAL CASES = 215,811
CASES/MILLION = 73,379
TOTAL DEATHS = 4,787
DEATHS/MILLION = 1,618
TOTAL TESTS = 1,730,435
TESTS/MILLION = 581,434
HOSPITALIZATIONS CURRENT = 1,463
HOSPITALIZATIONS CUMULATIVE = 8,145
IFR (INFECTION FATALITY RATE) = 2.22%
CFR (CASE FATALITY RATE) = 2.80%
POPULATION ON 03/01/20 = 2,989,260
POPULATION ON 12/31/20 = 2,976,149

NEBRASKA: YEAR-END STATS
CASE COUNT RANK = #35
TOTAL CASES = 166,798
CASES/MILLION = 86,227
TOTAL DEATHS = 1,651
DEATHS/MILLION = 853
TOTAL TESTS = 848,067
TESTS/MILLION = 438,412
HOSPITALIZATIONS CURRENT = 544
HOSPITALIZATIONS CUMULATIVE = 5,220
IFR (INFECTION FATALITY RATE) = 0.99%
CFR (CASE FATALITY RATE) = 1.51%
POPULATION ON 03/01/20 = 1,952,570
POPULATION ON 12/31/20 = 1,934,408

ARKANSAS: YEAR-END STATS
CASE COUNT RANK = #32
TOTAL CASES = 225,138
CASES/MILLION = 74,603
TOTAL DEATHS = 3,676
DEATHS/MILLION = 1,218
TOTAL TESTS = 2,297,510
TESTS/MILLION = 761,318
HOSPITALIZATIONS CURRENT = 1,195
HOSPITALIZATIONS CUMULATIVE = 11,358
IFR (INFECTION FATALITY RATE) = 1.63%
CFR (CASE FATALITY RATE) = 1.81%
POPULATION ON 03/01/20 = 3,038,099
POPULATION ON 12/31/20 = 3,017,804

CONNECTICUT: YEAR-END STATS
CASE COUNT RANK = #34
TOTAL CASES = 185,708
CASES/MILLION = 52,088
TOTAL DEATHS = 5,995
DEATHS/MILLION = 1,681
TOTAL TESTS = 4,309,664
TESTS/MILLION = 1,208,785
HOSPITALIZATIONS CURRENT = 1,136
HOSPITALIZATIONS CUMULATIVE = 12,257
IFR (INFECTION FATALITY RATE) = 3.23%
CFR (CASE FATALITY RATE) = 10.33%
POPULATION ON 03/01/20 = 3,563,077
POPULATION ON 12/31/20 = 3,565,287

NEW MEXICO: YEAR-END STATS
CASE COUNT RANK = #36
TOTAL CASES = 142,864
CASES/MILLION = 68,133
TOTAL DEATHS = 2,477
DEATHS/MILLION = 1,181
TOTAL TESTS = 1,970,212
TESTS/MILLION = 939,615
HOSPITALIZATIONS CURRENT = 803
HOSPITALIZATIONS CUMULATIVE = 9,689
IFR (INFECTION FATALITY RATE) = 1.73%
CFR (CASE FATALITY RATE) = 3.64%
POPULATION ON 03/01/20 = 2,096,640
POPULATION ON 12/31/2020 = 2,096,829

IDAHO: YEAR-END STATS
CASE COUNT RANK = #37
TOTAL CASES = 141,077
CASES/MILLION = 78,943
TOTAL DEATHS = 1,436
DEATHS/MILLION = 804
TOTAL TESTS = 859,851
TESTS/MILLION = 481,153
HOSPITALIZATIONS CURRENT = 375
HOSPITALIZATIONS CUMULATIVE = 5,567
IFR (INFECTION FATALITY RATE) = 1.02%
CFR (CASE FATALITY RATE) = 2.39%
POPULATION ON 03/01/20 = 1,826,156
POPULATION ON 12/31/20 = 1,787,065

SOUTH DAKOTA: YEAR-END STATS
CASE COUNT RANK = #39
TOTAL CASES = 99,164
CASES/MILLION = 112,093
TOTAL DEATHS = 1,488
DEATHS/MILLION = 1,682
TOTAL TESTS = 372,640
TESTS/MILLION = 421,224
HOSPITALIZATIONS CURRENT = 297
HOSPITALIZATIONS CUMULATIVE = 5,672
IFR (INFECTION FATALITY RATE) = 1.50%
CFR (CASE FATALITY RATE) = 1.59%
POPULATION ON 03/01/20 = 903,027
POPULATION ON 12/31/20 = 884,659

RHODE ISLAND: YEAR-END STATS
CASE COUNT RANK = #41
TOTAL CASES = 87,949
CASES/MILLION = 83,021
TOTAL DEATHS = 1,777
DEATHS/MILLION = 1,677
TOTAL TESTS = 1,974,498
TESTS/MILLION = 1,863,858
HOSPITALIZATIONS CURRENT = 426
HOSPITALIZATIONS CUMULATIVE = 6,506
IFR (INFECTION FATALITY RATE) = 2.02%
CFR (CASE FATALITY RATE) = 2.48%
POPULATION ON 03/01/20 = 1,056,161
POPULATION ON 12/31/20 = 1,059,361

OREGON: YEAR-END STATS
CASE COUNT RANK = #38
TOTAL CASES = 113,909
CASES/MILLION = 27,007
TOTAL DEATHS = 1,477
DEATHS/MILLION = 350
TOTAL TESTS = 2,652,670
TESTS/MILLION = 628,932
HOSPITALIZATIONS CURRENT = 524
HOSPITALIZATIONS CUMULATIVE = 6,498
IFR (INFECTION FATALITY RATE) = 1.30%
CFR (CASE FATALITY RATE) = N/A
POPULATION ON 03/01/20 = 4,301,089
POPULATION ON 12/31/20 = 4,217,737

NORTH DAKOTA: YEAR-END STATS
CASE COUNT RANK = #40
TOTAL CASES = 92,495
CASES/MILLION = 121,375
TOTAL DEATHS = 1,2925
DEATHS/MILLION = 1,695
TOTAL TESTS = 376,910
TESTS/MILLION = 494,592
HOSPITALIZATIONS CURRENT = 94
HOSPITALIZATIONS CUMULATIVE = 3,552
IFR (INFECTION FATALITY RATE) = 1.40%
CFR (CASE FATALITY RATE) = 1.43%
POPULATION ON 03/01/20 = 761,723
POPULATION ON 12/31/20 = 762,062

WEST VIRGINIA: YEAR-END STATS
CASE COUNT RANK = #42
TOTAL CASES = 85,334
CASES/MILLION = 49,003
TOTAL DEATHS = 1,338
DEATHS/MILLION = 759
TOTAL TESTS = 1,518,917
TESTS/MILLION = 847,540
HOSPITALIZATIONS CURRENT = 801
HOSPITALIZATIONS CUMULATIVE = N/A
IFR (INFECTION FATALITY RATE) = 1.57%
CFR (CASE FATALITY RATE) = 2.21%
POPULATION ON 03/01/20 = 1,778,070
POPULATION ON 12/31/20 = 1,792,147

MONTANA: YEAR END STATS
CASE COUNT RANK = #43
TOTAL CASES = 81,555
CASES/MILLION = 76,307
TOTAL DEATHS = 961
DEATHS/MILLION = 899
TOTAL TESTS = 791,589
TESTS/MILLION = 740,649
HOSPITALIZATIONS CURRENT = 203
HOSPITALIZATIONS CUMULATIVE = 3,568
IFR (INFECTION FATALITY RATE) = 1.18%
CFR (CASE FATALITY RATE) = 1.27%
POPULATION ON 03/01/20 = 1,086,759
POPULATION ON 12/31/20 = 1,068,778

ALASKA: YEAR-END STATS
CASE COUNT RANK = #45
TOTAL CASES = 45,461
CASES/MILLION = 62,144
TOTAL DEATHS = 205
DEATHS/MILLION = 280
TOTAL TESTS = 1,275,750
TESTS/MILLION = 1,743,912
HOSPITALIZATIONS CURRENT = 79
HOSPITALIZATIONS CUMULATIVE = 1,023
IFR (INFECTION FATALITY RATE) = 0.45%
CFR (CASE FATALITY RATE) = N/A
POPULATION ON 03/01/20 = 734,002
POPULATION ON 12/31/20 = 731,545

NEW HAMPSHIRE: YEAR-END STATS
CASE COUNT RANK = #47
TOTAL CASES = 44,028
CASES/MILLION = 32,380
TOTAL DEATHS = 759
DEATHS/MILLION = 558
TOTAL TESTS = 1,032,929
TESTS/MILLION = 759,668
HOSPITALIZATIONS CURRENT = 317
HOSPITALIZATIONS CUMULATIVE = 902
IFR (INFECTION FATALITY RATE) = 1.72%
CFR (CASE FATALITY RATE) = 1.99%
POPULATION ON 03/01/20 = 1,371,246
POPULATION ON 12/31/20 = 1,359,711

DELAWARE: YEAR-END STATS
CASE COUNT RANK = #44
TOTAL CASES = 57,456
CASES/MILLION = 59,004
TOTAL DEATHS = 926
DEATHS/MILLION = 951
TOTAL TESTS = 510,085
TESTS/MILLION = 523,828
HOSPITALIZATIONS CURRENT = 411
HOSPITALIZATIONS CUMULATIVE = N/A
IFR (INFECTION FATALITY RATE) = 1.61%
CFR (CASE FATALITY RATE) = N/A
POPULATION ON 03/01/20 = 982,895
POPULATION ON 12/31/20 = 973,764

WYOMING: YEAR-END STATS
CASE COUNT RANK = #46
TOTAL CASES = 44,409
CASES/MILLION = 76,731
TOTAL DEATHS = 438
DEATHS/MILLION = 757
TOTAL TESTS = 501,784
TESTS/MILLION = 867,000
HOSPITALIZATIONS CURRENT = 113
HOSPITALIZATIONS CUMULATIVE = 1,102
IFR (INFECTION FATALITY RATE) = 0.99%
CFR (CASE FATALITY RATE) = 1.02%
POPULATION ON 03/01/20 = 567,025
POPULATION ON 12/31/20 = 578,759

WASHINGTON D.C: YEAR-END STATS
CASE COUNT RANK = #(48)
TOTAL CASES = 28,963
CASES/MILLION = 41,448
TOTAL DEATHS = 786
DEATHS/MILLION = 1,117
TOTAL TESTS = 904,302
TESTS/MILLION = 1,281,337
HOSPITALIZATIONS CURRENT = 234
HOSPITALIZATIONS CUMULATIVE = N/A
IFR (INFECTION FATALITY RATE) = 2.71%
CFR (CASE FATALITY RATE) = 3.63%
POPULATION ON 03/01/20 = 720,687
POPULATION ON 12/31/20 = 705,749

MAINE: YEAR-END STATS
CASE COUNT RANK = #49 (48)
TOTAL CASES = 24,201
CASES/MILLION = 18,004
TOTAL DEATHS = 347
DEATHS/MILLION = 258
TOTAL TESTS = 1,207,730
TESTS/MILLION = 898,467
HOSPITALIZATIONS CURRENT = 177
HOSPITALIZATIONS CUMULATIVE = 1,065
IFR (INFECTION FATALITY RATE) = 1.43%
CFR (CASE FATALITY RATE) = 2.96%
POPULATION ON 03/01/20 = 1,345,790
POPULATION ON 12/31/20 = 1,344,212

VERMONT: YEAR-END STATS
CASE COUNT RANK = #51 (50)
TOTAL CASES = 7,276
CASES/MILLION = 11,878
TOTAL DEATHS = 136
DEATHS/MILLION = 218
TOTAL TESTS = 697,705
TESTS/MILLION = 1,118,137
HOSPITALIZATIONS CURRENT = 31
HOSPITALIZATIONS CUMULATIVE = N/A
IFR (INFECTION FATALITY RATE) = 1.87%
CFR (CASE FATALITY RATE) = 2.67%
POPULATION ON 03/01/20 = 628,061
POPULATION ON 12/31/20 = 623,989

HAWAII: YEAR-END STATS
CASE COUNT RANK = #50 (49)
TOTAL CASES = 21,397
CASES/MILLION = 15,112
TOTAL DEATHS = 288
DEATHS/MILLION = 203
TOTAL TESTS = 812,338
TESTS/MILLION = 573,737
HOSPITALIZATIONS CURRENT = 97
HOSPITALIZATIONS CUMULATIVE = 1,768
IFR (INFECTION FATALITY RATE) = 1.35%
CFR (CASE FATALITY RATE) = 2.14%
POPULATION ON 03/01/20 = 1,412,687
POPULATION ON 12/31/20 = 1,415,872

SECTION VI

REFERENCES
& RESOURCES

Introduction

1. South China Morning Post. Exclusive | Coronavirus: China's First Confirmed COVID-19 Case Traced Back to November 17. Josephine Ma. March 13, 2020. scmp.com.

2. World Health Organization. WHO Director-Generals' Opening Remarks at the Media Briefing on COVID-19. March 3, 2020. www.who.int.

3. CNBC. WHO Says Coronavirus Death Rates is 3.4% Globally, Higher than Previously Thought. Berkeley Lovelace Jr. and Noah Higgins-Dunn. March 3, 2020. www.cnbc.com.

4. Worldometers. worldometers.info/coronavirus.

5. CNet. The Twisted, Messy Hunt for COVID-19's Origin and the Lab Leak Theory. Jackson Ryan. February 6, 2021. www.cnet.com.

6. PBS Frontline. A Timeline of China's Response in the First Days of COVID-19. Priyanka Boghani. February 2, 2021. www.pbs.org.

7. Daily Mail. China Lab Leak Is the 'Most Credible' Source of the Coronavirus Outbreak, Says Top US Government Official, Amid Bombshell Claims Wuhan Scientist Has Turned Whistleblower. Abul Tahur. January 2, 2021. www.dailymail.co.uk.

8. JAMA Network. COVID-19 – New Insights on a Rapidly Changing Epidemic. Carlos del Rio, MD and Preeti N. Malani, MD, MSJ. February 28, 2020. www.jamanetwork.com.

9. South China Morning Post. No Link with Seafood Market in First Case of China Coronavirus, Chinese Scientists Revealed. Teddy Ng. January 25, 2020. www.scmp.com.

10. US News & World Report. China Government Spokesman Says U.S. Army Might Have Brought Virus to China. Reuters. March 12, 2020. www.usnews.com.

11. Centers for Disease Control and Prevention. SARS Basic Fact Sheet. www.cdc.gov.

12. BioSpace. Compare Update: 2003 SARS Pandemic Versus 2020 COVID-19 Pandemic. Gail Dutton. September 7, 2020. www.biospace.com.

13. Merck Manual. Sepsis and Septic Shock. Paul M. Maggio, MD. January, 2020. www.merckmanual.com.

14. Science Direct. Journal of Infection: Current Epidemiological and Clinical Features of COVID-19: a Global Perspective from China. Huilan Tu et al. www.sciencedirect.com.

15. Web MD. Symptoms of Coronavirus. www.webmd.com

16. CNN Health. Coronavirus Symptoms: A List and When to Seek Help. Sandee Lamotte. March 31, 2020. www.cnn.com.

17. Centers for Disease Control and Prevention. Symptoms of Coronavirus. May 13, 2020. www.cdc.gov.

18. UC Davis Health. Long Haulers: Why Some People Experience Long-Term Coronavirus Symptoms. January 15, 2021. www.health.ucdavis.edu.

19. Drugs.com. How Do COVID-19 Symptoms Progress and What Causes Death? Melisa Puckey. April 7, 2020. www.cnn.com.

20. Refinery 29. Let's Talk About COVID-19 Immunity. Elizabeth Gulino. November 5, 2020. www.refinery29.com.

21. Centers for Disease Control and Prevention. Emerging Infectious Diseases: High Contagiousness and Rapid Spread of Severe Acute Respiratory Syndrome Coronavirus 2. Steven Sanche et al. Vol. 26 No. 7. July 2020. www.cdc.gov.

22. Worldometers. Coronavirus Incubation period. March 12, 2020. www.worldometers.info.

23. CBS News. Pediatrician Says 80% of Kids Likely Have Coronavirus, but They're So Asymptomatic You'd Never Know. Christina Capatides. April 14, 2020. www.cbsnews.com.

24. BGR Science. The Coronavirus Might Not Spread Exactly How We Thought. Chris Smith. October 29, 2020. www.bgr.com.

25. Centers for Disease Control and Prevention. Emerging Infectious Diseases. COVID-19 Outbreak Associated with Air Conditioning in Restaurant, Guangzhou, China, 2020. Jianyun Lu et al. Vol. 26, No. 7, July 2020. www.cdc.gov.

26. Science News. Just Breathing or Talking May Be Enough to Spread COVID-19 After All. Tina Hesman Saey. April 2, 2020. www.sciencenews.org.

27. Worldometers. www.worldometers.info/coronavirus.

28. Daily Mail. How Did Covid REALLY Spread Around the World? Sam Blanchard. December 2, 2020. www.dailymail.co.uk.

29. CNet. Outbreak of Mysterious Illness in China Traced to Never-Before-Seen Virus. Amanda Kooser. January 9, 2020. www.cnet.com.
30. CIDRAP. China Releases Genetic Data on New Coronavirus, Now Deadly. Lisa Schnirring. January 11, 2020. www.cidrap.umn.edu.
31. History Link. First Confirmed Case of COVID-19 in the United States is Diagnosed in Snohomish County on January 20, 2020. Alan J. Stein. April 20, 2020. www.historylink.org.
32. Wikipedia. Timeline of the COVID-19 Pandemic in January 2020. en.wikipedia.org.
33. The Wall Street Journal. Trump Announces Coronavirus Task Force. Rebecca Ballhaus. January 29, 2020. www.wsj.com.
34. Reuters. Fact Check: Contaminated CDC COVID-19 Test Kits Recalled and Did Not Spread Virus. Reuters Staff. July 14, 2020. www.reuters.com.
35. Poynter. 'We Have It Totally Under Control.' A Timeline of President Donald Trump's Response to the Coronavirus Pandemic. John Greenberg. March 24, 2020. www.poynter.org.
36. USA Today. U.S. Passes Italy, China as Nation with the Most Confirmed Cases of COVID-19. Michael James. March 26, 2020. www.usatoday.com.
37. Washington State Department of Health. Non-Pharmaceutical Interventions (NPI) Implementation Guide. February 2020. www.dshs.wa.gov.
38. Pub Med. The Impact of Non-Pharmaceutical Interventions on SARS-CoV-2 Transmission Across 130 Countries and Territories. Lang Liu et al. Feb. 5, 2021. www.pubmed.ncbi.nlm.nih.gov.
39. Yahoo News. The Countries with the Best Coronavirus Success Stories and How They Did It. Katherine Chatfield. June 5, 2020. https://au.news.yahoo.com.
40. HHS.gov. Secretary Azar Declares Public Health Emergency for United States for 2019 Novel Coronavirus. January 31, 2020. www.hhs.gov.
41. The White House. Proclamation on Suspension of Entry as Immigrants and Nonimmigrants of Persons Who Pose a Risk of Transmitting 2019 Novel Coronavirus. January 31, 2020. www.whitehouse.gov.
42. Global Security. US' China Travel Ban an 'Overreaction' to WHO Declaration. January 31, 2020. www.globalsecurity.org.
43. NOQ Report. COVID-19 from the Start: The Definitive Coronavirus Timeline. Rich Weinstein. April 20, 2020. https://noqreport.com.
44. New York Times. 430,000 People Have Traveled from China to U.S. Since Coronavirus Surfaced. Steve Eder. April 4, 2020. www.nytimes.com.
45. JAMA Network. From Containment to Mitigation of COVID-19 in the U.S. Stephen M. Parodi, MD and Vincent X. Liu, MD, MSC. March 13, 2020. www.jamanetwork.com.
46. Live Science. Coronavirus: What Is 'Flattening the Curve,' and Will It Work? Brandon Specktor. March 16, 2020. www.livescience.com.
47. The Wall Street Journal. How the CDC's Restrictive Testing Guidelines Hid the Coronavirus Epidemic. Jessica Wang, et al. March 22, 2020. www.wsj.com.
48. Huff Post. How South Korea Succeeded Where the U.S. Has Failed on Coronavirus Testing. Chad Terhune, et al. March 18, 2020. www.huffpost.com.
49. NY Mag. Intelligencer. Why Has the Republican Response to the Pandemic Been So Mind-Bogglingly Disastrous? Jonathan Chait. July 20, 2020. www.nymag.com.
50. Breitbart. Poll: Nearly One-Third of Americans Do Not Believe Coronavirus Death Toll Is as High as Reported. Hannah Bleau. July 22, 2020. www.breitbart.com.
51. ABC News. Number of NY Nursing Home Residents Lost to COVID-19 Underreported by Up to 50%, Probe Says. Laura Romero. January 28, 2021. www.abcnews.go.com.
52. Centers for Disease Control and Prevention. "Excess Death" Data Point to Pandemic's True Toll. October 27, 2020. www.cdc.gov.
53. New York Times. 120,000 Missing Deaths: Tracking the True Toll of the Coronavirus Outbreak. Jin Wu et al. Updated regularly. www.nytimes.com.
54. Wikipedia. COVID-19 Pandemic in the United States. en.wikipedia.org.
55. Centers for Disease Control and Prevention. Emerging SARS-CoV-2 Variants. January 28, 2021. www.cdc.gov.

56. Vox. A Detailed Timeline of All the Ways Trump Failed to Respond to the Coronavirus. Cameron Peters. June 8, 2020. www.vox.com.
57. National Governor's Association. COVID-19: What You Need to Know. Updated regularly. https://www.nga.org/state-COVID-19-emergency-orders.
58: AARP. State-By-State Guide to Face Mask Requirements. Andy Markowitz. Updated regularly. www.aarp.org.
59. Centers for Disease Control and Prevention. National Center for Health Statistics. Excess Deaths Associated with COVID-19. www.cdc.gov/nchs.
60. Masks4All. What U.S. States Require Masks in Public? Updated daily. https://masks4all.co.
61. CNN Politics. Presidential Results. https://www.cnn.com/election/2020/results/president.
62. Centers for Disease Control and Prevention. Covid VIEW. Number of Specimens Tested and Percent Positive for SARS-CoV-2. www.cdc.gov.
63. The Covid Tracking Project. https://covidtracking.com/data.
64. Becker's Hospital Review. States Ranked by COVID-19 Test Positivity Rates. Updated Daily. www.beckershospitalreview.com.
65. Los Angeles Times. U.S. Deaths Are About 300,000 Higher than Expected Since the Coronavirus Arrived. Karen Kaplan. October 20, 2020. www.latimes.com.

Timeline: The Birth of a Pandemic.

1. South China Morning Post. Coronavirus: China's First Confirmed COVID-19 Case Traced Back to November 17. Josephine Ma. Mar. 13, 2020. www.scmp.com.
2. Science Magazine. Wuhan Seafood Market May Not Be Source of Novel Virus Spreading Globally. Jon Cohen. January 26, 2020. www.sciencemag.org.
3. Senator Tom Cotton. Cotton Op-Ed in the Wall Street Journal: 'Coronavirus and the Laboratories in Wuhan.' Tom Cotton. April 21, 2020. www.cotton.senate.gov.
4. New England Journal of Medicine. Early Transmission Dynamics in Wuhan, China, of Novel Coronavirus-Infected Pneumonia. Qun Li et al. March 26, 2020. www.nejm.org.
5. The Washington Post. Early Missteps and State Secrecy in China Probably Allowed the Coronavirus to Spread Farther and Faster. Gerry Shih et al. February 1, 2020. www.washingtonpost.com.
6. Conservative Firing Line. Did China Hide the Coronavirus to Help Get U.S.–China Trade Deal Done? Robert Romano. May 12, 2020. https://conservativefiringonline.com.
7. New York Post. Whistleblowing Coronavirus Doctor at Wuhan Hospital Mysteriously Vanishes. Amanda Woods. April 1, 2020. https://nypost.com.
8. CounterPunch. How China Learned About SARS-CoV-2 in the Weeks Before the Global Pandemic. Vijay Prashad et al. April 8, 2020. www.counterpunch.org.
9. The Lancet. Genomic Characterization and Epidemiology of 2019 Novel Coronavirus: Implications for Virus Origins and Receptor Binding. Xiang Zhao, MD et al. February 22, 2020. www.thelancet.com.
10. The Epoch Times. 100,000 Hospital Beds to Be Added in Hubei, China, Ground Zero of Coronavirus Outbreak." Evan Fu. January 27, 2020. www.theepochtimes.com.
11. CGTN. Everyone's in the Same Boat: Inside a Private Wuhan Hospital Taking on Coronavirus. Zhao Junzhu and Yu Jing. May 18, 2020. news.cgtn.com.
12. The New York Times. 430,000 People Have Traveled from China to U.S. Since Coronavirus Surfaced. Steve Eder, et al. April 4, 2020. www.nytimes.com.
13. Hudson Institute. Coronavirus Timeline. April 14, 2020. www.hudson.org.
14. CIDRAP. China Releases Genetic Data on New Coronavirus, Now Deadly. Lisa Schnirring. January 11, 2020. www.cidrap.umn.edu.
15. Vox. China Hid the Severity of Its Coronavirus Outbreak and Muzzled Whistleblowers – Because It Can. Julia Belluz. February 10, 2020. www.vox.com.
16. Daily Wire. Here's a Timeline of the Coronavirus Outbreak and China's Coverup. Ashe Schow. March 20, 2020. www.dailywire.com.
17. Axios. Timeline: The Early Days of China's Coronavirus Outbreak and Cover-Up. Bethany Allen-Ebrahimian. March 18, 2020. www.axios.com.

18. CCN. China, U.S. Discussed Coronavirus Threat in December—and Failed Us All. September 23, 2020. www.ccn.com.
19. Wikipedia. Timeline of the COVID-19 Pandemic in December 2019. https://en.wikipedia.org.
20. The Washington Post. The U.S. Was Beset by Denial and Dysfunction as the Coronavirus Raged. Yasmeen Abutaleb et al. April 4, 2020. www.washingtonpost.com.
21. The Lancet. A Familial Cluster of Pneumonia Associated with the 2019 Novel Coronavirus Indicating Person-to-Person Transmission: a Study of a Family Cluster. Jasper Fuk-Woo Chan, MD et al. www.thelancet.com.
22. TownHall. Here's the Timeline of The Trump Administration's Response to the Wuhan Coronavirus. Beth Baumann. April 13, 2020. www.townhall.com.
23. CNBC. Here's Why People Are Panic Buying and Stockpiling Toilet Paper to Cope with Coronavirus Fears. Chloe Taylor. March 11, 2020. www.cnbc.com.
24. Centers for Disease Control and Prevention. COVID-19 Travel Recommendations by Destination. Continually updated. www.cdc.gov.
25. Time Magazine. What Is Contact Tracing? Here's How It Could Be Used to Help Fight Coronavirus. Alejandro de la Garza. April 22, 2020. https://time.com.
26. World Health Organization. WHO Statement Regarding Cluster of Pneumonia Cases in Wuhan, China. January 9, 2020. www.who.int.
27. Worldometers. www.worldometers.info/coronavirus.
28. Mayo Clinic. COVID-19: Who's at Higher Risk of Serious Symptoms? www.mayoclinic.org.
29. Shine. China Shares Genetic Sequence of Novel Coronavirus from Wuhan: WHO. Xu Qing. January 13, 2020. www.shine.cn.
30. The Washington Times. Thai Officials Confirm First Case of Coronavirus Outside China. Shen Wu Tan. January 13, 2020. www.washingtontimes.com.
31. Daily Wire. Here's a Timeline of the Coronavirus Outbreak and China's Coverup. Ashe Schow. March 20, 2020. www.dailywire.com.
32. Technology Networks. Researchers Develop First Diagnostic Test for Novel Coronavirus in China. Original Story from DZIF. January 20, 2020. www.technologynetworks.com.
33. Associated Press. German Researchers Develop 1st Test for New Virus from China. January 16, 2020. www.apnews.com.
34. CDC Newsroom. Public Health Screening to Begin at 3 U..S. Airports for 2019 Novel Coronavirus ("2019-nCoV"). January 17, 2020. www.cdc.gov.
35. Centers for Disease Control and Prevention. Transcript of 2019 Novel Coronavirus Response Telebriefing. January 17, 2020. www.cdc.gov.
36. The Star. Wuhan Neighborhood Sees Infections after 40,000 Families Gather for Potluck. February 6, 2020. www.thestar.com.
37. The Daily Beast. Trump Didn't Like Azar's Warnings. So He Disappeared Him. Eleanor Clift. April 14, 2020. www.thedailybeast.com.
38. CNN. 'It's Going to Disappear'" A Timeline of Trump's Claims that COVID-19 Will Vanish. Daniel Wolfe and Daniel Dale. October 31, 2020. www.cnn.com.
39. AlJazeera. China Confirms Human-to-Human Transmission of New Coronavirus. January 20, 2020. www.aljazeera.com.
40. Wikipedia. National Responses to the COVID-19 Pandemic. en.wikipedia.org.
41. The New York Times. First Patient with Wuhan Coronavirus Is Identified in the U.S. Roni Caryn Rabin. January 21, 2020. www.nytimes.com.
42. Business Insider. 5 Million People Left Wuhan Before China Quarantined the City to Contain the Coronavirus Outbreak. Ashley Collman. January 27, 2020. www.businessinsider.com.
43. Global News. Where Did They Go? Millions Fled Wuhan, China, Before Coronavirus Lockdown." Erika Kinetz. The Associated Press. February 9, 2020. https://globalnews.ca.
44. FactCheck.org. Trump's Spin on 'Broken' Testing. Lori Robertson. April 1, 2020. www.factcheck.org.
45. Live5 News. Different Strains of Coronavirus Causing Confusion, Concerns. Patrick Phillips. January 31, 2020. www.live5news.com.

46. Daily Caller. FLASHBACK: January 21: Fauci Says Coronavirus 'Not a Major Threat' to U.S. William Davis. April 3, 2020.
47. The New York Times. A Complete List of Trump's Attempts to Play Down Coronavirus. David Leonhardt. March 15, 2020. www.nytimes.com.
48. NPR. A Timeline of Coronavirus Comments from President Trump and WHO. Tamara Keith and Malaka Gharib. April 15, 2020. www.npr.org.
49. The Atlantic. All the President's Lies about the Coronavirus. Christian Paz. May 28. www.theatlantic.com.
50. YouTube. NBC News. Timeline: Trump's Response to the Coronavirus Outbreak. March 31, 2020. www.youtube.com.
51. Vox. The US Was Offered Millions of Masks in January. The Trump Administration Turned the Offer Down. Riley Beggin. May 10, 2020. www.vox.com.
52. The Guardian. Coronavirus: China Mask Producers Work Overtime to Meet Demand. January, 2020. www.theguardian.com.
53. Markets Insider. These 3 Small Pharmaceutical Stocks Are Surging after Announcing Work on a Coronavirus Vaccine. Carmen Reinicke. January 27, 2020. https://markets.businessinsider.com.
54. Meaww. Wuhan Coronavirus: China Is Secretly Cremating Bodies and Lying in the Official Figures, Says Shocking Reports. Kunal Dey. January 31, 2020. www.meaww.com.
55. Watts Up With That. China Corona Virus Horror: Hospital Corridor of the Dead and Dying. Eric Worrall. January 24, 2020. www.wattsupwiththat.com.
56. Breitbart. Exclusive—Tom Cotton Urges Trump Administration to Consider Banning Travel from China over Coronavirus. Matthew Boyle. January 22, 2020. www.breitbart.com.
57. NPR. As Testing Quickly Ramps Up, Expect More U.S. Coronavirus Cases. Nell Greenfieldboyce. March 1, 2020. www.npr.org.
58. Politico. U.S. Health Officials Probe Coronavirus Test Problems at CDC. David Lim, et al. March 1, 2020. www.politico.com.
59. Politico. Wearing a Mask Is for Smug Liberals. Refusing to Is for Reckless Republicans. Ryan Lizza and Daniel Lippman. May 1, 2020. www.politico.com.
60. Science Direct. Psychological Factors Underlying Adherence to COVID-19 Regulations. January, 2020. Volume 2, Issue 1. www.sciencedirect.com.
61. Reuters. Wuhan Lockdown 'Unprecedented', Shows Commitment to Contain Virus: WHO Representative in China. January 23, 2020. www.reuters.com.
62. Wikipedia. COVID-19 Pandemic Lockdown in Hubei. https://en.wikipedial.org.
63. STAT. WHO Praises China's Response to Coronavirus, Will Reconvene Expert Committee to Assess Global Threat. Andrew Joseph and Megan Thielking. January 29, 2020. www.statnews.com.
64. BuzzFeed News. Trump's Biggest Supporters Think the Coronavirus Is a Deep State Plot. Ryan Broderick. February 26, 2020. www.buzzfeednews.com.
65. CNN Business. As Coronavirus Spreads, So Does Online Misinformation. Donnie O'Sullivan. January 30, 2020. www.edition.cnn.com.
66. CNN. These Countries Have Evacuated Citizens from Wuhan Because of the Coronavirus. Tara John and Tatiana Arias. January 29, 2020. www.edition.cnn.com.
67. Conservative Firing Line. Did China Hide the Coronavirus to Help Get U.S.–China Trade Deal Done? Robert Romano. May 12, 2020. https://conservativefiringonline.com.
68. The Washington Post. Early Missteps and State Secrecy in China Probably Allowed the Coronavirus to Spread Farther and Faster. Gerry Shih et al. February 1, 2020. www.washingtonpost.com.
69. The Epoch Times. 100,000 Hospital Beds to Be Added in Hubei, China, Ground Zero of Coronavirus Outbreak." Evan Fu. January 27, 2020. www.theepochtimes.com.
70. CNBC. In Pictures: China Is Building Two Hospitals in Less than Two Weeks to Combat Coronavirus. Hannah Miller. February 1, 2020. www.cnbc.com.
71. Politico. 15 Times Trump Praised China as Coronavirus Was Spreading Across the Globe. Myah Ward April 15, 2020. www.politico.com.
72. Forbes. How the CDC Botched Its Initial Coronavirus Response with Faulty Tests. Rachel Sandler. March 2, 2020. www.forbes.com.

73. Reuters. Over 100 Countries Ask South Korea for Coronavirus Testing Help. Hyonhee Shin and Ann Kauranen. April 1, 2020. www.reuters.com.
74. Vox. Hong Kong Declares a State of Emergency in Response to Five Confirmed Coronavirus Cases. Catherine Kim. January 25, 2020. www.vox.com.
75. Reuters. China Says Virus Ability to Spread Getting Stronger. January 26, 2020. www.reuters.com.
76. STAT. U.S. to Quarantine All American Citizens Evacuated from Wuhan, as CDC Raises Pandemic Possibility. Andrew Joseph. January 31, 2020. www.statnews.com.
77. Yahoo! News. China Races Against the Clock to Build Virus Hospitals. Sebastien Ricci. January 27, 2020. www.news.yahoo.com.
78. Yahoo! News. Confusion as WHO Corrects China Virus Global Risk Level. Dario Thuburn. January 27, 2020. www.news.yahoo.com.
79. The Spokesman Review. Stocks Tumble as Virus Fears Spark Sell-Off; Dow Falls 453 Points. Alex Veiga and Damian J. Troise. Associated Press. January 27, 2020. www.spokesman.com.
80. Yahoo! News. As Coronavirus Spreads, Biden Says Trump Is 'the Worst Possible Person' to Keep America Safe. Andrew Romano. January 28, 2020. www.news.yahoo.com.
81. South China Morning Post. Experts Estimate There Are Upwards of 44,000 Infected Residents in Wuhan. Victor Ting. January 27, 2020. www.scmp.com.
82. New York Times. 430,000 People Have Traveled from China to U.S. Since Coronavirus Surfaced. Steve Eder et al. April 4, 2020. www.nytimes.com.
83. CNBC. Elizabeth Warren Releases Plan to Prevent and Contain Infectious Diseases Amid Coronavirus Outbreak. Tucker Higgins. January 28, 2020. www.cnbc.com.
84. CBS News. Trump Creates Task Force to Lead U.S. Coronavirus Response. No author. January 30, 2020. www.cbsnews.com.
85. Market Watch. U.S. Health Officials Say Americans Shouldn't Wear Face Masks to Prevent Coronavirus. Elizabeth Buchwald. March 2, 2020. www.marketwatch.com.
86. Reuters. To Mask or Not to Mask: Confusion Spreads over Coronavirus Protection. John Geddie and Joseph Sipalan. January 31, 2020. www.reuters.com.
87. The New York Times. He Could Have Seen What Was Coming: Behind Trump's Failure on the Virus. Eric Lipton et al. April 11, 2020. www.nytimes.com.
88. Axios. Navarro Memos Warning of Mass Coronavirus Death Circulated in January. Jonathan Swan and Margaret Talev. April 7, 2020. www.axios.com.
89. NPR. A Timeline of Coronavirus Comments from President Trump and WHO. Tamara Keith and Malaka Gharib. April 15, 2020. www.npr.org.
90. Sup China. WHO Declares Public Health Emergency of International Concern. Jeremy Goldkorn. January 30, 2020. www.supchina.com.
91. Politico.com. Trump's 2020 Rallies, Twitter and an Expected Super Bowl Push. Anita Kumar. January 5, 2020. www.politico.com.
92. CNBC. Russia Closes Border with China to Prevent Spread of the Coronavirus. Holly Ellyatt. January 30, 2020. www.cnbc.com.
93. Politico. Trump Sticks Embattled Health Chief with Coronavirus Response. Nancy Cook and Dan Diamond. January 30, 2020. www.politico.com.
94. The White House. Proclamation on Suspension of Entry as Immigrants and Nonimmigrants of Persons Who Pose a Risk of Transmitting 2019 Novel Coronavirus. January 31, 2020. www.whitehouse.gov.
95. CNN. 'Mind-Boggling': How Pandemic Planning Never Accounted for a President Like Trump. April 14, 2020. www.cnn.com.
96. MDR Newswire. U.S. Companies Donate Nearly $27 Million in Medical Products to Aid in COVID-19 Outbreak in China. Ethan D. and Maria Fontanazza. February 27, 2020. www.mdrnewswire.com.
97. U.S. News & World Report. U.S. Announces Aid for China, Other countries Impacted by Coronavirus. Reuters. February 7, 2020. www.usnews.com.
98. HHS Health & Human Services. Secretary Azar Declares Public Health Emergency for United States for 2019 Novel Coronavirus. January 31, 2020. www.hhs.gov.
99. CNN Politics. Donald Trump Seems to Know Very Little About the Coronavirus. The Point with Chris Cillizza. February 25, 2020. www.cnn.com.

100. CNBC. Trump Says the Coronavirus Is the Democrats' 'New Hoax.' Thomas Franck. February 28, 2020. www.cnbc.com.

101. Global News. Japan Quarantines 3,700 on Cruise Ship after Positive Coronavirus Test. Josh K. Elliott. February 4, 2020. www.globalnews.ca.

102. Nature. Cell Research. Remdesivir and Chloroquine Effectively Inhibit the Recently Emerged Novel Coronavirus (2019-nCoV) in Vitro. Manli Wang, et al. February 4, 2020. www.nature.com.

103. CNBC. Trump Acquitted of Both Charges in Senate Impeachment Trial. Christina Wilkie and Kevin Breuninger. February 6, 2020. www.cnbc.com.

104. The Washington Post. A Faulty CDC Coronavirus Test Delays Monitoring of Disease's Spread. Carolyn Y. Johnson, et al. February 25, 2020. www.washingtonpost.com.

105. The New York Times. Chinese Doctor, Silenced after Warning of Outbreak, Dies from Coronavirus. Chris Buckley. February 6, 2020. www.nytimes.com.

106. American Hospital Association. Concerns Rise for PPE Shortages with Coronavirus. February 7, 2020. www.aha.org.

107. The New York Times. Deaths in China Surpass Toll from SARS. February 9, 2020. www.nytimes.com.

108. USA Today. Trump Says Coronavirus Will Be Gone by April When the Weather Gets Warmer, Doesn't Offer Scientific Explanation. Courtney Subramian, et al. February 10, 2020. www.usatoday.com.

109. Vox. The Life-and-Death Consequences of Naming the Coronavirus. Umair Ifran. February 14, 2020. www.vox.com.

110. Time. This Cruise Ship Has the Highest COVID-19 Infection Rate in the World. Hillary Leung. February 14, 2020. www.time.com.

111. ABC News. Coronavirus Has 'Pandemic Potential,' WHO Warns as U.S. Ramps Up Testing. Morgan Sinsor and Ivan Pereira. February 27, 2020. www.abcnews.go.com.

112. CNN Health. Coronavirus Outbreak in China Could Lead to 'Critical' Shortages of Medical Products in the US. Jen Christensen. February 26, 2020. www.cnn.com.

113. Yahoo! Finance. FDA Identified 20 Drugs with Shortage Risks Due to Coronavirus Outbreak. Reuters. February 25, 2020. www.finance.yahoo.com.

114. NPR. New World Health Organization Data Confirms Around 80% of Cases Are Mild. Maria Godoy. February 17, 2020. www.npr.org.

115. Forbes. IOC Must Consider Canceling or Postponing Tokyo Olympics Because of Coronavirus. Alex Reimer. February 27, 2020. www.forbes.com.

116. MedPage Today. Senators Grill HHS Secretary on Coronavirus Response. Joyce Frieden. February 25, 2020. www.medpagetoday.com.

117. Yahoo! News. South Korea Posts Surge in Coronavirus Cases Tied to Church. Jihye Lee and Peter Pae. February 19, 2020. www.news.yahoo.com.

118. The New York Times. Europe Confronts Coronavirus as Italy Battles an Eruption of Cases. Jason Horowitz and Elisabetta Povoledo. February 23, 2020. www.nytimes.com.

119. U.S. News & World Report. China Bans Trade, Consumption of Wild Animals Due to Coronavirus. Reuters. February 24, 2020. www.usnews.com.

120. PubMed. WHO Declares COVID-19 a Pandemic. Domenico Cucinotta and Maurizio Vanelli. March 11, 2020. www.pubmed.ncbi.nlm.nih.gov.

121. The Wall Street Journal. First COVID-19 Vaccine Given to U.S. Public. Peter Loftus and Melanie Grayce West. December 14, 2020. www.wsj.com.

122. Centers for Disease Control and Prevention. Pfizer-BioNTech COVID-19 Vaccine. www.cdc.gov.

123. MSN. Moderna Vaccine Vs. Pfizer Vaccine: Experts Say Both Are Safe and Effective. A.J. Nwoko. December 20, 2020. www.msn.com.

124. VeryWell Health. An Overview of the Johnson & Johnson COVID-19 Vaccine. Rachael Zimlich, BSN, RN and Andy Miller, MD. February 4, 2021. www.verywellhealth.com.

125. USA Today. 'Move Heaven and Earth': President-Elect Joe Biden's Covic-19 Plan Calls for 100 Million Shots in First 100 Days. Ken Alltucker. January 14, 2021. www.usatoday.com.

126. Centers for Disease Control and Prevention. New Variants of the Virus that Causes COVID-19. February 2, 2021. www.cdc.gov.

PANDEMIC 2020: The U.S. Edition

Statistics
Worldometers. www.worldometers.info/coronavirus.
National Governor's Association. COVID-19: What You Need to Know. Updated regularly.
   https://www.nga.org/state-COVID-19-emergency-orders.
AARP. State-By-State Guide to Face Mask Requirements. Andy Markowitz. Updated regularly.
   www.aarp.org.
Centers for Disease Control and Prevention. National Center for Health Statistics. Excess Deaths
   Associated with COVID-19. www.cdc.gov/nchs.
Masks4All. What U.S. States Require Masks in Public? Updated daily. https://masks4all.co.
CNN Politics. Presidential Results. https://www.cnn.com/election/2020/results/president.
Centers for Disease Control and Prevention. Covid VIEW. Number of Specimens Tested and Percent
   Positive for SARS-CoV-2. www.cdc.gov.
The Covid Tracking Project. https://covidtracking.com/data.
Becker's Hospital Review. States Ranked by COVID-19 Test Positivity Rates. Updated Daily.
   www.beckershospitalreview.com.
Los Angeles Times. U.S. Deaths Are About 300,000 Higher than Expected Since the Coronavirus Arrived.
   Karen Kaplan. October 20, 2020. www.latimes.com.

Year-End Summaries
Worldometers. www.worldometers.info/coronavirus.
The Covid Tracking Project. https://covidtracking.com/data.

Additional Resources
Live Science. Mysterious Blood Clots in COVID=19 Patients Have Doctors Alarmed. Rachael Rettner. April 23,
   2020. www.livescience.com.
USA Today. Inside America's Secretive Biolabs. Alison Young and Nick Penzenstadler. May 28, 2015.
   www.usatoday.com.
Centers for Disease Control and Prevention. Symptoms of Coronavirus. May 13, 2020. www.cdc.gov.
Centers for Disease Control and Prevention. Emerging Infectious Diseases. High Contagiousness and Rapid
   Spread of Severe Acute Respiratory Syndrome Coronavirus 2. Steven Sanche, et al. Vol. 26, No. 7. July,
   2020. www.cdc.gov.
Forbes. The COVID-19 Coronavirus Disease May Be Twice as Contagious as We Thought. Tara Haelle. April 7,
   2020. www.forbes.com.
Worldometers. Coronavirus Incubation Period. March 12, 2020. www.worldometers.info/coronavirus.
STAT. The New Coronavirus Can Likely Remain Airborne for Some Time. That Doesn't Mean We're Doomed.
   Sharon Begley. March 16, 2020. www.statnews.com.
New York Post. Coronavirus May Have Been Spreading in China Since August 2019: Study. Amanda Woods.
   June 9, 2020. www.nypost.com.
FactCheck.org. Baseless Conspiracy Theories Claim New Coronavirus Was Bioengineered. Jessica
   McDonald. February 7, 2020. www.factcheck.org.
Business Insider. The Chinese CDC Now Says the Coronavirus Didn't Jump to People at the Wuhan Wet
   Market – Instead, It Was the Site of a Superspreader Event. Aylin Woodward. May 28, 2020.
   www.businessinsider.com.
Associated Press. China Didn't Warn Public of Likely Pandemic for 6 Key Days. April 14, 2020.
   www.apnews.com.
Vox. The Evidence on Travel Bans for Diseases Like Coronavirus Is Clear: They Don't Work. Julia Belluz and
   Steven Hoffman. January 23, 2020. www.vox.com.
Coronavirus.gov. Underlying Conditions. FAQ. www.coronavirus.gov.
Centers for Disease Control and Prevention. CDC Updates, Expands List of People at Risk of Severe COVID-
   19 Illness. www.cdc.gov.

NBC News. More than 2,200 Coronavirus Deaths in Nursing Homes, but Federal Government Isn't Tracking Them. Suzy Khimm, et al. April 10, 2020. www.nbcnews.com.

The Epoch Times. Patients of Novel Coronavirus Show New Symptoms: Report. Nicole Hao. January 24, 2020. www.theepochtimes.com.

The Epoch Times. Chinese Social Media Depicts Chaos in Virus-Hit Wuhan. Eva Fu. January 24, 2020. www.theepochtimes.com.

Breitbart. China Closes Great Wall, Forbidden City to Contain Coronavirus. Bob Price. January 24, 2020. www.breitbart.com.

Real Conservatives Unite. Shocking Footage Inside China's Newly-Constructed Hospitals, 'Like Jail Cells Where You Go to Die.' February 4, 2020. www.realconservativesunite.com.

YouTube. Peak Prosperity. Coronavirus Is Worse than You've Been Told: Scientist Explains. Chris Martensen. February 24, 2020. www.youtube.com.

The New York Times. Coronavirus Spurs China to Suspend Tours Abroad and Xi to Warn of a 'Grave Situation.' January 25, 2020. www.nytimes.com.

CNN. China Says Coronavirus Can Spread Before Symptoms Show – Calling into Question U.S. Containment Strategy. Elizabeth Cohen. January 26, 2020. www.cnn.com.

The Epoch Times. Chinese Authorities Manipulate Tally of Confirmed Coronavirus Cases by Controlling the Supply of Diagnosis Kits. Olivia Li. January 27, 2020. www.theepochtimes.com.

The Epoch Times. China Underreporting True Scale of Deadly Virus Outbreak, Expert Says. Eva Fu. January 27, 2020. www.theepochtimes.com.

The New York Times. The 'Red Dawn' Emails: 8 Key Exchanges on the Faltering Response to the Coronavirus. Eric Lipton. April 11, 2020. www.nytimes.com.

Warren Democrats. Preventing, Containing and Treating Infectious Disease Outbreaks at Home and Abroad. Elizabeth Warren. January 28, 2020. www.elizabethwarren.com.

Politico. Azar: Coronavirus 'A Fast-Moving, Constantly Changing Situation.' Brianna Ehley. January 28, 2020. www.politico.com.

The Wall Street Journal. Act Now to Prevent an American Epidemic. Luciana Borio and Scott Gottlieb. January 28, 2020. www.wsj.com.

The Associated Press. China Delayed Releasing Coronavirus Info, Frustrating WHO. June 2, 2020. www.apnews.com.

Vice. You Can Now Go to Jail in China for Criticizing Beijing's Coronavirus Response. David Gilbert. January 30, 2020. www.vice.com.

Yahoo! News. China Accused of Cremating Bodies in Secret as Coronavirus Patient Numbers Spike. Yahoo News Staff. January 30, 2020. au.news.yahoo.com.

CNN. 'Mind-Boggling:' How Pandemic Planning Never Accounted for a President Like Trump. April 14, 2020. www.cnn.com.

The Associated Press. AP FACT CHECK: Trump's Inaccurate Boasts on China Travel Ban. Hope Yen. March 26, 2020. www.apnews.com.

The Washington Post. Trump's Claim that He Imposed the First 'China Ban.' Glenn Kessler. April 7, 2020. www.washingtonpost.com.

Reuters. Biden Slams Trump for Cutting Health Programs Before Coronavirus Outbreak. Trevor Hunnicutt. January 31, 2020. www.reuters.com.

Reuters. As Coronavirus Misinformation Spreads on Social Media, Facebook Removes Posts. Katie Paul. January 31, 2020. www.reuters.com.

CNET. Google, Facebook and Others Pressed to Stop Spread of Anti-Vax Information. Steven Musil. March 13, 2020. www.cnet.com.

The Epoch Times. Only 12 Days from Onset to Death, Pregnant Coronavirus Victim Had 'White Lungs.' Angela Bright. February 1, 2020. www.theepochtimes.com.

Breitbart. Navarro: Possible China Hoarding Coronavirus PPE for Profiteering, Diplomatic Weapon. Jeff Poor. May 7, 2020. www.breitbart.com.

Politifact. Fact-Checking Whether Biden Called Trump 'Xenophobic' for Restrictions on Travel from China. Miriam Valverde. March 27, 2020. www.politifact.com.

The Washington Times. Trump Never Actually Banned Flights from China or Europe. Why? Ethan Epstein. March 22, 2020. www.washingtontimes.com.

Mother Jones. Trump's 100 Days of Deadly Coronavirus Denial. Dave Gilson, et al. April 29, 2020. www.motherjones.com.

Time. Why We Are So Ill-Prepared for a Possible Pandemic Like Coronavirus. Michael T. Osterholm and Mark Olshaker. February 4, 2020. www.time.com.

YouTube. DW Documentary. Coronavirus in China | DW Documentary. March 17, 2020. www.youtube.com.

South China Morning Post. Coronavirus: China Tries to Contain Outbreak of Freedom of Speech, Closing Critics' WeChat Accounts. Kristin Huang. February 26, 2020. www.scmp.com.

The New York Times. They Documented the Coronavirus Crisis in Wuhan. Then They Vanished. Vivian Wang. February 14, 2020. www.nytimes.com.

CNET. Coronavirus Breakthrough: First 3D Protein Map Paves Way for Vaccine Design. Jackson Ryan. February 19, 2020. www.cnet.com.

National Geographic. Chinese Citizens Push to Abolish Wildlife Trade as Coronavirus Persists. Natasha Daly. January 30, 2020. www.nationalgeographic.com.

The Washington Post. Trump Tests His Most Promising Coronavirus Antidote: Lies. Dana Milbank. April 28, 2020. www.washingtonpost.com.

CNN. Fact Check: A List of 28 Ways Trump and His Team Have Been Dishonest about the Coronavirus. Daniel Dale and Tara Subramaniam. March 11, 2020.

Animal Equality. The Danger and Cruelty of Wet Markets. An Immediate Threat to Public Health. www.animalequality.org.

Politico. Wearing a Mask Is for Smug Liberals. Refusing to Is for Reckless Republicans. Ryan Lizza and Daniel Lippman. May 1, 2020. www.politico.com.

Reuters. Uncounted Among Coronavirus Victims, Deaths Sweep Through Italy's Nursing Homes. Emilio Parodi. March 18, 2020. www.reuters.com.

South China Morning Post. Coronavirus: Why Many Deaths Will Never Appear in Official Figures. Phoebe Zhang and Guo Rui. February 12, 2020. www.scmp.com.

U.S. News & World Report. AP Fact Check: Trump Says He Always Knew Virus Was a Pandemic. Associated Press. March 23, 2020. www.usnews.com.

Business Insider. China Took at Least 12 Strict Measures to Control the Coronavirus. They Could Work for the U.S., but Would Likely Be Impossible to Implement. Hilary Brueck, et al. March 24, 2020. www.businessinsider.com.

FactCheck.org. Trump's Spin on 'Broken' Testing. Lori Robertson. April 1, 2020. www.factcheck.org.

Law & Crime. Trump Was More Interested in Vaping than the Coronavirus in Late January: Report. Colin Kalmacher. March 21, 2020. www.lawandcrime.com.

Daily Wire. Here's a Timeline of the Coronavirus Outbreak and China's Coverup. Ashe Schow. March 20, 2020. www.dailywire.com.

MSN News. Chinese Laboratory that First Shared Coronavirus Genome with World Ordered to Close for 'Rectification.' Zhuang Pinghui. February 28, 2020. www.msn.com.

Health Policy Watch. Mystery Virus in Wuhan Identified as Novel Coronavirus; Researchers Still Searching for Animal Host. Grace Ren. January 13, 2020. www.healthpolicy-watch.org.

Wikipedia Pandemic Pages. Coronavirus Pandemic in [STATE]. en.wikipedia.org/wiki/COVID-19_Pandemic _in_[STATE].

Made in the USA
Middletown, DE
09 March 2021